✳   ✳   ✳

Presented To:

_____

From:

_____

Date:

_____

✳   ✳   ✳

A
Treasury of
Christmas
Joy

THE PROSE AND POETRY
OF THE SEASON

Honor Books
Tulsa, Oklahoma

Unless otherwise indicated, all Scripture quotations are taken from the *King James Version* of the Bible.

Scripture quotations marked NIV are taken from the *Holy Bible, New International Version* ®. NIV ®. Copyright © 1973, 1978, 1984 by International Bible Society. Used by permission of Zondervan Publishing House. All rights reserved.

Cover and interior design by Koechel Peterson & Associates.

Compiled and edited by Paul M. Miller.

Editor's Note: Some stories have been adapted, translated, or changed slightly for clarity or spacing. However, in all instances, every effort was made to maintain the original message and intent of the story.

Treasury of Christmas Joy:
The Prose and Poetry of the Season
ISBN 1-56292-639-X
Copyright © 1999 by Honor Books
P.O. Box 55388
Tulsa, Oklahoma 7415

2ⁿᵈ Printing

Contents

The Joys of Christmas

Just as Christmas is not merely *another* red-letter day on the calendar, so this collection of Christmas prose and poetry is not your ordinary book of holiday stuff. To the contrary, the readers of this treasury will be challenged by the many and varied uses of these Christmas resources.

Too often we search libraries and book-shops for just the right story or bit of verse to bring new light to a message or speech.

As storytellers, we search our files for a Christmas Eve narrative to entertain and inspire family and guests.

As parents, we are aware of the traditional and sacred, the fun-filled and the classic, the expendable and the eternal; all of which have a place in a Christmas anthology.

As believers, we want the spiritual meaning of Christmas to burn as brightly as the star on the top of your Christmas tree.

So find a quiet corner for yourself. . . .

Or gather the family around you. . . .

Or wrap this book in silvery tissue and present it to someone as a Yuletide gift for the soul and the mind and even the funny bone.

From the Editor

THE TWELVE JOYS OF CHRISTMAS

In the warm ambiance of Christmas tree lights and flickering candles we had just gobbled down our annual in-front-of-the-fireplace supper. The adults were making mental checklists of where the stocking stuffers were hidden and if we bought enough AA and AAA batteries, while the Grinch was in the process of stealing Christmas. This was a Kansas City suburb Christmas Eve in the late sixties when our son and daughter were still in elementary school and sugarplum visions were rampant.

While we are generally not a singing family, at this stage of her life our daughter Lisa was smitten by Barbra Streisand and was occasionally caught standing on the raised family room hearth with a wooden mixing spoon in front of her face, singing along with the diva. On this particular evening Lisa jumped to her feet and clicked off the TV with the announcement, "Let's sing songs!" Her older brother Tim groaned and tried to reach the TV power switch, but Lisa was too fast for him. "No more TV—we are going to sing!"

And sing we did. Accompanied by the Muppet Christmas album we hilariously warbled "The Twelve Days of Christmas." With great animation we imitated leaping lords and pear-tree partridges. Then Lisa getting serious, took the wooden-spoon microphone and, in her best Streisand voice, led us in "Joy to the world, the Lord is come . . ." and on to "Joy to the world, the Savior reigns."

Then Dad found some Christmas words to an old hymn set to the tune of Beethoven's "Ode to Joy":

Joyful, joyful we adore You,
God of glory, Lord of light;
Angels lifting praise before You
Sing throughout this holy night.
In a manger lies a Baby—
Child of Mary, Son of God.
Voices joined in joyful chorus
Praise You for Your gift of love.

What single word describes this season of Jesus' birth? Not fun, though it certainly is; not gifts, though they are a part of it; not even food or *The Nutcracker* or mistletoe. The Christmas word is JOY! That's the common denominator of Christ's birth. Whether shepherd, innkeeper, wise man, or blessed mother, joy is the result of the Christmas event. Fortunate are those who celebrate the twelve days of Christmas—with enough joy to last a lifetime. To those and to all of us, consider the "Twelve Joys of Christmas" that you will discover in this treasury.

PAUL M. MILLER

of Anticipation

Of the twelve joys of Christmas, few are more appropriate to the season than the joy of anticipation. Just ask any child why Mom says the closet in the guest room is off limits and why Daddy has taken some big bike-size cartons from the car into the basement. The reason? That's simple—Christmas is coming!

Why is it that snow gets shoveled, home-work done, and rooms are picked up without moaning?—Christmas is coming!

For us on this side of Bethlehem, a celebra-tion of the season is the knowledge that Jesus the Christ came into the world more than 2,000 years ago. With Him came eternal life and the anticipation of a day when He will come again.

Before the First Advent, the world looked for a savior. The Prophet Isaiah heightened that hope when he announced, "His name shall be called Wonderful, Counselor, The mighty God, The Everlasting Father—The Prince of Peace" (Isaiah 9:6).

Come Thou quickly Lord Jesus!

Anticipating the Day

BY A CHRISTMAS FANATIC

As the year comes full circle, it comes time to make ready, once again, for Christmas. In a sense, the preparations have gone on for months and, for suppliers the planning may have started years in advance. Christmas catalogues close up tight in the spring; the Christmas rush to order merchandise shows up in July, and promotionally we are hotfooting it toward Christmas even before the Thanksgiving turkey grows cold on the table.

Emotionally, however, the spirit of Christmas moves at a more deliberate pace, in a gathering torrent of delightful anticipation. The memories come flooding in.

The warmth of the kitchen with the summer harvest of jellies and relishes bubbling on top of the stove, with gleaming gift jars arranged to receive them. The "may I lick the spoon?" tastes of the spicy, fruit-stuffed batters of fall, mounded into loaf pans or onto cookie sheets to be baked as presents. The oven itself, the kitchen's heart, with the special once-a-year foods taking shape within it, adding their unique scents to an atmosphere already electric with excitement.

The thrill of opening the tiny door to December 1st on the Advent calendar and seeing the first of a succession of surprise pictures, gradually increasing in size and splendor to the wonders of the 25th.

The stifled giggles and whispers behind closed doors and the rushing of mysterious parcels in plain brown wrappers up the stairs to the secret hiding place (which it turned out years later, everyone knew about).

In the days of our blissful belief, when were very young, our adrenaline would be in overdrive by the time we had to go to bed on Christmas Eve. We would leave cookies and milk, or perhaps an orange, near the fireplace for Santa Claus with a last written reminder of what we wanted most to find in the stockings hanging limply from the mantel.

Once in bed, we would toss and turn, then sit up to listen for the tiny hoofbeats of Santa's reindeer landing on the roof. Sleep seemed as if it would never come . . . and the sound of talk and laughter would float up from downstairs. Why did the grown-ups take so long going to bed? Santa couldn't possibly come while anyone was still awake.

Eventually, of course, sleep would come and we wouldn't even know it . . . until that magical moment when our eyes suddenly blinked open and it was, it truly was, Christmas Day!

So Christmas comes again—and despite all the changes we have made in it and the commercial advantages we have found in it, we cannot remove the loving spirit from this dearest of holidays, nor abate our sense of awe that this splendid celebration had its beginnings so simply and humbly in a stable with a tiny Baby lying on a bed of hay.

✳ ✳ ✳

The Church has identified the anticipation

of Christmas and the coming of Christ

Advent

as Advent. There are four Sundays in

the Advent season, which begins four weeks

before Christmas. The following are

Scripture readings that can be shared

by you and others during this season.

✳ ✳ ✳

First Sunday

OUR MESSIAH WILL COME

[The Lord God of Israel said,]
"I will send my messenger,
who will prepare the way before me."
A voice of one calling:
"In the dessert prepare the way for the LORD;
make straight in the wilderness a highway for our God.
Every valley shall be raised up,
every mountain and hill made low;
The rough ground shall become level,
the rugged places plain.
And the glory of the LORD will be revealed,
and all mankind together will see it.
For the mouth of the LORD has spoken."
The sovereign LORD comes with power,
and his arm rules for him.
See, his reward is with him,
and his recompense accompanies him.
He tends his flock like a shepherd:
he gathers the lambs in his arms
and carries them close to his heart.

MALACHI 3:1; ISAIAH 40:3-5, 10-11 NIV

Second Sunday

OUR MESSIAH WILL BRING PEACE

A shoot will come up from the stump of Jesse;

from his roots a Branch will bear much fruit.

The Spirit of the LORD will rest on him—

the Spirit of wisdom and of understanding,

the Spirit of counsel and of power,

the Spirit of knowledge and of the fear of the LORD—

and he will delight in the fear of the LORD.

He will not judge by what he sees with his eyes,

or decide by what he hears with his ears;

but with righteousness he will judge the needy,

with justice he will give decisions for the poor of the earth.

The wolf will live with the lamb.

the leopard will lie down with the goat.

They will neither harm nor destroy on all my holy mountain,

for the earth will be full of the knowledge of the LORD

as the waters cover the sea.

ISAIAH 11:1-4, 6, 9 NIV

Third Sunday

OUR MESSIAH WILL BRING SALVATION

The Spirit of the Sovereign LORD is on me,

because the LORD has anointed me to preach good news to the poor.

He has sent me to bind up the brokenhearted,

to proclaim freedom for the captives

and release from darkness for the prisoners,

to proclaim the year of the LORD's favor.

To comfort all who mourn,

and provide for those who grieve in Zion—

to bestow on them a crown of beauty instead of ashes,

the oil of gladness instead of mourning,

and a garment of praise instead of a spirit of despair.

They will be called oaks of righteousness,

a planting of the LORD for the display of his splendor.

Shout aloud and sing for joy, people of Zion,

For great is the Holy One of Israel among you.

ISAIAH 61:1-3; 12:6 NIV

Fourth Sunday

The people walking in darkness have seen a great light;

on those living in the land of the shadow of death

a light has dawned.

For to us a child is born,

to us a son is given,

and the government will be on his shoulders.

And he will be called Wonderful Counselor,

Mighty God,

Everlasting Father,

Prince of Peace.

Of the increase of his government and peace

there will be no end.

He will reign on David's throne

and over his kingdom,

establishing and upholding it with justice and righteousness

from that time on and forever.

The zeal of the LORD Almighty will accomplish this.

ISAIAH 9:2, 6-7 NIV

Christmas Eve
In the Back of the Bus
BY PAUL M. MILLER

"The 6:00 bus for Harrisonville, Peculiar, Butler, Grandview, Kansas City and points west will not depart until 8:36. Trailways is sorry for the delay. Merry Christmas."

Well, so much for Christmas Eve with my nieces. By the time I reach Jeff and Debbie's, the girls will be in bed—in fact, everybody will be in bed. This is really a disappointment; for the past month Brianna and Alissa have gotten on the phone and giggled in excitement and anticipation of our being all together for Christmas.

"Uncle George, we just can't wait!"

They can't wait! I've been like a kid, looking forward to being with those girls. I got them each some Barbie stuff and a couple of books that the saleslady said six and four year olds would like. She even wrapped . . .

"Excuse me, is anyone sitting here?"

I look up and discover a pregnant young woman standing in front of me.

"No. Here, sit down." I scoot over to give her more room.

"Did I hear that announcement correctly? The Kansas City bus won't be leaving until 8:30?"

"8:36 to be exact."

The young woman eases herself down onto the bench. "That means my husband will have to wait two and a half hours at the Wichita bus depot—and on Christmas Eve." There is an awkward pause for a moment, then she adds, "He probably won't be happy."

"Will this be your first child?" I ask.

Her eyes light up for a second and a fleeting smile passes across her face. "Yes, this is our first. It's going to be a boy."

"Oh, you know already!"

"My husband doesn't like surprises."

"Are you excited?"

"Of course. I've anticipated having a baby for so long. My parents are really excited, too—becoming grandparents and all."

We smile at each other. I introduce myself. Her name turns out to be Marion and she's been visiting her parents. Conversation comes to an end and we slip back into our own private worlds. I find my C. S. Lewis paperback in my knapsack and Marion, my seatmate, reads something called *Modern Motherhood*.

I doze off for a few minutes and then am awakened by the bus announcer's tinny voice; "Passengers for the Kansas City local are advised that the 8:36 departure has been pushed back to 7:30. We will be leaving in 20 minutes. Merry Christmas!"

By the time the passengers gather up their kids and their belongings and are settled on the bus, we pull away from the depot at just about 7:38.

Marion and I sit in the last row at the back of the bus. I let her have the seat next to the window; for some reason she feels safer there.

"Where are you spending Christmas?" she asks.

"I'm going to be with my brother and sister-in-law, and their two girls just outside Kansas City."

"That's nice." Marion turns her face toward the window. Because of the blackness of the night outside, I can see her face reflected in the window, as clearly as in a mirror. It's obvious she is upset. I can see a tear coursing down her cheek.

"Is everything okay?" I ask lamely. "I mean if I can help you in some way . . ."

She shakes her head and stares out the window. Finally after many minutes, during which I return to my paperback, Marion speaks again.

"Can I ask you a question?"

"Sure, fire away."

Jerking away from the window she asks, "Why does everyone get so worked up over Christmas?" Before I can venture a reaction, Marion confesses, "Since I've been an adult and married, it's always such a let-down. Christmas never lives up to what I think it ought to be."

For the next who-knows-how-many-miles Marion and I talk. I try to tell her about Christmas when I was growing up in Lamar; how I was hardly ever disappointed in the gift department, but more than that, how in our family, anticipating Christmas was half of the experience. I describe our Advent wreath and the five candles; how for the four weeks before Christmas we'd light the candles and read the promises of Messiah's coming; how we'd set up the Bethlehem stable and empty manger on our coffee table, and then add the figures week by week during the season. Of course the culmination was Christmas Eve when one of us got to place Baby Jesus in the manger.

"The Baby made a difference, Marion."

Touching her tummy, the dark-eyed soon-to-be mother looks at me wistfully and adds, "I sure hope this baby makes a difference—in our home." Turning back to the window, she is quiet the rest of the way to Kansas City. I turn off my reading light and the driver lowers the interior lights.

People are settling down for the last hour of the journey. A little girl across the aisle asks, "When are we going to get there mama?"

"Pretty soon, honey."

"I just can't wait!"

"Well, just relax and shut your eyes—it'll make us get there faster."

"Will Santa have already come, mama?"

"Guess we'll just have to wait to see."

The next thing I know, the bus is pulling into a Trailways depot and the driver's voice is calling out, "Kansas City. There will be a 45 minute layover. If you are leaving here, don't forget to take all of your belongings. Your checked baggage will be available by the door. Good night and Merry Christmas."

Marion turns to look at me while I pull my backpack off the overhead rack and stuff C. S. Lewis inside. She gives me another wistful smile and reaches up with her hand to shake mine. "Thanks for the encouragement. I liked our conversation."

My instinct is to kiss her on the cheek and remind her that a Baby made a difference back then, and maybe it will now. But I don't; instead I shake her hand and mumble a "Merry Christmas." Then I push my way down the aisle. When I step out of the bus I hear two piping voices call out, "There's Uncle George!" and I have an armful of nieces.

Glancing at the window above me I see Marion. She offers me a slight wave of the hand and I shout out to her, "A Baby makes a difference!" She frowns that she can't hear me. I shout again, "A Baby makes a difference!" She catches my words and smiles and makes the okay sign with her thumb and forefinger.

Then Alissa jumps up into my arms and Brianna tugs at my sweater, "Uncle George, whose baby makes a difference?"

"God's Baby, Jesus. Merry Christmas, my sweethearts!"   ✳

"Everywhere, everywhere

Christmas tonight!

For the Christ Child

Who comes is the Master of all;

No palace too great—

No cottage too small."

PHILLIPS BROOKS

Shepherds,
Shake Off Your Drowsy Sleep

People, look East. The time is near
Of the crowning of the year.
Make your house fair as you are able,
Trim the hearth and set the table.
People, look East, and sing today;
Love the Guest is on the way.

Furrows, be glad. Though earth is bare.
One more seed is planted there:
Give up your strength the seed to nourish,
That in turn the flower may flourish.
People, look East, and sing today:
Love the Rose is on the way.

Birds, though ye long have ceased to build.
Guard the nest that must be filled.
Even the hour when wings are frozen
He for fledgling-time has chosen.
People, look East, and sing today:
Love the Bird is on the way.

Stars, keep the watch. When night is dim
One more light the bowl shall brim.
Shining beyond the frosty weather.
People, look East, and sing today:
Love the Star is on the way.

Angels announce to man and beast
Him who cometh from the East.
Set every peak and valley humming
With the word, the Lord is coming.
People, look East, and sing today:
Love the Lord is on the way.[1]

ELEANOR FARJEON

* * *

The Christmas gift list is as traditional

gift list

as all the other accessories of the season.

In anticipation of our potential holiday

excesses, Pastor Charles Swindoll holds up

the following admonition.

* * *

A Christmas List
BY CHARLES R. SWINDOLL

Our lovely land of plenty drifts dangerously near insanity three or four weeks every year. If you doubt that, consider these statistics: Americans spend 8.5 billion dollars during the Christmas season; 150 million dollars will go for wrappings alone, most of which will be immediately discarded; 100 million dollars will be spent on trees; 200 million dollars will be spent on postage; 2 million telegrams will be sent between the 23rd and 25th of December. (My figures are slightly out of date, but if anything, each could be increased this year.)

Along with all this, emotions, unpredictable and undisciplined, begin to run wild. Nostalgia mixed with eleven months of guilt can prompt illogical and extravagant purchases. Neighborhood pressure can cause perfectly normal people to mount extravagant displays and string hundreds of lights on their houses. Television advertising, Christmas bank accounts, and special "wish books" only increase the pull of the magnet that inevitably ends with the sound of cash registers or the hollow snap of the credit card.

While we think we may be immune to all this, we Christians need to be especially alert to the dangers and think through a strategy that allows us to combat each one. I'll mention only four.

Doctrinal Danger . . . substituting the temporal for the eternal. A couple of Scriptures give needed counsel here: ". . . keep seeking the things above, where Christ is. . . . Set your mind on the things above, not on the things that are on earth. . . . And do not be conformed to this world, but be transformed . . . Col.3:1-2; Rom. 12:2).

It is important that we understand exactly what we are celebrating. It is our Savior's arrival, not Santa's. The significance of giving presents is to be directly related to God's presenting us the gift of His Son.

Personal Danger . . . impressing but not imparting. We represent the King. We are His chosen ambassadors, doing His business "in season and out of season." So let's do it this season! People are wide open to the Gospel these days.

Economical Danger . . . spending more than you have. Before every purchase think: *Is this within my budget? Is it appropriate? Is it really saying what I want it to say?* And remember, homemade gifts are often more appreciated and much less expensive.

Psychological Danger . . . getting built up for a letdown. One of the most effective maneuvers of the world system is to create a false sense of excitement. The Christian can get "high" very easily on the crest of Christmas, and the afterglow can be a dangerous, depressing experience.

Guard yourself. Keep a firm hand on the controls. Don't be deceived. Enjoy the 25th . . . but not at the expense of the 26th.[2]   ✳

A Christmas Carol

"What means this glory round our feet,"

    The Magi mused, "more bright than morn?"

And voices chanted clear and sweet,

    "Today the Prince of Peace is born."

"What means that star," the Shepherds said,

    "That brightens through the rocky glen?"

And angels answering overhead,

    Sang, "Peace on earth, goodwill to men!"

It's eighteen hundred years and more

    Since those sweet oracles were dumb;

We wait for Him, like them of yore;

    Alas, He seems so slow to come!

But it was said, in words of gold

    No time or sorrow ever shall dim,

That little children might be bold

    In perfect trust to come to Him.

All round about our feet shall shine

    A light like that the Wise Men saw,

If we our loving wills incline

    To that sweet Life which is the Law.

So shall we learn to understand

    The simple faith of shepherds then,

And, clasping kindly hand in hand,

    Sing, "Peace on earth, goodwill to men."

And they who do their souls no wrong,

    But keep at eve the faith of morn,

Shall daily hear the angel-song,

    "Today the Prince of Peace is born!"[3]

JAMES RUSSELL LOWELL

*   *   *

Laura Ingalls Wilder is probably

best known for her Little House books.

Christmas

In 1991 Stephen Hines discovered a collection

anticipation

of Ms. Wilder's reminiscences, written journal style.

Included is this memory of Christmas anticipation

when Laura was a sixteen-year-old schoolteacher

living twelve miles from home.

*   *   *

Christmas When I Was Sixteen

By Laura Ingalls Wilder

The snow was scudding low over the drifts of the white world outside the little claim shanty. It was blowing through the cracks in its walls and forming little piles and miniature drifts on the floor, and even on the desks before which several children sat, trying to study: for this abandoned claim shanty, which had served as the summer home of a homesteader on the Dakota prairie, was being used as a schoolhouse during the winter.

The walls were made of one thickness of wide boards with cracks between, and the enormous stove that stood nearly in the center of the one room could scarcely keep out the frost, though its sides were glowing red. The children were dressed warmly and had been allowed to gather closely around the stove following the advice of the county superintendent of schools who, on a recent visit said that the only thing he had to say to them was to keep their feet warm.

This was my first school: I'll not say how many years ago. But I was only sixteen years old and twelve miles from home during a frontier winter. I walked a mile over unbroken snow from my boarding place to school every morning and back at night. There were only a few pupils, and on this particular snowy afternoon, they were restless, for it was nearing 4 o'clock and tomorrow was Christmas. "Teacher" was restless too, though she tried not to show it, for she was wondering if she could get home for Christmas Day.

It was almost too cold to hope for Father to come, and a storm was hanging in the northwest which might mean a blizzard at any minute. Still, tomorrow was Christmas—and then there was a jingle of sleigh bells outside. A man in a huge fur coat in a sleigh full of robes passed the window. I was going home after all!

When one thinks of twelve miles now, it is in terms of motor cars and means only a few minutes. It was different then, and I'll never forget that ride. The bells made a merry jingle, and the fur robes were warm: but the weather was growing colder, and the snow was drifting so that the horses must push their way through the drifts.

We were facing the strong wind, and every little while he placed his hands over each horse's nose in turn and thawed the ice from them where breath had frozen over their nostrils. Then he would get back into the sled and on we'd go until once more the horses could not breathe for the ice.

When we reached the journey's end, it was 40 degrees below zero; the snow was blowing so thickly that we could not see across the street; and I was so chilled that I had to be half carried into the house. But I was home for Christmas, and cold and danger were forgotten.

Such magic there is in Christmas to draw the absent ones home. Our hearts grow tender with childhood memories and love of kindred, and we are better through the year for having, in spirit, become a child again at Christmastime.[4]   ✳

The Meaning of Christmas

BY FRANCIS CARDINAL SPELLMAN

*H*oliday and Holy Day, Christmas is more than a Yule log, holly, or a tree. It is more than natural good cheer and the giving of gifts. Christmas is even more than the feast of the home and of children, the feast of love and friendship. It is more than all these together. Christmas is Christ, the Christ of justice and charity, of freedom and peace.

The joy of Christmas is a joy that war cannot kill, for it is a joy no earthly wealth can give. Time cannot wither Christmas, for it belongs to eternity. The world cannot shatter it, for it is union with Him Who has overcome the world.

The leaders and peoples of nations must understand these fundamental truths if we are ever to have freedom and peace. Unless charters and pacts have a divine sanction, unless "God is the Paramount Ruler of the world," then again and again, as the waves upon the shore, must catastrophe follow catastrophe. Not until men lay aside greed, hatred, pride, and the tyranny of evil passions, to travel the road that began at Bethlehem, will the star of Christmas peace illuminate the world. Christmas is the birthday of freedom, for it is only the following of Christ that makes men free.[5] ✳

* * *

Ever wonder how that announcing angel

in the Christmas narrative felt during that time of

anticipation, just before some shepherds would

hear his mighty "for unto you is born" speech?

Film writer and playwright Larry Enscoe

takes us to a warm-up room in Heaven,

where Gabriel with his horn is pacing,

getting his chops ready, and rehearsing

his spoken announcement.

* * *

The Word Is Given

A MONOLOGUE FOR GABRIEL

BY LAWRENCE G. ENSCOE

(GABRIEL *enters carrying a horn case and a white angel robe over his arm. Starts to open case, then looks up . . .*)

Hi.

So it's finally the Big Night. I've been anticipating this for a long time. (*Stares out over the audience.*) Look at all of 'em out there, pushing and shoving. Not a pretty sight. It's been crazy like this all day. People have been running their heads off. Packing themselves into the city. Filling up all the shops, the restaurants. I don't think anyone's said a civil word to one another all day. And now that it's night, nothing's gotten any better. Colder than the North Pole out there, and some folks still haven't got a place to sleep. It's not right. Peace on earth looks like a long ways off from where I'm standing. And if something like tonight can't turn things around, I don't know what will. Strange. What people have got right under their noses and they don't even know it. They're always looking for something in the future.

(*Paces some more, then picks up his horn case.*)

Come on. I'm ready. I've been waiting for this forever. I don't know what He's doing in there. What's the delay? I need to get out there. I've got to get to work This gig is really important tonight. Probably the most important one I'll ever play.

(*Goes over to an anteroom door and listens.*)

Is He . . . ? No, I know He'll tell me when He's ready. I'm just antsy about it, that's all. The wait feels like its killing me. You have any idea how—? I know (<u>laughs.</u>) Well, He knows where to find me.

(*Paces.*)

I shouldn't be complaining, I suppose. (*Jerks a thumb at the door.*) He likes to take His time with people. He cares about them as individuals is the point. That's why I stay with Him. People just don't know how fortunate they are to have someone like Him love them so much.

(*Softly we hear "It Came Upon the Midnight Clear."*)

Yeah. Tonight's the Big Night. Oh, and it's a beautiful one, too. All the stars are out. That makes it just right, I think. Look at that star over there! That's perfect. This whole night is going to turn out perfect. I can feel it already. What a holiday we're going to have! Everything is on track so far. Except for this hurry-up-and-wait routine. You don't think He's forgotten about me in there?

(*Strides to the door and speaks through the crack.*)

Sorry to bother You again, but I don't know how much longer I can wait. The suspense is getting to me out here. No, I'm not trying to rush anyone. I'm just . . . excited. Well, You know what night this is. Everybody's excited around here. Everybody just can't wait to get out there. (*Smiles.*) OK. Sure, I understand. Just give me the high sign, will You?

(*He opens the horn case and takes out some speaking notes. Begins mouthing the words, quietly as if memorizing something. Nods and puts the paper away.*)

What I have to do won't take long. I just need to get out there and do it. (*Pause. Sits and thinks for a few seconds.*) It's really something to think about, though, isn't it? The whole thing. Not the crowds, the smells in the air, the jam-packed businesses. I'm talking about the heart of the whole thing. I'm talking about a poor carpenter. His poor young wife. Trudging all those miles on a donkey. And then tonight, there's no place but a stable. A poor woman has a shivering baby in a filthy manger. Animals are the only witnesses to what should have been the greatest birth in history. And they're only watching because they're waiting to see if they're going to get their bedroom back.

(*Pause.*)

The whole thing turned out so different than I first thought. What did I expect? A warm reception? They're not exactly known for rolling out the red carpet out there.

(*Pause.*)

Still, I'm wondering if this whole thing isn't just a bit too . . . subtle, though. I'm just wondering if people, in all the bustle today, if anyone'll catch a sense of the bittersweet melody of the whole scene. I mean, a baby born in a stable in a one-horse town. Is that going to make an impression on anyone? It might be a little under-played. You know how sometimes you have to hit people over the head with stuff. (*Pause. Smiles.*) But I think it really sings, though. I think it strikes chords in people who really listen. I think the dirty manger has a grace all its own. Shows His way of surprising people by finding power in the small things . . . the, ah, commonplace things. It just proves nobody has to be anything special to join in the music. I don't know. I'm not sure people will hear a new song like that, is all I'm saying. (*Looks around. Loudly.*)

And nobody's going to hear anything if I don't get out of here and to work.

(*Pulls notes out of a pocket and goes over them. We begin to hear "Angels We Have Heard on High" play softly. Suddenly Gabriel looks at the door.*)

Wha . . . what? Did you—? Oh sorry. Thought I heard you . . . Oh I know. All in the right time. No. no. I want to do this right, that's for sure. It's an important night. There's no doubt about that.

(*He paces. Stops.*)

I just thought of something. I sure hope I'm going out in front of the right people. We need just the right kind of audience for this, I think. We need people who can spread the word. People with some connections. Or who know how to put things together right so other people'll see the pictures. I just hope we're booked in the right place, is all I have to say. This isn't something You can do over again. (*Laughs.*) Listen to me, I'm second-guessing everything, as if He didn't know what He was doing. That's my problem. I've got too much time to think in here. I'm starting to let the nerves get to me. OK. (*Takes a breath.*) I'm just going to go in and talk to Him. Tell Him that I think the moment is now. Remind Him how much these people need to know what tonight is really about. (*Heads for the door.*) I'll tell Him I'm ready to—(*Stops dead. Smiles.*) Oh, hello Sir. Oh, no, I'm all ready. Yes, I'm sure about it. I've rehearsed a little too. So, is this it, then? I mean . . . is the word given?

(*Pause.*)

The word is given. (*Claps his hands.*) That's wonderful! No, we're all set. That's right. (*Puts on his white angel robe and grabs the battered horn case.*) No, the others are ready, too. (*Heads for the door.*) Yes, we know the place. Got the address somewhere. (*Pats himself.*) Anyway, we're playing at Bethlehem Fields, right? To the left of the city. Yes, we've got the right music picked out. We're all set. This is going to be great! You arranged this whole thing just perfect, I think. But I got to tell You, it sure isn't the way anybody'd expect it all to happen. No, no! That's the beauty of it, though! (*Looks out.*) They're so lucky. You love them very much, don't You? Yeah. I wish they knew it, too. But, what can You do? You've already done it.

(*Pauses at door.*)

I just thought of something, Sir. I'm sure we're going to scare the daylights out of 'em down there. Give 'em a real shaking. We always seem to do that, don't we. Even when we look like one of them. (*Pulls out the piece of paper.*) I'll make a change here, huh? (*Writes.*) Right here at the top, I'll add an intro. "Don't be afraid. I'm bringing you good news of great joy!" That should do it.

(*"Hark the Herald Angels Sing" begins to play, loudly. GABRIEL walks through the door still reading.*)

"Tonight in Bethlehem a Savior has been born to you. He is Christ the Lord! And this will be a sign to you. You will find the Baby—"Oh, they're going to love to hear this. It's music to the ears. They've waited a long time to hear a song like this.

(*Blackout.*)[6]

✳

Mr. Edwards Meets Santa Claus

BY LAURA INGALLS WILDER

The days were short and cold, the wind whistled sharply, but there was no snow. Cold rains were falling. Day after day the rain fell, pattering on the roof and pouring from the eaves.

Mary and Laura stayed close by the fire, sewing their nine-patch quilt blocks, or cutting paper dolls from scraps of wrapping-paper, and hearing the wet sound of the rain. Every night was so cold that they expected to see snow next morning, but in the morning they saw only sad, wet grass.

They pressed their noses against the squares of glass in the windows that Pa had made, and they were glad they could see out. But they wished they could see snow.

Laura was anxious because Christmas was near, and Santa Claus and his reindeer could not travel without snow. Mary was afraid that, even if it snowed, Santa Claus could not find them, so far away in Indian Territory. When they asked Ma about this, she said she didn't know.

"What day is it?" they asked her, anxiously. "How many more days till Christmas?" And they counted off the days on their fingers, till there was only one more day left.

Rain was still falling that morning. There was not one crack in the gray sky. They felt almost sure there would be no Christmas. Still, they kept hoping.

Just before noon the light changed. The clouds broke and drifted apart, shining white in a clear blue sky. The sun shone, birds sang, and thousands of drops of water sparkled on the grasses. But when Ma opened the door to let in the fresh, cold air, they heard the creek roaring.

They had not thought about the creek. Now they knew they would have no Christmas, because Santa Claus could not cross that roaring creek.

Pa came in, bringing a big fat turkey. If it weighed less than twenty pounds, he said, he'd eat it, feathers and all. He asked Laura, "How's that for a Christmas dinner? Think you can manage one of those drumsticks?"

She said, yes, she could. But she was sober. Then Mary asked him if the creek was going down, and he said it was still rising.

Ma said it was too bad. She hated to think of Mr. Edwards eating his bachelor cooking all alone on Christmas day. Mr. Edwards had been asked to eat Christmas dinner with them, but Pa shook his head and said a man would risk his neck, trying to cross that creek now.

"No," he said. "That current's too strong. We'll just have to make up our minds that Edwards won't be here tomorrow."

Of course that meant that Santa Claus could not come, either.

Laura and Mary tried not to mind too much. They watched Ma dress the wild turkey, and it was a very fat turkey. They were lucky little girls, to have a good house to live in, and a warm fire to sit by, and such a turkey for their Christmas dinner. Ma said so, and it was true. Ma said it was too bad that Santa Claus couldn't come this year, but they were such good girls that he hadn't forgotten them; he would surely come next year.

Still, they were not happy.

After supper that night they washed their hands and faces, buttoned their red-flannel nightgowns, tied their night-cap strings, and soberly said their prayers. They lay down in bed and pulled the covers up. It did not seem at all like Christmas time.

Pa and Ma sat silent by the fire. After a while Ma asked why Pa didn't play the fiddle, and he said, "I don't seem to have the heart to, Caroline."

After a longer while, Ma suddenly stood up.

"I'm going to hang up your stockings, girls," she said. "Maybe something will happen."

Laura's heart jumped. But then she thought again of the creek and she knew nothing could happen.

Ma took one of Mary's clean stockings and one of Laura's, and she hung them from the mantel-shelf, on either side of the fireplace. Laura and Mary watched her over the edge of their bed-covers.

"Now go to sleep," Ma said, kissing them good night. "Morning will come quicker if you're asleep."

She sat down again by the fire and Laura almost went to sleep.

Then she heard Jack growl savagely. The door-latch rattled and someone said, "Ingalls! Ingalls!" Pa was stirring up the fire, and when he opened the door Laura saw that it was morning. The outdoors was gray.

"Great fishhooks, Edwards! Come in, man! What's happened?" Pa exclaimed.

Laura saw the stockings limply dangling, and she scrooged her shut eyes into the pillow.

She heard Pa piling wood on the fire, and she heard Mr. Edwards say he had carried his clothes on his head when he swam the creek. His teeth rattled and his voice shivered. He would be all right, he said, as soon as he got warm.

"It was too big a risk, Edwards," Pa said. "We're glad you're here, but that was too big a risk for a Christmas dinner."

"Your little ones had to have a Christmas," Mr. Edwards replied. "No creek could stop me, after I fetched them their gifts from Independence."

Laura sat straight up in bed. "Did you see Santa Claus?" she shouted.

"I sure did," Mr. Edwards said.

"Where? When? What did he look like? What did he say? Did he really give you something for us?" Mary and Laura cried.

"Wait, wait a minute!" Mr. Edwards laughed. And Ma said she would put the presents in the stockings, as Santa Claus intended. She said they mustn't look.

Mr. Edwards came and sat on the floor by their bed, and he answered every question they asked him. They honestly tried not to look at Ma, and they didn't quite see what she was doing.

When he saw the creek rising, Mr. Edwards said, he had known that Santa Claus could not get across it. ("But you crossed it," Laura said. "Yes," Mr. Edwards replied, "but Santa Claus is too old and fat. He couldn't make it, where a long, lean razor-back like me could do so.") And Mr. Edwards reasoned that if Santa Claus couldn't cross the creek, likely he would come no farther south than Independence. Why should he come forty miles across the prairie, only to be turned back? Of course he wouldn't do that!

So Mr. Edwards had walked to Independence. ("In the rain?" Mary asked. Mr. Edwards said he wore his rubber coat.) And there, coming down the street in Independence, he had met Santa Claus. ("In the daytime?" Laura asked. She hadn't thought that anyone could see Santa Claus in the daytime. No, Mr. Edwards said; it was night, but light shone out across the street from the saloons.)

Well, the first thing Santa Claus said was, "Hello, Edwards!" ("Did he know you?" Mary asked, and Laura asked, "How did you know he was really Santa Claus?" Mr. Edwards said that Santa Claus knew everybody. And he had recognized Santa at once by his whiskers. Santa Claus had the longest, thickest, whitest set of whiskers west of the Mississippi.)

So Santa Claus said, "Hello, Edwards! Last time I saw you you were sleeping on a corn-shuck bed in Tennessee." And Mr. Edwards well remembered the little pair of red-yarn mittens that Santa Claus had left for him that time.

Then Santa Claus said, "I understand you're living now down along the Verdigris River. Have you ever met up, down yonder, with two little young girls named Mary and Laura?"

"I surely am acquainted with them," Mr. Edwards replied.

"It rests heavy on my mind," said Santa Claus. "They are both of them sweet, pretty, good little young things, and I know they are expecting me. I surely do hate to disappoint two good little girls like them. Yet with the water up the way it is, I can't ever make it across that creek. I can figure no way whatsoever to get to their cabin this year Edwards," Santa Claus said. "Would you do me the favor to fetch them their gifts this one time?"

"I'll do that, and with pleasure," Mr. Edwards told him.

Then Santa Claus and Mr. Edwards stepped across the street to the hitching-posts where the pack-mule was tied. ("Didn't he have his reindeer?" Laura asked. "You know he couldn't," Mary said. "There isn't any snow." "Exactly," said Mr. Edwards. Santa Claus traveled with a pack-mule in the southwest.)

And Santa Claus uncinched the pack and looked through it, and he took out the presents for Mary and Laura.

"Oh, what are they?" Laura cried; but Mary asked, "Then what did he do?"

Then he shook hands with Mr. Edwards, and he swung up on his fine bay horse. Santa Claus rode well, for a man of his weight and build. And he tucked his long, white whiskers under his bandana. "So long, Edwards," he said, and he rode away on the Fort Dodge trail, leading his pack-mule and whistling. Laura and Mary were silent an instant, thinking of that. Then Ma said, "You may look now, girls."

Something was shining bright in the top of Laura's stocking. She squealed and jumped out of bed. So did Mary, but Laura beat her to the fireplace. And the shining thing was a glittering new tin cup. Mary had one exactly like it.

These new tin cups were their very own. Now they each had a cup to drink out of. Laura jumped up and down and shouted and laughed, but Mary stood still and looked with shining eyes at her own tin cup.

Then they plunged their hands into the stockings again. And they pulled out two long, long sticks of candy. It was peppermint candy, striped red and white. They looked and looked at that beautiful candy, and Laura licked her stick, just one lick. But Mary was not so greedy. She didn't take even one lick of her stick.

Those stockings weren't empty yet. Mary and Laura pulled out two small packages. They unwrapped them, and each found a little heart-shaped cake. Over their delicate brown tops was sprinkled white sugar. The sparkling grains lay like tiny drifts of snow.

The cakes were too pretty to eat. Mary and Laura just looked at them. But at last Laura turned hers over, and she nibbled a tiny nibble from underneath, where it wouldn't show. And the inside of that little cake was white!

It had been made of pure white flour, and sweetened with white sugar.

Laura and Mary never would have looked in their stockings again. The cups and the cakes and the candy were almost too much. They were too happy to speak. But Ma asked if they were sure the stockings were empty.

Then they put their arms down inside them, to make sure.

And in the very toe of each stocking was a shining bright, new penny!

They had never even thought of such a thing as having a penny. Think of having a whole penny for your very own. Think of having a cup and a cake and a stick of candy and a penny.

There never had been such a Christmas.

Now of course, right away, Laura and Mary should have thanked Mr. Edwards for bringing those lovely presents all the way from Independence. But they had forgotten all about Mr. Edwards. They had even forgotten Santa Claus. In a minute they would have remembered, but before they did, Ma said, gently, "Aren't you going to thank Mr. Edwards?"

"Oh, thank you, Mr. Edwards! Thank you!" they said, and they meant it with all their hearts. Pa shook Mr. Edwards' hand, too, and shook it again. Pa and Ma and Mr. Edwards acted as if they were almost crying. Laura didn't know why. So she gazed again at her beautiful presents.

She looked up again when Ma gasped. And Mr. Edwards was taking sweet potatoes out of his pockets. He said they had helped to balance the package on his head when he swam across the creek. He thought Pa and Ma might like them, with the Christmas turkey.

There were nine sweet potatoes. Mr. Edwards had brought them all the way from town, too. It was just too much. Pa said so. "It's too much, Edwards," he said. They never could thank him enough.

Mary and Laura were much too excited to eat breakfast. They drank the milk from their shining new cups, but they could not swallow the rabbit stew and the cornmeal mush.

"Don't make them, Charles," Ma said. "It will soon be dinnertime."

For Christmas dinner there was the tender, juicy, roasted turkey. There were the sweet potatoes, baked in the ashes and carefully wiped so that you could eat the good skins, too. There was a loaf of salt-rising bread made from the last of the white flour.

And after all that there were stewed dried blackberries and little cakes. But these little cakes were made with brown sugar and they did not have white sugar sprinkled over their tops.

Then Pa and Ma and Mr. Edwards sat by the fire and talked about Christmas times back in Tennessee and up north in the Big Woods. But Mary and Laura looked at their beautiful cakes and played with their pennies and drank water out of their new cups. And little by little they licked and sucked their sticks of candy, till each stick was sharp-pointed on one end.

That was a happy Christmas.[7]

✳

The Joy

# of Realization

"How many days till Christmas, Daddy?"

"Five more, honey."

"Daddy?"

"Hmm?"

"Daddy, how will I know it's Christmas?"

"Well, we'll go to church Christmas Eve; then we'll come home and have Mom's special supper."

"But Daddy, how do we really know that it's Christmas? That Jesus came?"

"When your brother places the Christ Child figure in the empty manger we will be reminded that Jesus came."

"But daddy . . ."

So, how did shepherds realize that the baby Mary placed in the manger was the Christ Child? And the wise men—how did they come to understand that the child they sought was God's only begotten Son?

An angel announced the good news, a heavenly choir sang His praises, and a shining star pointed the way. Christmas is the realization that God is in Christ.

That's a *real* realization.

Let's Keep Christmas

A SERMON BY PETER MARSHALL
NOTED MINISTER AND PAST CHAPLAIN
OF THE UNITED STATES SENATE.

WITH AN INTRODUCTION BY CATHERINE MARSHALL

INTRODUCTION

Soon after Peter Marshall came to the United States, he had an experience which he never forgot. What person can forget the moments when life is lifted above the ordinary and the splendor of God shines into human hearts?

It happened on Christmas Eve. New-found friends had opened their hearts and their home to the immigrant boy from Scotland. Joyously, Peter had helped decorate a fragrant spruce tree. Then he sat on a kitchen stool and carefully cut out cookies, decorating them with cherries and nuts.

Later there had been a family sing around the piano—"Silent Night, Holy Night," "God Rest Ye Merry, Gentlemen," "The Holly and the Ivy," and "O Little Town of Bethlehem." As they sang, into the house there came the unmistakable feeling of a Presence. Everyone felt it. It was something more than just the spirit of Christmas, that spirit of expectancy which warms the heart and melts into nothingness the arid practicability of other days. It was as if Christ Himself had entered that home and quietly joined the family circle.

Finally Peter said, "I must go . . . I've got a long drive ahead." The look on his face clearly revealed his reluctance to leave.

"If you must go," his host said, "I have just one request to make of you. Would you have a little prayer with us before you leave?"

So, as the family stood around the open fire, the voice with the pleasant Scottish burr had crowned a perfect evening with a prayer of gratitude that the Christ-child had come into the world.

Later, as Peter drove steadily through the clear moonlight night toward Birmingham, his thoughts were there with his friends in the little white house. Friendship was there—and love; joy and oneness and goodwill—and God. For that family the angel's prophecy had come true. For them, there was indeed "on earth peace, good will toward men."

And for other families too, who lived along the white ribbon of a road, the prophecy had become fact. Frosty stars seem to lean close over the rooftops of little homes. Lights streamed from the windows. Christmas lights twinkled on lawns. Once, as Peter drove along, he heard children caroling. From an open doorway came snatches of laughter. These people, too, were caught up in the all-pervading spirit of Christmas.

Suddenly, Peter was filled with a great wistfulness. It brought tears to his eyes. Even then, in other parts of the world, there was anything but music and laughter—only strikes and bread lines, hunger marches, rebellion, and bloodshed.

The thought in Peter's mind became a prayer on his lips . . . "Oh, God, why can't more people, all of us, open our hearts to the wonderful spirit abroad in the world tonight—not just on Christmas, but on every day? What a happy place this old earth could be if—oh God, if only we could keep Christmas the whole year through."   ✳

The Sermon

I thank God for Christmas. Would that it lasted all year. For on Christmas Eve, and Christmas Day, all the world is a better place, and men and women are more lovable. Love itself seeps into every heart, and miracles happen.

When Christmas doesn't make your heart swell up until it nearly bursts . . . and fill your eyes with tears . . . and make you all soft and warm inside . . . then you'll know that something inside of you is dead.

We hope that there will be snow for Christmas. Why? It is not really important, but it is so nice, and old-fashioned, and appropriate, we think.

Isn't it wonderful to think that nothing can really harm the joy of Christmas? . . .

Although your Christmas tree decorations will include many new gadgets, such as lights with bubbles in them, it's the old tree decorations that mean the most, the ones you save carefully from year to year . . . the crooked star that goes on the top of the tree . . . the ornaments that you've been so careful with.

And you'll bring out the tiny manger, and the shed, and the little figures of the Holy Family, and lovingly arrange them on the mantel or in the middle of the dining room table.

And getting the tree will be a family event, with great excitement for the children. . . .

And there will be a closet into which you'll forbid your husband to look, And he will be moving through the house mysteriously with bundles under his coat, and you'll pretend not to notice.

There will be the fragrance of cookies baking, spices and fruitcake . . . and the warmth of the house shall be melodious with the lilting strains of "Silent Night, Holy Night."

And you'll listen to the wonderful Christmas music on the radio, Some of the songs will be modern—good enough music perhaps—

but it will be the old carols, the lovely old Christmas hymns that will mean the most.

And forests of fir trees will march right into our living rooms. . . . There will be bells on our doors and holly wreaths in our windows . . . And we shall sweep the Noel skies for their brightest colors and festoon our homes with stars.

There will be a chubby stocking hung by the fireplace . . . and with finger to lip you will whisper and ask me to tiptoe, for a little tousled head is asleep and must not be awakened until after Santa has come.

And finally Christmas morning will come. Don't worry—you'll be ready for it—You'll catch the spirit all right, or it will catch you, which is even better.

And then you will remember what Christmas means . . . the beginning of Christianity . . . the Second Chance for the world . . . the hope for peace . . . and the only way.

The promise that the angels sang is the most wonderful music the world has ever heard. "Peace on earth and good will toward men."[8] ✳

The Shepherd Speaks

Out of the midnight sky a great dawn broke,

And a voice singing flooded us with song.

In David's city was He born, it sang,

A Saviour, Christ the Lord. Then while I sat

Shivering with the thrill of that great cry,

A mighty choir a thousandfold more sweet

Suddenly sang, Glory to God, and Peace—

Peace on the earth; my heart, almost unnerved

By the swift loveliness, would hardly beat.

Speechless we waited till the accustomed night

Gave us no promise more sweet surprise;

Then scrambling to our feet, without a word

We started through the fields to find the Child.[9]

JOHN ERSKINE

How Far to Bethlehem?

"How far is it to Bethlehem town?"
   Just over the Jerusalem hills adown,
Past lovely Rachel's white-domed tomb—
   Sweet shrine of motherhood's young doom.

It isn't far to Bethlehem town—
   Just over the dusty roads adown,
Past Wise Men's well, still offering
   Cool draughts from welcome wayside spring;
Past shepherds with their flutes of reed
   That charm the wooly sheep they lead;

Past boys with kites on hill-tops flying,
   And soon you're there where Bethlehem's lying,
Sunned white and sweet on olived slopes,
   Gold-lighted still with Judah's hopes.

And so we find the Shepherd's field
   The plain that gave rich Boaz yield;
And look where Herod's villa stood.
   We thrill that earthly parenthood
Could foster Christ who was all good;
   And thrill that Bethlehem town today
Looks down on Christian homes that pray.

It isn't far to Bethlehem town!
   It's anywhere that Christ comes down
And finds in people's friendly face
   A welcome and abiding place.

The road to Bethlehem runs right through
   The homes of folks like me and you.[10]

MADELEINE SWEENY MILLER

A Gift From the Heart

BY NORMAN VINCENT PEALE

New York City, where I live, is impressive at any time, but as Christmas approaches, it's overwhelming. Store windows blaze with light and color, furs and jewels. Golden angels, forty feet tall, hover over Fifth Avenue. Wealth, power, opulence . . . nothing in the world can match this fabulous display.

Through the gleaming canyons, people hurry to find last-minute gifts. Money seems to be no problem. If there's a problem, it's that the recipients so often have everything they need or want that it's hard to find anything suitable, anything that will really say "I love you."

Last December, as Christ's birthday drew near, a stranger was faced with just that problem. She had come from Switzerland to live in an American home and perfect her English. In return, she was willing to act as secretary, mind the grandchildren, do anything she was asked. She was just a girl in her late teens. Her name was Ursula.

One of the tasks her employers gave Ursula was keeping track of Christmas presents as they arrived. There were many, and all would require an acknowledgement. Ursula kept a faithful record, but with a growing sense of concern. She was grateful to her American friends; she wanted to show her gratitude by giving them a Christmas present. But nothing that she could buy with her small allowance could compare with the gifts she was recording daily. Besides, even without these gifts, it seemed to her that her employer already had everything.

At night, from her window, Ursula could see the snowy expanse of Central Park, and beyond it the jagged skyline of the city. Far below, in the restless streets, taxis hooted and traffic lights winked red and green. It was so different from the silent majesty of the Alps that at times she had to blink back tears of the homesickness she was careful never to show. It was in the solitude of her little room, a few days before Christmas, that her secret idea came to Ursula.

It was almost as if a voice spoke clearly, inside her head. "It's true," said the voice, "that many people in this city have much more than you do. But surely there are many people who have far less. If thou will think about this, you may find a solution to what's troubling you."

Ursula thought long and hard. Finally on her day off, which was Christmas Eve, she went to a great department store. She moved slowly along the crowded aisles, selecting and rejecting things in her mind. At last she bought something, and had it wrapped in gaily colored paper. She went out into the gray twilight and looked helplessly around. Finally she went up to a doorman, resplendent in blue and gold. "Excuse, please," she said in her hesitant English, "can you tell me where to find a poor street?"

"A poor street, miss?" said the puzzled man.

"Yes, a very poor street. The poorest in the city."

The doorman looked doubtful. "Well, you might try Harlem. Or down in the Village. Or the Lower East Side, maybe."

But these names meant nothing to Ursula. She thanked the doorman and walked along, threading her way through the stream of shoppers until she came to a tall policeman. "Please," she said, "can you direct me to a very poor street in . . . in Harlem?"

The policeman looked at her sharply and shook his head. "Harlem's no place for you, miss." And he blew his whistle and sent the traffic swirling past.

Holding her package carefully, Ursula walked on, head bowed against the sharp wind. If a street looked poorer than the one she was on, she took it. But none seemed like the slums she had heard about. Once she stopped a woman, "Please, where do the very poor people live?" But the woman gave her a stare and hurried on.

Darkness came sifting from the sky. Ursula was cold and discouraged and afraid of becoming lost. She came to an intersection and stood forlornly on the corner. What she was trying to do suddenly seemed foolish, impulsive, absurd. Then, through the traffic's roar, she heard the cheerful tinkle of a bell. On the corner opposite, a Salvation Army man was making his traditional Christmas appeal.

At once Ursula felt better; the Salvation Army was a part of life in Switzerland, too. Surely this man could tell her what she wanted to know. She waited for the light, then crossed over to him. "Can you help me? I'm looking for a baby. I have here a little present for the poorest baby I can find." And she held up the package with the green ribbon and the gaily colored paper.

Dressed in gloves and overcoat a size too big for him, he seemed a very ordinary man. But behind his steel-rimmed glasses his eyes were kind. He looked at Ursula and stopped ringing his bell. "What sort of present?" he asked.

"A little dress. For a small, poor baby. Do you know of one?"

"Oh, yes," he said. "Of more than one, I'm afraid."

"Is it far away? I could take a taxi, maybe?"

The Salvation Army man wrinkled his forehead. Finally he said, "It's almost six o'clock. My relief will show up then. If you want to wait, and if you afford a dollar taxi ride, I'll take you to a family in my own neighborhood who needs just about everything."

"And they have a small baby?"

"A very small baby."

"Then," said Ursula joyfully, "I wait!"

The substitute bell-ringer came. A cruising taxi slowed. In its welcome warmth, she told her new friend about herself, how she came to be in New York, what she was trying to do. He listened in silence, and the taxi driver listened too. When they reached their destination, the driver said, "Take your time, missy, I'll wait for you."

On the sidewalk, Ursula stared up at the forbidding tenement— dark, decaying, saturated with hopelessness. A gust of wind, iron-cold, stirred the refuse in the street and rattled the reeling trash cans. "They live on the third floor," the Salvation Army man said. "Shall we go up?"

But Ursula shook her head. "They would try to thank me, and this is not from me." She pressed the package into his hand. "Take it up for me, please. Say it's from . . . from someone who has everything."

The taxi bore her swiftly from dark streets to lighted ones, from misery to abundance. She tried to visualize the Salvation Army man climbing the stairs, the knock, the explanation, the package being opened, the dress on the baby. It was hard to do.

Arriving at the apartment house on Fifth Avenue where she lived, she fumbled in her purse. But the driver flicked the flag up. "No charge, miss."

"No charge?" echoed Ursula, bewildered.

"Don't worry," the driver said. "I've been paid." He smiled at her and drove away.

Ursula was up early the next day. She set the table with special care. By the time she had finished, the family was awake, and there was all the excitement and laughter of Christmas morning. Soon the living room was a sea of gay discarded wrappings. Ursula thanked everyone for the presents she received. Finally, when there was a lull, she began to explain hesitantly why there seemed to be none from her. She told about going to the department store. She told about the Salvation Army man. She told about the taxi driver. When she finished, there was a long silence. No one seemed to trust himself to speak. "So you see," said Ursula, "I try to do a kindness in your name. And this is my Christmas present to you. . . ."

How do I happen to know all this? I know it because ours was the home where Ursula lived. Ours was the Christmas she shared. We were like many Americans, so richly blessed that to this child from across the sea there seemed to be nothing she could add to the material things we already had. And so she offered something of far greater value: a gift from the heart, an act of kindness carried out in our name.

Strange, isn't it? A shy Swiss girl, alone in a great impersonal city. You would think that nothing she could do would affect anyone. And yet, by trying to give away love, she brought the true spirit of Christmas into our lives, the spirit of selfless giving. That was Ursula's secret—and she shared it with us all.[11] ✳

The Road to Bethlehem

Above the road to Bethlehem
    When I was very young,
A twilight sky of tender blue
    With golden stars was hung;

And kneeling at the stable door,
    I happily confessed
My humble worship of the Child
    Who slept at Mary's breast.

But now the road to Bethlehem
    Seems cold and steep and far;
It wanders through a wilderness
    Unlit by any star.

The earth I tread is frozen hard;
    The winter chills my breath;
On either hand rise evil shapes
    From valleys dark with death.

The air is tense with moans of pain
  And cries of bitter hate,
Where bloodstained hills and
    shattered stones
Lie black and desolate.

How can the sacred heart of God
  Heal all this guilt and grief?
Lord, I believe, And yet, this night,
  Help Thou mine unbelief!

Purge Thou mine eyes, that they may see
  Thy Star across the gloom!
Touch Thou my heart, that I may lose
  These agonies of gloom!

Now in the darkness guide my feet,
  Give holy strength to them
To walk with childlike faith once more
  The road to Bethlehem![12]

WATSON KIRKCONNELL

*　*　*

When the Word declares that Mary pondered

all that happened in the birth of Jesus,

does that mean she fully realized who

the Child was Who lay in the crook of her arm?

Did she fully realize His mission?

Creative preacher and writer Max Lucado

helps us appreciate what Mary may

have pondered that night.

*　*　*

Mary's Prayer

BY MAX LUCADO

God. Infant—God. Heaven's fairest child. Conceived by the union of divine grace with our disgrace. Sleep well.

Sleep well. Bask in the coolness of this night bright with diamonds. Sleep well, for the heat of anger simmers nearby. Enjoy the silence of the crib, for the noise of confusion rumbles in your future. Savor the sweet safety of my arms, for a day is soon coming when I cannot protect you.

Rest well, tiny hands. For though you belong to a king, you will touch no satin, own no gold. You will grasp no pen, guide no brush. No, your tiny hands are reserved for works more precious:

to touch a leper's open wound,
to wipe a widow's weary tear,
to claw the ground of Gethsemane.

Your hands, so tiny, so tender, so white—clutched tonight in an infant's fist. They aren't destined to hold a scepter nor wave from a palace balcony. They are reserved instead for a Roman spike that will staple them to a Roman cross.

Sleep deeply, tiny eyes. Sleep while you can. For soon the blurriness will clear and You will see the mess we have made of Your world.

You will see our nakedness, for we cannot hide.

You will see our selfishness, for we cannot give.

You will see our pain, for we cannot heal.

O eyes that will see hell's darkest pit and witness her ugly prince . . . sleep, please sleep; sleep while You can.

Lay still, tiny mouth. Lay still mouth from which eternity will speak.

Tiny tongue that will soon summon the dead,

>   that will define grace,

>   that will silence our foolishness.

Rosebud lips—upon which ride a starborn kiss of forgiveness to those who believe in you, and of death to those who deny You—lay still.

And tiny feet cupped in the palm of my hand, rest. For many difficult steps lie ahead for You.

Do You taste the dust of the trails You will travel?

Do You feel the cold sea water upon which You will walk?

Do You wrench at the invasion of the nails You will bear?

Do You fear the steep descent down the spiral staircase into Satan's domain?

Rest, tiny feet. Rest today so that tomorrow You might walk with power. Rest. For millions will follow in Your steps.

And little heart . . . holy heart . . . pumping the blood of life through the universe: How many times will we break You?

You'll be torn by the thorns of our accusations.

You'll be ravaged by the cancer of our sin.

You'll be crushed under the weight of Your own sorrow.

And You'll be pierced by the spear of our rejection.

Yet in that piercing, in that ultimate ripping of muscle and membrane, in that final rush of blood and water, You will find rest. Your hands will be freed, Your eyes will see justice, Your lips will smile, and Your feet will carry You home.

And there You'll rest again—this time in the embrace of Your Father.[13]

Judean Hills Are Holy

Judean hills are holy,
Judean fields are fair,
For one can find the footprints
Of Jesus everywhere.

One finds them in the twilight
Beneath the singing sky,
Where shepherds watch in wonder
White planets wheeling by.

His trails are on the hillsides
And down the dales and deeps;
He walks the high horizons
Where vesper silence sleeps.
He haunts the lowly highways
Where human hopes have trod
The Via Dolorosa
Up to the heart of God.

He looms, a lonely figure,
Along the fringe of night,
As lonely as a cedar
Against the lonely light.

Judean hills are holy,
Judean fields are fair,
For one can find the footprints
Of Jesus everywhere.[14]

WILLIAM L. STIDGER

Christmas Prayer

Let not our hearts be busy inns,
That have no room for Thee,
But cradles for the living Christ
And His nativity.

Still driven by a thousand cares
The pilgrims come and go;
The hurried caravans press on;
The inns are crowded so!

Here are the rich and busy ones,
With things that must be sold,
No room for simple things within
This hostelry of God.

Yet hunger dwells within these walls,
These shining walls and bright,
And blindness groping here and there
Without a ray of light.

Oh, lest we starve, and lest we die,
In our stupidity,
Come, Holy Child, within and share
Our hospitality.

Let not hearts be busy inns,
That have no room for Thee,
But cradles for the living Christ
And His nativity.[15]

RALPH SPAULDING CUSHMAN

An Offertory

Oh, the beauty of the Christ Child
The gentleness, the grace,
The smiling, loving tenderness,
The infantile embrace!
All babyhood he holdeth,
All motherhood enfoldeth—
Yet who hath seen his face?

Oh, the nearness of the Christ Child,
When, for a sacred space,
He nestles in our very homes—
Light of the human race!
We know him and we love him,
No man to us need prove him—
Yet who hath seen his face?[16]

MARY MAPES DODGE

Dear God

Dear God
    help me to have Christmas
in my heart every day
    so that I may give gifts
of summer dandelions
    or winter pine boughs
and know joy.

Help me to see
    a snowflake
or a grain of sand,
    a blade of grass
or a turning leaf
that I may know beauty.

Help me to hear
    silence and church bells,
laughter and music
    that I may know
the sound of Your voice.

Help me to feel
    someone else's smile or tear
that I might know
    understanding.

Help me to learn
    about different people
and religions,
    different customs
and lands
    that I may know
the width
    of Your kingdom.

Help me to receive
    Your gift of love.[17]

Deborah Killip

The Consecration of the Common Way

The hills that had been long and lean

Were pricking with a tender green,

And flocks were whitening over them

From all the folds of Bethlehem.

The King of Heaven had come our way,

And in a lowly stable lay:

He had descended from the sky

In answer to the world's long cry—

Descended in a lyric burst

Of high archangels, going first

Unto the lowest and the least,

To humble bird and weary beast.

His palace was a wayside shed;

A battered manger was his bed:

An ox and ass with breathings deep

Made warm the chamber of his sleep.

Three sparrows with a friendly sound

Were picking barley from the ground:

An early sunbeam, long and thin,

Slanted across the dark within

And brightened in its silver fall

A cart-wheel leaning to the wall.

An ox-yoke hung upon a hook:

A worn plow with a clumsy crook

Was lying idly by the wheel.

And everywhere there was the feel

Of that sweet peace that labor brings—

The peace that dwells with homely things.

Now have the homely things been made

Sacred, and a glory on them laid,

For He whose shelter was a stall,

The King was born among them all.

He came to handle saw and plane,

To use and hallow the profane:

Now is the holy not afar

In temples lighted by a star,

But where the loves and labors are.

Now the King has gone away,

Great are the things of everyday![18]

EDWIN MARKHAM

Love can cause mere mortals
or a nice young couple to disregard personal
sacrifice—until comes the realization . . .

The Gift of the Magi

BY O. HENRY

One dollar and eighty-seven cents. That was all. And sixty cents of it was in pennies. Pennies saved one and two at a time by bull-dozing the grocer and the vegetable man and the butcher until one's cheeks burned with the silent imputation of parsimony that such close dealing implied. Three times Della counted it. One dollar and eighty-seven cents. And the next day would be Christmas.

There was clearly nothing to do but flop down on the shabby little couch and howl. So Della did it. Which instigates the moral reflection that life is made up of sobs, sniffles, and smiles, with sniffles predominating.

While the mistress of the home is gradually subsiding from the first stage to the second, take a look at the home. A furnished flat at $8 per week. It did not exactly beggar description, but it certainly had that word on the lookout for the mendicancy squad.

In the vestibule below was a letter-box into which no letter would go, and an electric button from which no mortal finger could coax a ring. Also appertaining hereunto was a card bearing the name "Mr. James Dillingham Young."

The "Dillingham" had been flung to the breeze during a former period of prosperity when its possessor was being paid $30 per week. Now, when the income was shrunk to $20, the letters of "Dillingham" looked blurred, as though they were thinking seriously of contracting to a modest and unassuming D. But whenever Mr. James Dillingham Young came home and reached his flat above he was called "Jim" and greatly hugged by Mrs. James Dillingham Young, already introduced to you as Della. Which is all very good.

Della finished her cry and attended to her cheeks with the powder rag. She stood by the window and looked out dully at a gray cat walking a gray fence in a gray backyard. Tomorrow would be Christmas Day, and she had only $1.87 with which to buy Jim a present. She had been saving every penny she could for months, with this result. Twenty dollars a week doesn't go far. Expenses had been greater than she had calculated. They always are. Only $ 1.87 to buy a present for Jim. Her Jim. Many a happy hour she had spent planning for something nice for him. Something fine and rare and sterling— something just a little bit near to being worthy of the honor of being owned by Jim.

There was a pier-glass between the windows of the room. Perhaps you have seen a pier-glass in an $8 flat. A very thin and very agile person may, by observing his reflection in a rapid sequence of longitudinal strips, obtain a fairly accurate conception of his looks. Della, being slender, had mastered the art.

Suddenly she whirled from the window and stood before the glass. Her eyes were shining brilliantly, but her face had lost its color within twenty seconds. Rapidly she pulled down her hair and let it fall to its full length.

Now, there were two possessions of the James Dillingham Youngs in which they both took a mighty pride. One was Jim's gold watch that had been his father's and his grandfather's. The other was Della's hair. Had the Queen of Sheba lived in the flat across the airshaft, Della would have let her hair hang out the window some day to dry just to depreciate Her Majesty's jewels and gifts. Had King Solomon been the janitor, with all his treasures piled up in the basement, Jim would have pulled out his watch every time he passed, just to see him pluck at his beard from envy.

So now Della's beautiful hair fell about her rippling and shining like a cascade of brown waters. It reached below her knee and made itself almost a garment for her. And then she did it up again nervously and quickly. Once she faltered for a minute and stood still while a tear or two splashed on the worn red carpet.

On went her old brown jacket; on went her old brown hat. With a whirl of skirts and with the brilliant sparkle still in her eyes, she fluttered out the door and down the stairs to the street.

Where she stopped the sign read: "Mme. Sofronie. Hair Goods of All Kinds." One flight up Della ran, and collected herself, panting. Madame, large, too white, chilly, hardly looked the "Sofronie."

"Will you buy my hair?" asked Della.

"I buy hair," said Madame. "Take yer hat off and let's have a sight at the looks of it."

Down rippled the brown cascade.

"Twenty dollars," said Madame, lifting the mass with a practiced hand.

"Give it to me quick," said Della.

Oh, and the next two hours tripped by on rosy wings. Forget the hashed metaphor. She was ransacking the stores for Jim's present.

She found it at last. It surely had been made for Jim and no one else. There was no other like it in any of the stores, and she had turned all of them inside out. It was a platinum fob chain simple and chaste in design, properly proclaiming its value by substance alone and not by meretricious ornamentation—as all good things should do. It was even worthy of The Watch. As soon as she saw it she knew that it must be Jim's. It was like him. Quietness and value—the description applied to both. Twenty-one dollars they took from her for it, and she hurried home with the 87 cents. With that chain on his watch Jim might be properly anxious about the time in any company. Grand as the watch was, he sometimes looked at it on the sly on account of the old leather strap that he used in place of a chain.

When Della reached home her intoxication gave way a little to prudence and reason. She got out her curling irons and lighted the gas and went to work repairing the ravages made by generosity added to love. Which is always a tremendous task, dear friends—a mammoth task.

Within forty minutes her head was covered with tiny, close-lying curls that made her look wonderfully like a truant schoolboy. She looked at her reflection in the mirror long, carefully, and critically.

"If Jim doesn't kill me," she said to herself, "before he takes a second look at me, he'll say I look like a Coney Island chorus girl. But what could I do—oh! what could I do with a dollar and eighty-seven cents?"

At 7 o'clock the coffee was made and the frying-pan was on the back of the stove hot and ready to cook the chops.

Jim was never late. Della doubled the fob chain in her hand and sat on the corner of the table near the door that he always entered. Then she heard his step on the stairway down on the first flight, and she turned white for just a moment. She had a habit of saying little silent prayers about the simplest everyday things, and now she whispered: "Please God, make him think I am still pretty."

The door opened and Jim stepped in and closed it. He looked thin and very serious. Poor fellow, he was only twenty-two—and to be burdened with a family! He needed a new overcoat and he was without gloves.

Jim stopped inside the door, as immovable as a setter at the scent of quail. His eyes were fixed upon Della, and there was an expression in them that she could not read, and it terrified her. It was not anger, nor surprise, nor disapproval, nor horror, nor any of the sentiments that she had been prepared for. He simply stared at her fixedly with that peculiar expression on his face.

Della wriggled off the table and went for him.

"Jim, darling," she cried, "don't look at me that way. I had my hair cut off and sold it because I couldn't have lived through Christmas without giving you a present. It'll grow out again—you won't mind, will you? I just had to do it. My hair grows awfully fast. Say 'Merry Christmas!' Jim, and let's be happy. You don't known what a nice— what a beautiful, nice gift I've got for you."

"You've cut off your hair?" asked Jim, laboriously, as if he had not arrived at that patent fact yet even after the hardest mental labor.

"Cut it off and sold it," said Della. "Don't you like me just as well, anyhow? I'm me without my hair, ain't I?"

Jim looked about the room curiously.

"You say your hair is gone?" he said, with an air almost of idiocy.

"You needn't look for it," said Della. "It's sold, I tell you—sold and gone, too. It's Christmas Eve, boy. Be good to me, for it went for you. Maybe the hairs of my head were numbered," she went on with a sudden serious sweetness, "but nobody could ever count my love for you. Shall I put the chops on, Jim?"

Out of his trance Jim seemed quickly to wake. He enfolded his Della. For ten seconds let us regard with discreet scrutiny some inconsequential object in the other direction. Eight dollars a week or a million a year—what is the difference? A mathematician or a wit would give you the wrong answer. The magi brought valuable gifts, but that was not among them. This dark assertion will be illuminated later on.

Jim drew a package from his overcoat pocket and threw it upon the table.

"Don't make any mistake, Dell," he said, "about me. I don't think there's anything in the way of a haircut or a shave or a shampoo that could make me like my girl any less. But if you'll unwrap that package you may see why you had me going a while at first."

White fingers and nimble tore at the string and paper. And then an ecstatic scream of joy; and then, alas! a quick feminine change to hysterical tears and wails, necessitating the immediate employment of all the comforting powers of the lord of the flat.

For there lay The Combs—the set of combs, side and back, that Della had worshipped for long in a Broadway window. Beautiful combs, pure tortoise shell, with jewelled rims—just the shade to wear in the beautiful vanished hair. They were expensive combs, she knew, and her heart had simply craved and yearned over them without the least hope of possession. And now, they were hers, but the tresses that should have adorned the coveted adornments were gone.

But she hugged them to her bosom, and at length she was able to look up with dim eyes and a smile and say: "My hair grows so fast, Jim!"

And then Della leaped up like a little singed cat and cried, "Oh, oh!"

Jim had not yet seen his beautiful present. She held it out to him eagerly upon her open palm. The dull precious metal seemed to flash with a reflection of her bright and ardent spirit.

"Isn't it a dandy, Jim? I hunted all over town to find it. You'll have to look at the time a hundred times a day now. Give me your watch. I want to see how it looks on it."

Instead of obeying, Jim tumbled down on the couch and put his hands under the back of his head and smiled. "Dell," said he, "let's put our Christmas presents away and keep 'em a while. They're too nice to use just at present. I sold the watch to get the money to buy your combs. And now suppose you put the chops on."

The magi, as you know, were wise men—wonderfully wise men— who brought gifts to the Babe in the manger. They invented the art of giving Christmas presents. Being wise, their gifts were no doubt wise ones, possibly bearing the privilege of exchange in case of duplication. And here I have lamely related to you the uneventful chronicle of two foolish children in a flat who most unwisely sacrificed for each other the greatest treasures of their house. But in a last word to the wise of these days let it be said that of all who give gifts these two were the wisest. Of all who give and receive gifts, such as they are wisest. Everywhere they are wisest. They are the magi.[19]   ✳

The Joy

Giving

# of Giving

Some say it was the generosity of the Wise Men from the East that initiated the practice of Christmas gift-giving. Others believe gift-giving is recognition of a Heavenly Father Who gave His Son to a needy world. Whichever is the motivation behind our delightful tradition of giving gifts at Christmas, it is important to remember that the new tie or the electric train set is a way of saying "because we love, we give—not get!"

When any of us think of Christmas morning we see "children's faces looking up, holding wonder like a cup." The wonder of giving to those we love . . . to those we have never met . . . to those into whose lives the Bethlehem Babe must be born anew!

Remember this verse by Christina Rossetti?

> What can I give Him
> Poor as I am?
> If I were a Shepherd,
> I would give Him a lamb
> If I were a Wise Man,
> I would do my part,—
> But what I can I give Him,
> I give Him my heart.

Christmas Gifts

Some packages are lovely
With fancy bow and tie;
The paper looks so glossy
It captivates the eye.

It's not the pretty ribbon
Or cover bright and bold,
But the spirit of the giver
Hidden in the fold.

Wrap a little of yourself
And tie it with a smile,
Fill it full of warmth and love
And give a gift worthwhile.[20]

BETTY COOKE

Christian Paradox

It is in loving—not in being loved,—
　　The heart is blest;
It is in giving—not in seeking gifts,—
　　We find our quest.

If thou art hungry, lacking heavenly food,—
　　Give hope and cheer.
If thou art sad and wouldst be comforted,—
　　Stay sorrow's tear.

Whatever be thy longing and thy need,—
　　That do thou give;
So shall thy soul be fed, and thou indeed,
　　Shalt truly live.

AUTHOR UNKNOWN

* * *

Christmas hospitality can be a gift

without equal. In a 1907 book of holiday

suggestions, a writer known only as

H. H. presents a dinner menu that

should warm the heart of any guest.

* * *

A Simple Bill of Fare for a Christmas Dinner

BY H. H.

All good recipe books give bills of fare for different occasions, bills of fare for grand dinners, bills of fare for little dinners; dinner to cost so much per head; dinners "which can be easily prepared with one servant," and so on. They give bills of fare for one week; bills of fare for each day in a month, to avoid too great monotony in diet.

There are bills of fare for dyspeptics; bills of fare for consumptives, bills of fare for fat people, and bills of fare for thin; and bills of fare for hospitals, asylums, and prisons, as well as for gentlemen's houses. But among them all, we never saw the one which we give below. It has never been printed in any book; but it has been used in families. We are not drawing on our imagination for its items. We have sat at such dinner; we have helped prepare such dinners; we believe in such dinners; they are within everyone's means.

In fact the most marvelous thing about this bill of fare is that the dinner does not cost a cent. Ho! All ye that are hungry and thirsty, and would like so cheap a Christmas dinner, listen to this:

BILL OF FARE FOR A CHRISTMAS DINNER

FIRST COURSE—GLADNESS.

This must be served hot. No two housekeepers make it alike; no fixed rule can be given for it. It depends, like so many of the best things, chiefly on memory; but strangely enough, it depends quite as much on proper forgetting as it does on proper remembering. Worries must be forgotten. Troubles must be forgotten. Yes, even sorrow itself must be denied and shut out. Perhaps this is not quite possible. Ah! We have all seen

Christmas Days on which sorrow would not leave our hearts nor our houses. But even sorrow can be compelled to look away from its sorrowing for a festival which is so joyous at Christ's birthday.

Memory can be filled full of other things to be remembered. No soul is entirely destitute of blessings, absolutely without comfort. Perhaps we have but one. Very well; we can think steadfastly on that one. But the probability is that we have more than we can count. We are all richer than we think.

Gladness, then is the first item, the first course on our bill of fare for a Christmas dinner.

ENTRÉES—LOVE GARNISHED WITH SMILES.

Gentleness. Serve with sweet wine sauce of Laughter.

Gracious Speech. Cook with any fine savory herbs, such as Frollery, which is always in season, or Pleasant Reminiscence, which no one needs to be without.

SECOND COURSE—HOSPITALITY.

In some houses Hospitality is brought on surrounded with Relatives. This is very well. In other houses, it is dished up with Dignitaries of all sorts. This gives a fine effect to the eye, but cools quickly.

In the third class, which is best of all, hospitality is served in simple shapes, but with a great variety of Unfortunate Persons—those who need Love, Gentleness, and Hospitality.

DESSERT—MIRTH

Gratitude and Faith beaten together and piled up in snowy shapes. These will look light if run over night in the molds of Solid Trust and Patience.

Consider providing a dish of the bon bons of Good Cheer and Kindliness.

This is a short and simple bill of fare. There is not a costly thing in it.

Note: If meat is desired, it can be added. That is another reason the bill of fare is so excellent; there is nothing about it that makes it incongruent with the richest or the plainest of fare.[21]   ✳

* * *

Just about as long as author Catherine often

can remember, one of the best Christmas

presents Mama ever gave

her family was her gift of Christmas

"bountifulness" that was the result

of a long-time family secret.

* * *

And For As Long As I Can Remember . . .

BY CATHERINE OTTEN

Mama wasn't stingy—far from it—but I never saw her spend a dime. When we were young, I suppose we didn't notice her thrifty quirk, but as we grew up, we all worried about Mama's concern with dimes.

Mama ran our house like a tight little ship. She and Papa set the course for their young crew, which was made up of my two sisters, my two brothers, and me.

The term "good old days" could have originated in our home. Mama never ran out of energy or food and we seldom ate Sunday suppers alone. Unexpected company usually dropped in, and there was always enough food to go around—Mama's Saturday baking binge took care of that. Little did we youngsters know or care that those were the days of the Depression. But we never felt deprived.

Years slipped by, and one by one we left home to start families of our own. When Papa retired, he and Mama moved into our summer cottage.

During our visits, we became more aware of Mama's obsession with dimes. When we shopped with her, she refused to use a single dime, even if it meant breaking a dollar bill to pay for a ten-cent item. What was wrong with our mother?

Christmas was the time we all gathered for a big family dinner. Mama would have it no other way.

"Dinner is at four o'clock," Mama would say. "Just bring yourselves, and don't be late."

Dad would be busy for weeks making wreaths from the pine trees in the yard. One Christmas every window boasted a small wreath, and a huge one decorated the door.

By the time the last family arrived with their treasures, the pile of gifts resembled a pyramid, competing in height and beauty with the shining Christmas tree.

The Christmas dinner table was another picture that we shall never forget. It had been pulled out into the living room, and stretched to its full length. The shining dishes and silverware had been polished to the hilt for the occasion.

The centerpiece was always the same—little wax candles skaters, snowmen, angels, animals and trees carefully placed on the raised round reflector. The sparkling wine glasses and water goblets resembled a picket fence around the relish dishes, salads, cranberries, biscuits, mints, and nuts.

The hot dishes were brought in with ceremony. The huge, golden-brown turkey was placed in front of Papa. Then came platters of buttery vegetables and heaping bowls of mashed and sweet potatoes. Papa led grace as our eyes feasted on the picture before us. We toasted everyone's welfare in the coming year, and the feast began.

One Christmas, as we put away the dishes and the leftovers, we girls ganged up on Mama and insisted on sharing the expenses of the day. She was quiet for a bit, and then she revealed her secret.

"Don't worry children," she laughed. "I pay for it all with a year of dimes that I've saved."

We looked at each other guiltily. Our concern over Mama's thing with dimes melted into relief. The joke was on us!

Years have passed since that Christmas. Now my children are grown and raising families of their own, passing on the giving-traditions that our parents gave to us.[22]   ✳

✳ ✳ ✳

There was a kinder and gentler Christmas

kindler,

season that may have been lost in the flurry

gentler,

of commerce and the entertainment industry.

Christmas

These words were discovered in a 1911

scrapbook of favorite clippings.

✳ ✳ ✳

In the Glow
of Christmas

BY JOE MITCHELL CHAPPLE

*I*n the glow of Christmas giving and merriment our hearts become suffused with the Christ-like impulse of kindly, gentle greeting, and respect for the rights of others, obedience to the most lofty ideals of human exchanges, and deference to our fellow-beings as life seems illuminated by the ineffable and softened light of the Star of Bethlehem.

Let us sit down, in the twilight, by the flickering firelight, and think over for a moment just how much we owe to others for whatever happiness we enjoy. Think a moment—think reflectively, as did Sidney Lanier when he wrote:

I shut myself in with my soul,
And the shapes come eddying forth.

Think tenderly and lovingly—and forms and faces crowd upon the vision that perhaps have been long forgotten in the tumult of life. Among the first are those of mother and father, from whose ideals, years ago, were gained the impulses that led to honorable achievement. Here is a vision of the passing friend, whose memory is only preserved in a yellow bundle of letters—letters from whose fading sentences came the inspiration that influences a life career.

Nor are all faces those of the dead. Many, indeed, are still seen in everyday life. Our friends—the people we meet in business or join in pleasure—how many have helped to mold our lives as we reckon them up in the fading light of the Christmas fire!

I am reminded of the famous painting which hangs for universal inspiration in Watts' room in the Wallace collection, on the Thames embankment in London. A great world circling through infinite space is represented—surmounted by a harp with but one string; but that string vibrates with the spirit of Hope, and underneath is a motto especially appropriate for Christmastide—

"To give is to gain."

And unless Christmas can be kept as a time of giving; unless that giving means some sacrifice and some radiance of joy and comfort and hope to a human being, it will indeed be a dull and cheerless Yuletide.

Let this Christmas be one of happiness, and the new year will be radiant with hope and filled with impulse of doing something for someone every day. The books will balance if the impulse be actuated by fair play—fair play to every fellow being.

With this sublimation will come the great consciousness of peace and benediction from Him who having lived a perfect life on earth now reigns over that universal kingdom toward which the heart and soul of man have ever turned for the "peace that passeth understanding" and the good will whose primal chord vibrates the harp strings of Hope.[23]　　　✳

I can only give myself, I have nothing left but this.

Advent

I have no more gold;
I spent it all on foolish songs,
Gold I cannot give to you.

Incense, too, I burned
To the great idols of this world;
I must come with empty hands.

Myrrh I lost
In that darker sepulcher
Where another Christ
Died for man in vain.—

I can only give myself,
I have nothing left but this.
Naked I wait, naked I fall
Into Your Hands, Your Hands.

JOHN GOULD FLETCHER

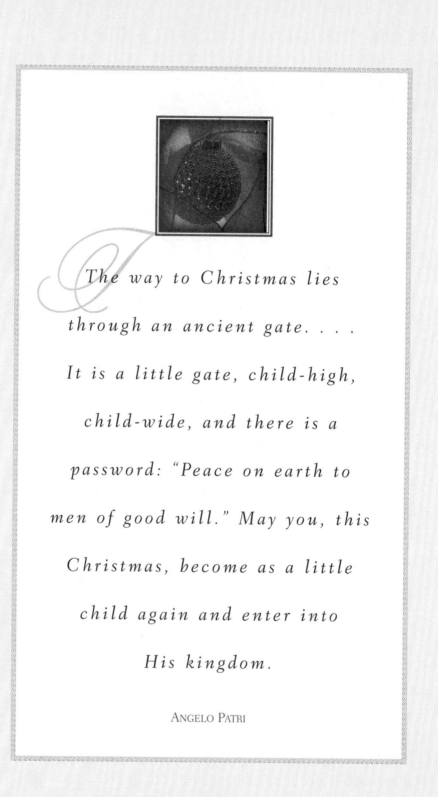

The way to Christmas lies through an ancient gate. . . . It is a little gate, child-high, child-wide, and there is a password: "Peace on earth to men of good will." May you, this Christmas, become as a little child again and enter into His kingdom.

ANGELO PATRI

My Christmas Miracle

BY TAYLOR CALDWELL

*F*or many of us, one Christmas stands out from all the others, the one when the meaning of the day shone clearest.

Although I did not guess it, my "truest" Christmas began on a rainy, spring day in the bleakest year of my life. Recently divorced, I was in my twenties, had no job, and was on my way downtown to go the rounds of the employment offices. I had no umbrella, for my old one had fallen apart, and I could not afford another one. I sat down in the streetcar, and there against the seat was a beautiful silk umbrella with a silver handle inlaid with gold and flecks of bright enamel. I had never seen anything so lovely.

I examined the handle and saw a name engraved among the golden scrolls. The usual procedure would have been to turn the umbrella to the conductor, but on impulse, I decided to take it with me and find the owner myself. I got off the streetcar in a downpour and thankfully opened the umbrella to protect myself. Then I searched a telephone book for the name on the umbrella and found it. I called, and a lady answered.

Yes, she said in surprise, that was her umbrella, which her parents, now dead, had given her for a birthday present. But, she added, it had been stolen from her locker at school (she was a teacher) more than a year before. She was so excited that I forgot I was looking for a job and went directly to her small house. She took the umbrella, and her eyes filled with tears.

The teacher wanted to give me a reward, but—though $20 was all I had in the world—her happiness at retrieving this special possession was such that to have accepted money would have spoiled something. We talked for a while, and I must have given her my address. I don't remember.

The next six months were wretched. I was able to obtain only temporary employment here and there, for a small salary, though this is what is now called the Roaring Twenties. But I put aside twenty-five or fifty cents when I could afford it for my little girl's Christmas presents. (It took me six months to save eight dollars.) My last job ended the day before Christmas, my thirty dollar rent was soon due, and I had fifteen dollars to my name—which Peggy and I would need for food. She was home from her convent boarding school and was excitedly looking forward to her gifts the next day, which I had already purchased. I had bought a small tree, and we were going to decorate it that night.

The stormy air was full of the sound of Christmas merriment. Bells rang and children shouted in the bitter dusk of the evening, and windows were lighted and everyone was running and laughing. But there would be no Christmas for me, I knew, no gifts, no remembrance whatsoever. As I struggled through the snowdrifts, I just about reached the lowest point in my life. Unless a miracle happened I would be homeless in January, foodless, jobless. I had prayed steadily for weeks, and there had been no answer but this coldness and darkness, this harsh air, this abandonment. God and men had completely forgotten me. I felt old as death, and as lonely. What was to come of us?

I looked in my mailbox. There were only bills in it, a sheaf of them, and two white envelopes which I was sure contained more bills. I went up three dusty flights of stairs, and I cried, shivering in my thin coat. But I made myself smile so I could greet my little daughter with a pretense of happiness. She opened the door for me and threw herself in my arms, screaming joyously and demanding that we decorate the tree immediately.

Peggy was not yet six years old, and had been alone all day while I worked. She had set our kitchen table for our evening meal, proudly, and put pans out and the three cans of food which would be our dinner. For some reason, when I looked at those pans and cans, I felt brokenhearted. We would have only hamburgers for our Christmas dinner tomorrow, and gelatin. I stood in the cold little kitchen, and misery overwhelmed me. For the first time in my life, I doubted the existence of God and His mercy, and the coldness in my heart was colder than ice.

The doorbell rang, and Peggy ran fleetly to answer it, calling that it must be Santa Claus. Then I heard a man talking heartily to her and went to the door. He was a delivery man, and his arms were full of big parcels, and he was laughing at my child's frenzied joy and her dancing. "This is a mistake," I said, but he read the name on the parcels, and they were for me. When he had gone I could only stare at the boxes. Peggy and I sat on the floor and opened them. A huge doll, three times the size of the one I bought for her. Gloves. Candy. A beautiful leather purse. Incredible! I looked for the name of the sender. It was the teacher, the address simply "California," where she had moved.

Our dinner that night was the most delicious I had ever eaten. I could only pray to myself, "Thank you, Father." I forgot I had no money for the rent and only $15 in my purse and no job. My child and I ate and laughed together in happiness. Then we decorated the little tree and marveled at it. I put Peggy to bed and set up her gifts around the tree, and a sweet peace flooded me like a benediction. I had some hope again. I could even examine the sheaf of bills without cringing. Then I opened the two white envelopes. One contained a check for $30 from a company I had worked for briefly in the summer. It was, said a note, my "Christmas bonus." My rent!

The other envelope was an offer of a permanent position with the government—to begin two days after Christmas. I sat with the letters in my hand and the check on the table before me, and I think that was the most joyful moment of my life up to that time.

The church bells began to ring. I hurriedly looked at my child, who was sleeping blissfully, and ran down to the street. Everywhere people were walking to church to celebrate the birth of the Savior. People smiled at me and I smiled back. The storm had stopped, the sky was pure and glistening with stars.

"The Lord is born!" sang the bells to the crystal night and the laughing darkness. Someone began to sing, "Come all ye faithful!" I joined in and sang with the strangers all about me.

I am not alone at all, I thought. I was never alone at all.

And that, of course, is the message of Christmas. We are never alone. Not when the night is darkest, the wind coldest, the world seemingly most indifferent. For this is still the time God chooses.[24]   ✳

Washington's Christmas List

George Washington himself prepared this list of presents he planned to give to his five-year-old stepson, Jackie, and his three-year-old step-daughter, Patsy, on Christmas Day, 1759.

- A bird on Bellows
- A Cuckoo
- A turnabout Parrot
- A Grocers Shop
- An Aviary
- A Prussian Dragoon
- A Tunbridge Tea Sett

- 3 Neat Tunbridge Toys
- A Neat Book-Fashioned Tea Chest
- A box best Household Stuff
- A straw Patch box with a Glass
- A neat dress'd Wax Baby

The Joy

Christ

# of Children

When rehearsals began for the annual children's Christmas program my son, Tim, began making excuses and developed strange Sunday maladies that came on just before kids' choir practice. One happy Sunday evening on the way home from church Tim announced

"I'm going to be in the Christmas program—and I don't have to sing!"

"What's that in your hand, Tim?"

"It's an oatmeal carton, Dad."

"What's it for?"

"You'll see."

The night of the children's Christmas program . . .

"Where's Tim?" his younger sister asked after eyeballing the children's chorus.

"Guess we'll have to wait to find out."

The next number on the program was the popular "Little Drummer Boy" song with its "Pa-rum-pa-pum-pum." And who was making his own "Pa-rum-pa-pum-pums"? Tim Miller, dressed like a shepherd boy and playing on his oatmeal carton drum with all the concentration he gave anything he was proud of doing. Afterward, he bounded up to his family,

"That's the best Christmas program I have never had to sing in!"

"Why's that Tim?"

"I like the idea of giving Jesus a gift for his birthday. That's what I got to do with my drum."

The ABC's of Christmas

BY JEANNE BLOMQUEST

A Angels from the realms of glory,
Telling of the Christmas story.

B Bethlehem beckons with joyful accord;
Come hither, come see, and worship the Lord.

C Christ was born on Christmas Day,
Asleep in a manger, a bed made of hay.

D Divine and holy is Thy birth;
Wing Your flight o'er all the earth.

E Everlasting Father, and Father of all,
Look with mercy and love us all.

F "Fear not," said the angel, one night long ago.
"I bring you good tidings, for this I know."

G "Glory to the Son," we sing,
"Christ, our Prophet, Priest and King."

H Heavenly hosts, their watch are keeping,
Precious child so sweetly sleeping.

I Immanuel, we sing Thy praise,
Thou Prince of Life, Thou Fount of Grace.

J Joy to the world, the Lord is come,
Born in a manger, God's only son.

K King of Kings, prophets foretold,
Now all men His love behold.

L Love is a gift, He gives to all,
To each of us, both great and small.

M Messiah and Savior—for this He came—
Live in our hearts and there remain.

N Night so holy, silent and still,
   Proclaiming joy, peace and good will.

O Odors of Edom and offerings divine,
   Myrrh from the forest and gold from the mine.

P Peace on earth, good will from heaven,
   Souls redeemed and sins forgiven.

Q Quietly He came to earth
   To give us all a second birth.

R Rejoice, give thanks and loudly sing,
   Glory to the new-born King.

S Shepherds watched their flocks by night
   While Wise Men followed the heavenly light.

T Tidings of great joy I bring;
   Good news from heaven the angels sing.

U Unto us a child is born
   On this happy Christmas Morn.

V Virgin-born, Immanuel,
   Let every tongue Thy praises tell.

W Wise Men from the East, they came
   To worship and praise His holy name.

X X is for Christ when in Greek it is read;
   A Savior, the Lord, so the angel said.

Y Yonder shines brightly the heavenly star
   Showing the way to those from afar.

Z Zeal was bestowed on God's only Son
   From His childhood years till His work was done.[25]

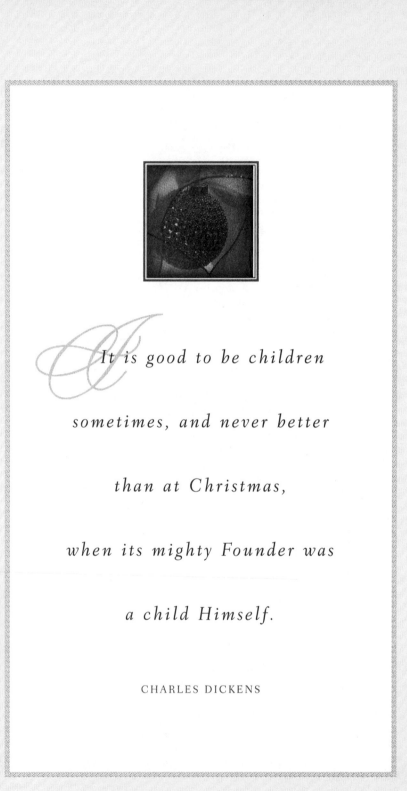

It is good to be children

sometimes, and never better

than at Christmas,

when its mighty Founder was

a child Himself.

CHARLES DICKENS

Another European Hans Christian
Andersen short story abridged
for today's children.

The Fir Tree

BY HANS CHRISTIAN ANDERSEN

In a small cottage on the borders of a forest lived a poor laborer, who gained a scanty living by cutting wood. He had a wife and two children who helped him in his work. The boy's name was Valentine, and the girl was called Mary. They were obedient, good children, and a great comfort to their parents. One winter evening, this happy little family were sitting quietly round the hearth, the snow and the wind raging outside, while they ate their supper of dry bread, when a gentle tap was heard on the window, and a childish voice cried from outside; "Oh, let me in, I pray! I am a poor child, with nothing to eat, and no home to go to, and I shall die of cold and hunger unless you let me in."

Valentine and Mary jumped up from the table and ran to open the door, saying: "Come in, poor little child! We have not much to give you, but whatever we have we will share with you."

The stranger-child came in and warmed his frozen hands and feet at the fire, and the children gave him the best they had to eat saying: "You must be tired, too, poor child! Lie down on our bed; we can sleep on the bench for one night."

Then said the little stranger-child: "Thank God for all your kindness to me!"

So they took their little guest into their sleeping-place, laid him on the bed, covered him over, and said to each other: "How thankful we ought to be! We have warm rooms and a cozy bed, while this poor child has only heaven for his roof and the cold earth for his sleeping-place."

When the father and mother went to bed, Mary and Valentine lay quite contentedly on the bench near the fire, saying, before they fell asleep: "The stranger-child will be happy tonight in his warm bed."

These kind children had not slept many hours before Mary awoke, and softly whispered to her brother: "Valentine, dear brother, wake, and listen to the sweet music under the window."

Then Valentine rubbed his eyes and listened. It was sweet music indeed, and sounded like beautiful voices singing to the tones of a harp:

> *"Oh holy Child, we greet thee! bringing*
> *Sweet strains of harp to aid our singing."*
> *"Thou holy Child, in peace art sleeping,*
> *While we our watch without are keeping."*
> *"Blest be the house wherein thou liest,*
> *Happiest on earth, to heaven the nighest."*

The children listened, while a solemn joy filled their hearts: then they stepped softly to the window to see who was singing.

In the east was a streak of rosy dawn, and in its light they saw a group of children standing in front of the house, clothed in sparkling garments and holding golden harps. Amazed at the sight, the brother and sister were still gazing out the window when they heard a sound behind them. Turning they discovered the stranger-child standing before them. "I am the little Christ-child," he said, "I wander through the world bringing peace and happiness to children. You took me in and cared for me when you though I was a poor child, and now you shall have my blessing for what you have done."

A fir tree grew near the little house; and from this the Christ-child broke a twig and planted it in the ground. He looked directly at Valentine and Mary and said, "This twig shall become a tree, and shall bring forth fruit year by year for you."

No sooner had he done this than he vanished, and with him the choir of angels. The fir-branch grew and became a Christmas tree, and on its branches hung golden apples and silver nuts every Christmas.

Such is the story told to German children concerning their beautiful Christmas trees, though we know that this is only a fable. The real Christ-child can never be wandering cold and homeless in our world, because he is safe in heaven by his Father's side; yet we may gather from this story the same truth which the Bible plainly tells us—that anyone who helps another person, it will be counted to them as if he had done it to Christ himself. "In as much as ye have done it unto the least of these my brethren, ye have done it unto me."[26] ✳

***

Let's shelve the Santa Claus

known-by-

controversy long enough to include

every-child

this much-loved and

Christmas

known-by-every-child Christmas

classic

classic. The same can be said

for other pieces that follow.

***

A Visit from St. Nicholas

By Clement Moore

'Twas the night before Christmas, when all through the house

Not a creature was stirring, not even a mouse;

The stockings were hung by the chimney with care,

In hopes that St. Nicholas soon would be there;

The children were nestled all snug in their beds,

While visions of sugar-plums danced in their heads;

And Mamma in her kerchief, and I in my cap,

Had just settled our brains for a long winter's nap,

When out on the lawn there arose such a clatter,

I sprang from the bed to see what was the matter.

Away to the window I flew like a flash,

Tore open the shutters and threw up the sash.

The moon on the breast of the new-fallen snow

Gave the lustre of midday to objects below,

When what to my wondering eyes should appear,

But a miniature sleigh, and eight tiny reindeer,

With a little old driver, so lively and quick,

I knew in a moment it must be St. Nick.

More rapid than eagles his coursers they came,

And he whistled, and shouted, and called them by name:

Now, Dasher! now Dancer! now Prancer and Vixen!

On, Comet! on, Cupid! on, Donner and Blitzen!

To the top of the porch! to the top of the wall!

Now dash away! dash away! dash away all!'

As dry leaves that before the wild hurricane fly,

When they meet with an obstacle, mount to the sky,

So up to the house-top the coursers they flew,

With the sleigh full of toys and St. Nicholas too.

And then, in a twinkling, I heard on the roof

The prancing and pawing of each little hoof.

As I drew in my head, and was fuming around,

Down the chimney St. Nicholas came with a bound.

He was dressed all in fur, from his head to his foot,

And his clothes were all famished with ashes and soot;

A bundle of toys he had flung on his back,

And he looked like a peddler just opening his pack.

His eyes—how they twinkled! his dimples how merry!

His cheeks were like roses, his nose like a cherry!

His droll little mouth was drawn up like a bow,

And the beard of his chin was as white as the snow;

The stump of a pipe he held tight in his teeth,

And the smoke it encircled his head like a wreath;

He had a broad face and a little round belly,

That shook when he laughed, like a bowl full of jelly.

He was chubby and plump, a right jolly old elf,

And I laughed when I saw him, in spite of myself;

A wink of his eye and a twist of his head

Soon gave me to know I had nothing to dread.

He spoke not a word, but went straight to his work,

And filled all the stockings; then turned with a jerk,

And laying his finger aside of his nose,

And giving a nod, up the chimney he rose;

He sprang to his sleigh, to his team gave a whistle,

And away they all flew like the down of a thistle.

But I heard him exclaim, ere he drove out of sight,

Happy Christmas to all and to all a good night.[27]

Yes, Virginia, There Is a Santa Claus

FIRST PRINTED IN THE NEW YORK SUN, SEPTEMBER 21, 1897

Dear Editor:

I am 8 years old.

Some of my little friends say there is no Santa Claus. Papa says, "If you see it in *The Sun* it's so." Please tell me the truth, is there a Santa Claus?

Virginia O'Hanlon, 115 West 95th Street

Virginia, your little friends are wrong. They have been affected by the skepticism of a skeptical age. They do not believe except they see. They think that nothing can be which is not comprehensible by their little minds.

All minds, Virginia, whether they be men's or children's, are little. In this great universe of ours man is a mere insect, an ant, in his intellect as compared with the boundless world about him, as measured by the intelligence capable of grasping the whole truth and knowledge.

Yes, Virginia, there is a Santa Claus. He exists as certainly as love and generosity and devotion exist, and you know that they abound and give to your life its highest beauty and joy. Alas! how dreary would be the world if there were no Santa Claus! It would be as dreary as if there were no

Virginias. There would be no child-like faith then, no poetry, no romance to make tolerable this existence. We should have no enjoyment, except in sense and sight. The eternal light with which childhood fills the world be extinguished.

Not believe in Santa Claus! You might as well not believe in fairies! You might get your Papa to hire men to watch in all the chimneys on Christmas Eve to catch Santa Claus, but even if they did not see Santa Claus coming down, what would that prove? Nobody sees Santa Claus, but that is no sign that there is no Santa Claus. The most real things in the world are those that neither children nor men can see. Did you ever see fairies dancing on the lawn? Of course not, but that's no proof that they are not there. Nobody can conceive or imagine all the wonders that are unseen and unseeable in the world.

You tear apart the baby's rattle and see what makes the noise inside, but there is a veil covering the unseen world which not the strongest man, nor even the united strength of all the strongest men that ever lived, could tear apart. Only faith, fancy, poetry, love, romance, can push aside that curtain and view and picture the supernal beauty and glory beyond. Is it all real? Ah, Virginia, in all this world there is nothing else real and abiding. No Santa Claus! Thank God he lives and he lives forever. A thousand years from now, Virginia, nay ten times ten thousand years from now, he will continue to make glad the heart of childhood.

* * *

And I do come home at Christmas.

We all do, or we all should.

We all come home,

or ought to come home,

for a short holiday—the longer,

the better. . . .

CHARLES DICKENS

* * *

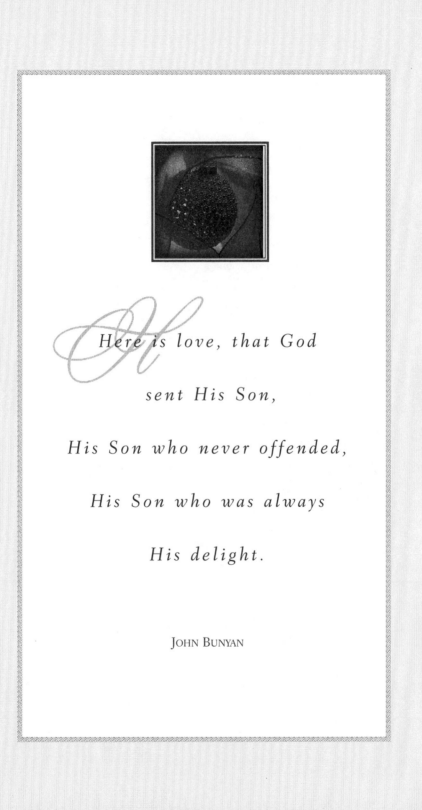

Here is love, that God

sent His Son,

His Son who never offended,

His Son who was always

His delight.

JOHN BUNYAN

The Lamb

Little lamb, who made thee?
Dost thou know who made thee.
Gave thee life, and bid thee feed
By the streams and o'er the mead;
Gave thee clothing of delight,
Softest clothing, wooly, bright;
Gave thee such a tender voice,
Making all the valleys rejoice?
    Little lamb, who made thee?
    Dost thou know who made thee?

Little lamb, I'll tell thee;
Little lamb, I'll tell thee.
He is called by thy name,
For He calls Himself a lamb;
He is meek and He is mild,
He became a little child.
I a child, and thou a lamb,
    Little lamb, God bless thee!
    Little lamb, God bless thee.

WILLIAM BLAKE

God Bless Us Every One

"God bless us every one!" prayed Tiny Tim,
　　Crippled, and dwarfed of body, yet so tall
Of soul, we tiptoe earth to look on him,
　　High towering over all.

He loved the loveless world, nor dreamed, indeed,
　　Then it, as best, could give to him, the while,
But pitying glances, when his only need
　　Was but a cheery smile.

And thus he prayed, "God bless us every one!"
　　Enfolding all the creeds within the span
Of his child-heart; and so, despising none,
　　Was nearer saint than man.

I like to fancy God in Paradise,
　　Lifting a finger o'er the rhythmic swing
Of chiming harp and song, with eager eyes
　　Turned earthward, listening—
The Anthem stilled—the angels leaning there
　　Above the golden walls—the morning sun
Of Christmas bursting flower-like with the prayer,
　　"God bless us Every One!"[28]

JAMES WHITCOMB RILEY

Santa's List

'Tis a week before Christmas
And far, far away,
In a land full of magic
Where the polar bears play,
Stands a small cozy
All covered with snow,
Where the lights from the windows
Make the countryside glow.

The smoke from the chimney
Rises billowed and curled
To greet the new moon
As it brightens the world.

In front of the cottage
Stands a little red sleigh,
And behind, frolic reindeer
In a moonlit ballet.

A peek through the window
Is a vision supreme,
With the color and warmth
Of a fairyland dream,
A fireplace blazing
That flickers and glows
On a room full of toys
And boxes and bows.

There are Teddy bears, baseballs
And dolls by the score,
And sleds, skis and ice skates
From ceiling to floor.

There are bugles and sailboats
And shiny new trains,
And piles of books
And all kinds of games.
And there in the corner
Near the clock on the shelf
Sits a little round man
Who looks like an elf.

His beard is pure white
And his suit is bright red,
From his pipe smokes a halo
That circles his head.

A smile on his face
And a glint in his eye
Show his work is progressing
As the seconds tick by.

A huge book before him
And a pen in his hand,
And he hums while he puffs,
'Cause he's feeling so grand.

He's thinking of Christmas,
Just one week away,
And the joy he will bring
On that wonderful day.

And his eyes seem to sparkle
As he looks at the toys,
And he writes in his ledger
Of good girls and good boys.

And soon he is finished,
His volume complete,
And he looks at the schedule
That he has to meet.
Then he rounds up the reindeer
And packs up the sleigh,
And, with his book on his belly,
He's up and away.
High o'er the treetops
And soon out of sight,
He follows the stars
That lead him in flight.
Over the oceans
And over great lands,
The strong winter winds
Are like delicate hands,
That lift him and guide him
As his journey takes birth,
While he carefully starts
To circle the earth.
And at each town and village,
A call very brief,
He lands on each rooftop
Like a new-fallen leaf.
Just enough time to visit
Each girl and each boy
And answer their dreams
With a new Christmas toy.

And then in a flash
He's off into space,
Like an eagle returning
To a far distant place.
But if quickly you peek
Through the frost on the pane,
You can see in the moonlight
As he checks off a name.
Then he waves Merry Christmas,
As you take your last look
At this magical man
And his wonderful book.
And just for that moment
All time takes a pause,
And you'll never forget
That you'll see Santa Claus!

DONALD R. STOLTZ

Tough Questions for Santa Claus in a Tough No-nonsense World

HE KNOWS IF YOU'VE BEEN BAD OR GOOD

1. How do you know? Did my little brother snitch on me?

2. How can you visit every kid's house all over the world in one night?

3. How can you remember the names and addresses of every little kid and recall what each one asked for? Do you have all this on a computer?

4. How can you get zillions of gifts into that one dinky little sack?

5. How can a chubby guy like you fit through the chimney?

6. Don't you ever get tired of the milk and cookies kids leave out? How would you feel about a grilled cheese and cocoa?

7. What do your reindeer like for a snack?

8. Don't you get cold living at the North Pole?

9. What's Mrs. Claus like? How come you never had kids of your own?

10. How come I saw you at three different department stores? Then again out at the corner of Main and 4th? How can you be in all those places at one time?

11. If there's no snow on Christmas Eve, will the sleigh still be able to land on our roof?

* * *

Rachel Field has authored a score

of children's books, some of them winners

Scandinavian

of the prized Cauldecott award for excellence

in children's literature. Her interest in

traditions

Scandinavian traditions is reflected

by this Swedish and Norwegian

Minnesotan's celebration of Christmas.

* * *

Christmas in the Heart

BY RACHEL FIELD

Years ago and years ago two little girls trudged up a long hill in the twilight of late December. They carried a basket between them, and one was I, and one was Helga Swanson. The smell of warm coffeecake and braided cinnamon bread and little brown twists like deer horns comes back to me now from that remembered basket. Sweeter than all the perfumes of Arabia that fragrance reached our half-frozen noses, yet we never lifted the folded napkin, for we took our responsibility hard. Helga's mother and grandmother had spent the better part of three days over that Christmas baking, and we had been chosen to deliver it and help trim the tree at the Lutheran Home on the hill above Fallen Leaf Lake.

"We must hurry," Helga said. "They've lighted the parlors already."

I could hardly see Helga's face for the darkness, but I felt her warm, vigorous presence beside me in her tightly buttoned coat and knitted tam that half covered her fair braids. I would be seven in another month and she had been eight last March when we had moved from the state of Maine to Minnesota. It had seemed strange and a little frightening to me then to hear so many people speaking to one another in words I couldn't understand. Helga, herself, could drop into Swedish if it seemed worth her while to join in such conversations.

"It's nothing. I'll teach you," she had promised. But her

enthusiasm had waned after a few attempts. So Helga became my inter-
preter as well as my most intimate friend. Without her I should never
have known the old men and women in the red brick house who were our
hosts that night. I should never have seen Pastor Hanson bending over
the melodeon or heard old Christine Berglund tell about the star.

"Merry Christmas!" we called even before the door was thrown open
and the spiciness of cooking food came out to us as from the gates of
heaven.

There were sixteen of us, counting Helga and me, round that table
with its white cloth, and its soup tureen at one end and round yellow
cheese and the other. We all stood at our places while Pastor Hanson said
a blessing in Swedish.

"There is a church in every man's heart," I remember he said in
English at the end of his prayer, "but let us be sure that it is always God
who preaches the sermon."

The smell from those bowls of pea soup stays with me yet! Golden
and smooth and rich to the last spoonful, we ate it with slices of fresh rye
bread and home-churned butter. Pastor Hanson, himself, sliced the
cheese with a knife that shaved it into one yellow curl after another.
Cinnamon and coffee and hot bread and molasses mingled in one delicious scent as dishes and cups and plates passed from hand to hand.

At last we gathered in the parlor and another scuttle of coal went into
the big stove. The time had come for decorating the tree, and everyone
took a hand in it except old Mrs. Berglund, who stayed in a wheel chair
because of her rheumatism. But even she gave advice about where more
strings of popcorn were needed and if the candles were placed where they
would show best among the green branches. Mr. Johnson had made birds
out of pine cones, and there were cranberries in long strings as red as the
popcorn was white. There were hearts and crescents of tinfoil and balls

made out of bright bits of worsted. But there was no star anywhere and I wondered about that, for no Christmas tree could be complete without a star to light its tip. But I need not have been troubled about that, as it turned out.

Pastor Hanson went over to the melodeon against the wall and began to play a Christmas carol. When we had finished, someone went over and whispered to old Mrs. Berglund in her wheel chair. From under her shawl she took out a small box that she held fast in her hands, which were thin and crooked as apple twigs. It was very still in the room for a moment, the kind of stillness that makes you know something exceedingly important is going to happen.

"Well, Pastor Hanson," she said, and held out the little box, "I did not think God would spare me for another year, but here I am, and here is the Christmas star."

"You must tell the children," he said. "It is right that they should hear before we hang it on the tree."

"Yust like tonight it vas," Christine Berglund began, and I felt grateful that she was telling it so for my sake, even though her j's and y's and v's and w's had a way of changing places as she said them. " I vere eleven year old then and sick in my heart because Christmas is coming and I am so far from my mother and my brothers and sisters—"

I could see that big country estate as she told us about it—the stone walls and courtyard, the park with its thick woods; the tiled floors and great fireplaces; the heavy, carved furniture, the enormous beds that would have held her whole family of brothers and sisters. She was young to be sent away into service, and everything and everyone in that house was old, from the mistress to the servants who had tended her for many years.

"They had need of my young knees and quick fingers," she explained, "for they had grown too stiff to bend and dust under all the tables and chairs."

Pastor Lange came once each month to hold service in the stone chapel, because his parish church was too far away for the servants to attend. Pastor Lange was a very kind old man, and Christine did not feel so lonely on the days when he came. He always spent the night there and, though the mistress of the house never went into the chapel, after the service was over she sent for him and they ate supper together and talked before the fire until bedtime. Christine knew this because once she was sent with a tray from the kitchen to set before them.

"God bless you, my child," Pastor Lange had said. "May you rest well."

But the old lady had kept her lips shut in a thin line and she would not let her eyes rest on her young serving maid. It was the next morning that Pastor Lange answered Christine's questions. Their mistress had hardened her heart against every living thing because years ago she had lost her only child, a daughter as good as she was gay and beautiful. When death had taken her child the mother had turned as cold and gray as a boulder. She had ordered the girl's room closed and the birds let out of their cages. She had had a cloth hung over her portrait and every reminder of her presence taken from each nook and corner. Worst of all, she had summoned Pastor Lange and told him that she would live if she must, but he need never look for her in the family pew again. God had forsaken her, and Sunday and Easter and Christmas would be for her as any other days.

And she had kept her vow, though Pastor Lange had never ceased to pray that a miracle might turn her bitterness into faith once more.

"And did it?" Helga and I interrupted in our impatience.

But the story could not be hurried.

"Christmas it is the vorst," old Christine went on, "for in that big house there is not one cake baked or one bit of green hung on any door. At home ve are poor, but ve put out grain for the birds and have our candles to light and our songs to sing."

Each night she cried as the holiday drew near. She thought of her mother and brothers and sisters all together in a house that was small but savory with holiday cooking. She thought also of the little church on Christmas Eve, with its lighted windows, and the graves outside, each with a torch set there to burn through the long hours till Christmas morning. It was right, her mother had told her, that even the dead should join with the living on that Holy Night. And there was nothing that Christine could do, a half-grown girl in that house of silence and old, old people, to show that Christmas was in her heart.

But once she had noticed near the chapel some tilted gravestones and among them one not so old and gray as the others. Lichens covered the letters cut upon it. She was afraid to scrape away the moss to read the name, but there could be no harm, she thought, in putting a branch of green upon it. Perhaps she might even take her own candle out there to burn and say a prayer and sing a carol. The thought of that made her feel less lonely. She hummed a Christmas hymn as she went back to her work, and it was as she crossed the courtyard that something bright caught her eye in a crack between two flagstones. She bent to pick it up and there, half hidden by moss, was a pin, star-shaped and shining and giving out jets of color as she turned it in the sun.

"Like the Star of Bethlehem," she thought, and her heart beat fast under the apron she wore, for surely it seemed like a sign to comfort her.

She pinned it where no one would see it under her dress, and all day she felt it close to her heart as she went about her duties. That night she slept with it beneath her pillow, and she thought of the Wise Men of old who had seen that other star in the East and followed it to Bethlehem.

Next day she slipped out and stopped by the gravestones. On the smallest stone she set a green branch of fir with cones. It stood straight and fine—almost, Christine Berglund told us, like the Christmas tree we had just trimmed.

"That night is Christmas Eve," she went on, "and I think there can be no harm if I go out after it is dark and light my candle and set the star there to keep watch till it is morning."

But, as the afternoon passed and twilight came, Christine did not feel so happy. The hidden star pricked her with its points, almost as if it were her own conscience telling her that stars were not meant to be hidden, that what we pick up is not ours merely for the finding. She tried to tell herself that it would be different if she had found her treasure in the house, not out there between the stones of the courtyard.

So darkness fell and it was Christmas Eve. Some of the old servants remembered and spoke of other times when there had been laughter and festivity in those rooms, and the chapel bell ringing to call them to midnight service. Christine sat quiet until she could slip away to her little room. It was chill there in the darkness because she dared not waste her candle.

At last the fires were banked and the house grew silent. Then Christine put on her cloak and crept down the stairs. She let herself into the courtyard, where nothing stirred but the shadows of trees beyond the walls. The moon was high above the stone turrets. She and it seemed to be the only things which moved in that world of winter quiet. She passed the chapel where no bells pealed from the dark belfry. There were the old tilted gravestones and the one with the bit of green to mark it. Her fingers shook as she set her candle on the headstone and tried to light it.

Twice it went out before the small flame shone clear. Her hands still trembled as she took out the star and pinned it among the green needles of the fir bough.

"And then I get down on my knees and first I say 'Our Father.' Then I make another one that is mine, so God shall know that I do not forget the night of our Saviour's birth. It is hard for me to find the words for my prayer and my teeth are chattering like little hammers, so I don't hear someone come tap-tapping on the stones—"

"Oh!" Helga and I drew sharp breaths. "Who was it?"

But old Christine must tell the story in her own way.

"There I am on my knees," she repeated, "praying to God, and my candle is still burning. Yes, that is how she found me."

We dared not interrupt her again, but our eyes never left her face.

"'Mistress,' I said," she went on, "'forgive me.' But she don't answer me; she yust stand there and turn it in her hands, and she act like she is seeing a ghost."

They must have stood so a long time. The candle burned out on the headstone before the old mistress took Christine back to the house. She did not speak until they reached the great hall, though tears ran down her cheeks at each step they took. Her hands reached for the bell rope and the house echoed to her frantic ringing. Christine could hear the servants hurrying to and fro upstairs in answer to the summons.

"I think she send for them because I have done a bad thing," old Christine told us, "so I stand and shiver there and don't know what is going to happen to me. And then they come down, all so sleepy they forget to make their curtsies. And Mistress point to me, and I cry so I don't see her face any more. But she say to them, 'Go; make a fire in the blocker room. Spread linen and blankets on the bed and warm it, and bring food, that this child may eat and be comforted.' I think I don't hear her right, but they take me there, and I see the fire lighted and the bed vaiting, so I don't try to think anymore. I yust lie down with the flowers spread over me, and I sleep and sleep. And there is no one to come and shake me at sunrise to help in the kitchen. I vake, and it is Christmas morning and bells are ringing so sweet I think I dream them from home. But they are ringing in the chapel. Then the maids come and bring me a beautiful warm dress that smells of cloves and lavender. And they dress me in it, and I ask them the meaning of all this; but they yust smile and say, 'Pastor Lange, he vill tell you.'"

And, sure enough, Pastor Lange and the old mistress came from the chapel. He had driven since sunrise in the carriage she had sent to bring him there.

"You shall see for yourself, Pastor," the old coachman had said, "that the day of miracles is not past."

So Christine went down to meet them in the dress that was heavy with gold embroidery and slippers so soft she seemed to be walking on snow. These rooms were no longer gray and gloomy but warm with leaping fires. The covers were gone from the portrait of a laughing girl no older than she. Her dress was the same that Christine wore, and the star showed plainly on the painted folds. Christine marveled at each change she saw about her, most of all at her mistress's face, which was still sad, but no longer set like stone.

Then Pastor Lange put his hand on Christine's head and blessed her in God's name. But to the old woman he said, "Blessed are they that mourn, for they shall be comforted."

And Christine sat between them at dinner, and felt strange that she should now be served who had so lately carried in the dishes.

"And after dinner is over Pastor Lange he tells me that it is indeed a miracle God has worked through me to bring faith to our mistress. I don't understand how that can be, for it was not right that I keep the pin and tell no one. But Pastor Lange does not know how to explain that to me. So he says, 'Christine, it must have been that God vas in your heart to do this thing.' 'No, Pastor,' I tell him the truth; 'it was Christmas in my heart.' And Pastor Lange he don't scold me, he yust say maybe that is the same thing."

Old Christine was growing tired. Her voice had dwindled to a thin thread of sound by the time she had answered our questions. . . . Yes, the pin had belonged to her mistress's daughter. She had lost it one winter day and grown so chill hunting for it in the courtyard that she had fallen ill and died. It was her gravestone by the chapel that Christine had chosen to light and decorate with green. So great had been that mother's grief that it was more than thirty years since she had spoken her daughter's name or let anything be a reminder. But Christine's candle shining on Christmas Eve had been like a sign sent from her dead child by a living one on that most happy night of the year.

So Christine no longer served as a maid in that great house. She lived as the old woman's daughter, and in winter the rooms were warm and bright with fires and laughter, and in summer sweet with flowers and the singing of birds.

"And see, here is the star to hang on the tree."

"The same one? The very same?"

"Yes, the same. It goes with me always since that night."

We touched the five shining points with wonder in our finger tips before Christine's old fingers lifted it from the bed of cotton.

"Real diamonds and not one missing," she said proudly as she handed it to Captain Christiansen, because he was tall enough to set it on the topmost tip.

"But I never think it vould come all the way to America. I never think I come all that vay myself."

We watched it send out little jets of brightness when the candles were lighted below and all the old faces shining in the loveliest of light. We sang another carol all together, and then it was time to go home with Helga's father, who had come for us.

"Good night." Their voices followed us to the door. "God Jul! Merry Christmas!"

"Merry Christmas!" Helga and I called back before we turned to follow her father's lantern into the wintry dark.[29]

Christmas Morning

If Bethlehem were here today,
Or this were very long ago,
There wouldn't be a winter time
Nor any cold or snow.

I'd run out through the garden gate,
And down along the pasture walk;
And off beside the cattle barns
I'd hear a kind of gentle talk.

I'd move the heavy iron chain
And pull away the wooden pin:
I'd push the door a little bit
And tiptoe very softly in.

The pigeons and the yellow hens
And all the cows would stand away;
Their eyes would open wide to see
A lady in the manger hay,
If this were very long ago.
And Bethlehem were here today.

And mother held my hand and smiled—
I mean the lady would—and she
Would take the wooly blankets off
Her little boy so I could see.

His shut-up eyes would be asleep,
And he would look just like our John,
And he would be all crumpled too,
And have a pinkish color on.

I'd watch his breath go in and out,
His little clothes would all be white.
I'd slip my finger in his hand
To feel how he could grasp it tight.

And she would smile and say, "Take care,"
The mother, Mary, would say, "Take care";
And I would kiss his little hand
And touch his hair.

While Mary put the blankets back,
The gentle talk would soon begin.
And when I'd tiptoe softly out
I'd meet the wise man going in.[30]

ELIZABETH MADOX ROBERTS

＊　＊　＊

*William Dean Howells was born in Martins Ferry,
Ohio, in 1837; he died in 1920. Very much a man of
his era, Howells was a self-made and self-educated
denizen of the literary circles of the time, serving in
various editorial positions on the* Atlantic Monthly
*from 1866 to 1881. He is recognized as a major influ-
ence on the American novel, being one of the first to
depart from the earlier oratorical style that so domi-
nated nineteenth-century fiction. His literary voice
was at once clear-sighted and warmhearted as is evident in the following story. Christmas comes but once
a year and as Howells' fanciful tale implies, there is
something to be said for that.*

＊　＊　＊

Christmas Every Day

By William Dean Howells

The little girl came into her papa's study, as she always did Saturday morning before breakfast, and asked for a story. He tried to beg off that morning, for he was very busy, but she would not let him. So he began:

"Well, once there was a little pig—"

She put her hand over his mouth and stopped him at the word. She said she had heard little pig stories till she was perfectly sick of them.

"Well, what kind of story shall I tell, then?"

"About Christmas. It's getting to be the season. It's past Thanksgiving already."

"It seems to me," argued her papa, "that I've told as often about Christmas as I have about little pigs."

"No difference! Christmas is more interesting."

"Well!" Her papa roused himself from his writing by a great effort. "Well, then, I'll tell you about the little girl that wanted it Christmas every day in the year. How would you like that?"

"First-rate!" said the little girl; and she nestled into comfortable shape in his lap, ready for listening.

"Very well, then, this little pig—Oh, what are you pounding me for?"

"Because you said little pig instead of little girl."

"I should like to know what's the difference between a little pig and a little girl that wanted it Christmas every day!"

"Papa," said the little girl, warningly, "if you don't go

on, I'll give it to you!" And at this her papa darted off like lightning, and began to tell the story as fast as he could.

Well, once there was a little girl who liked Christmas so much that she wanted it to be Christmas every day in the year; and as soon as Thanksgiving was over she began to send postal cards to the old Christmas Fairy to ask if she mightn't have it. But the old Fairy never answered any of the postals; and, after a while, the little girl found out that the Fairy was pretty particular, and wouldn't even notice anything but letters, not even correspondence cards in envelopes; but real letters on sheets of paper, and sealed outside with a monogram—or your initial, any way. So, then, she began to send her letters; and in about three weeks—or just the day before Christmas, it was—she got a letter from the Fairy, saying she might have it Christmas every day for a year, and then they would see about having it longer.

The little girl was a good deal excited already, preparing for the old-fashioned, once-a-year Christmas that was coming the next day, and perhaps the Fairy's promise didn't make such an impression on her as it would have made at some other time. She just resolved to keep it to herself, and surprise everybody with it as it kept coming true; and then it slipped out of her mind altogether.

She had a splendid Christmas. She went to bed early, so as to let Santa Claus have a chance at the stockings, and in the morning she was up the first of anybody and went and felt them, and found hers all lumpy with packages of candy, and oranges and grapes, and pocket-books and rubber balls and all kinds of small presents, and her big brother with nothing but the tongs in them, and her young lady sister's with a new silk umbrella, and her papa's and mamma's with potatoes and pieces of coal wrapped up in tissue paper, just as they always had every Christmas. Then she waited around till the rest of the family were up, and she was the first to burst into the library, when the doors were opened, and look at the large presents laid out on the library-table—books, and portfolios, and boxes of stationery, and breast-pins, and dolls, and little stoves, and dozens of handkerchiefs, and inkstands, and skates, and snow-shovels, and photograph frames, and little easels, and boxes of watercolors, and Turkish paste, and nougat, and candied cherries, and dolls' houses, and waterproofs—and the big Christmas tree, lighted and standing in a waste-basket in the middle.

She had a splendid Christmas all day. She ate so much candy that she did not want any breakfast; and the whole forenoon the presents kept pouring in that the expressman had not had time to deliver the night before; and she went 'round giving the presents she had got for other people, and came home and ate turkey and cranberry for dinner, and plum-pudding and nuts and raisins and oranges and more candy, and then went out and coasted and came in with a stomach ache, crying; and her papa said he would see if his house was turned into that sort of fool's paradise another year; and they had a light supper, and pretty early everybody went to bed cross.

Here the little girl pounded her papa in the back, again.

"Well, what now? Did I say pigs?"

"You made them act like pigs."

"Well, didn't they?"

"No matter; you oughtn't to put it into a story."

"Very well, then, I'll take it all out."

Her father went on:

The little girl slept very heavily, and she slept very late, but she was wakened at last by the other children dancing 'round her bed with their stockings full of presents in their hands.

"What is it?" said the little girl, and she rubbed her eyes and tried to rise up in bed.

"Christmas! Christmas! Christmas!" they all shouted, and waved their stockings.

"Nonsense! It was Christmas yesterday."

Her brothers and sisters just laughed. "We don't know about that. It's Christmas today, anyway. You come into the library and see."

Then all at once it flashed on the little girl that the Fairy was keeping her promise, and her year of Christmases was beginning. She was dreadfully sleepy, but she sprang up like a lark—a lark that had overeaten itself and gone to bed cross—and darted into the library. There it was again! Books, and portfolios, and boxes of stationery, and breast-pins—

"You needn't go over it all, Papa; I guess I can remember just what was there," said the little girl.

Well, and there was the Christmas tree blazing away, and the family picking out their presents, but looking pretty sleepy, and her father perfectly puzzled, and her mother ready to cry.

"I'm sure I don't see how I'm to dispose of all these things," said her mother, and her father said it seemed to him they had had something just like it the day before, but he supposed he must have dreamed it. This struck the little girl as the best kind of joke; and so she ate so much candy she didn't want any breakfast, and went 'round carrying presents, and had turkey and cranberry for dinner, and then went out and coasted, and . . . came in with a—

"Papa!"

"Well, what now?"

"What did you promise, you forgetful thing?"

"Oh! oh, yes!

Well, the next day, it was just the same thing over again, but everybody getting crosser; and at the end of a week's time so many people had lost their tempers that you could pick up lost tempers everywhere; they perfectly strewed the ground. Even when people tried to recover their tempers they usually got somebody else's, and it made the most dreadful mix.

The little girl began to get frightened, keeping the secret all to herself; she wanted to tell her mother, but she didn't dare to; and she was ashamed to ask the Fairy to take back her gift, it seemed ungrateful and ill-bred. So it went on and on, and it was Christmas on St. Valentine's Day, and Washington's Birthday just the same as any day, and it didn't skip even the First of April, though everything was counterfeit that day, and that was some little relief.

After a while turkeys got to be awfully scarce, selling for about a thousand dollars apiece. They got to passing off almost anything for turkeys—even half-grown hummingbirds. And cranberrie—well, they asked a diamond apiece for cranberries. All the woods and orchards were cut down for Christmas trees. After a while they had to make Christmas trees out of rags. But there were plenty of rags, because people got so poor, buying presents for one another, that they couldn't get any new clothes, and they just wore their old ones to tatters. They got so poor that everybody had to go to the poorhouse, except the confectioners, and the storekeepers, and the booksellers; and they all got so rich and proud that they would hardly wait upon a person when he came to buy. It was perfectly shameful!

After it had gone on about three or four months, the little girl, whenever she came into the room in the morning and saw those great ugly, lumpy stockings dangling at the fireplace, and the disgusting presents around everywhere, used to sit down and burst out crying. In six months she was perfectly exhausted; she couldn't even cry anymore.

And how it was on the Fourth of July! On the Fourth of July, the first boy in the United States woke up and found out that his firecrackers and toy pistol and two-dollar collection of fireworks were nothing but sugar and candy painted up to look like fireworks. Before ten o'clock every boy in the United States discovered that his July Fourth things had turned into Christmas things and was so mad. The Fourth of July orations all turned into Christmas carols, and when anybody tried to read the Declaration of Independence, instead of saying, "When in the course of human events it becomes necessary," he was sure to sing, "God rest you merry gentlemen." It was perfectly awful.

About the beginning of October the little girl took to sitting down on dolls wherever she found them — she hated the sight of them so; and by Thanksgiving she just slammed her presents across the room. By that time people didn't carry presents around nicely anymore. They flung them over the fence or through the window, and, instead of taking great pains to write "For dear Papa," or "Mama," or "Brother," or "Sister," they used to write, "Take it, you horrid old thing!" and then go and bang it against the front door.

Nearly everybody had built barns to hold their presents, but pretty soon the barns overflowed, and then they used to let them lie out in the rain, or anywhere. Sometimes the police used to come and tell them to shovel their presents off the sidewalk or they would arrest them.

Before Thanksgiving came it had leaked out who had caused all these Christmases. The little girl had suffered so much that she had talked about it in her sleep, and after that hardly anybody would play with her, because if it had not been for her greediness it wouldn't have happened. And now, when it came Thanksgiving, and she wanted them to go to church, and have turkey, and show their gratitude, they said that all the turkeys had been eaten for her old Christmas dinners, and if she would stop the Christmases, they would see about the gratitude. And the very next day the little girl began sending letters to the Christmas Fairy, and then telegrams, to stop it. But it didn't do any good; and then she got to calling at the Fairy's house, but the girl that came to the door always said, "Not at home," or "Engaged," or something like that; and so it went on till it came to the old once-a-year Christmas Eve. The little girl fell asleep, and when she woke up in the morning —

"She found it was all nothing but a dream," suggested the little girl.

"No, indeed!" said her papa. "It was all every bit true!"

"What did she find out, then?"

"Why, that it wasn't Christmas at last, and wasn't ever going to be, anymore. Now it's time for breakfast."

The little girl held her papa fast around the neck.

"You shan't go if you're going to leave it so!"

"How do you want it left?"

"Christmas once a year."

"All right," said her papa; and he went on again.

Well, with no Christmas ever again, there was the greatest

rejoicing all over the country. People met together everywhere and kissed and cried for joy. Carts went around and gathered up all the candy and raisins and nuts, and dumped them into the river; and it made the fish perfectly sick. And the whole United States, as far out as Alaska, was one blaze of bonfires, where the children were burning up their presents of all kinds. They had the greatest time!

The little girl went to thank the old Fairy because she had stopped its being Christmas, and she said she hoped the Fairy would keep her promise and see that Christmas never, never came again. Then the Fairy frowned, and said that now the little girl was behaving just as greedily as ever, and she'd better look out. This made the little girl think it all over carefully again, and she said she would be willing to have it Christmas about once in a thousand years; and then she said a hundred, and then she said ten, and at last she got down to one. Then the Fairy said that was the good old way that had pleased people ever since Christmas began, and she was agreed. Then the little girl said, "What're your shoes made of?" And the Fairy said, "Leather." And the little girl said, "Bargain's done forever," and skipped off, and hip-pity-hopped the whole way home, she was so glad.

"How will that do?" asked the papa.

"First-rate!" said the little girl; but she hated to have the story stop, and was rather sober. However, her mama put her head in at the door and asked her papa:

"Are you never coming to breakfast? What have you been telling that child?"

"Oh, just a tale with a moral."

The little girl caught him around the neck again.

"We know! Don't you tell what, papa! Don't you tell what!" ✳

＊　＊　＊

Those of us who know Charles Dickens

as the creator of Victorian greats

like David Copperfield, Little Nell, Mr. Pickwick,

and Oliver Twist *need to get acquainted*

with another side of his personality—

a father who made sure his children

knew Jesus Christ. Here is Jesus' birth account

from Dickens' Victorian point of view.

＊　＊　＊

The Life of Our Lord
For My Dear Children

BY CHARLES DICKENS

CHAPTER THE FIRST

I am very anxious that you should know something about the History of Jesus Christ. For everyone ought to know about Him. No one ever lived who was so good, so kind, so gentle, and so sorry for all people who did wrong, or were in any way ill or miserable as He was. And as He is now in Heaven, where we hope to go, and all to meet each other after we are dead, and there be happy always together, you never can think what a good place Heaven is, without knowing who He was and what He did.

He was born a long, long time ago—nearly two-thousand years ago—at a place called Bethlehem. His father and mother lived in a city called Nazareth, but they were forced by business to travel to Bethlehem. His father's name was Joseph, and His mother's name was Mary. And the town being very full of people, also brought there by business, there was no room for Joseph and Mary in the Inn or in any house; so they went into a stable to lodge, and in this stable Jesus Christ was born. There was no cradle or anything of that kind there, so Mary laid her pretty little boy in what is called a manger, which is a place the horses eat of. And there He fell asleep.

While He was asleep, some shepherds who were watching sheep in the fields saw an Angel from God, all light and beautiful, come moving over the grass towards them. At first they were afraid and fell down and hid their faces. But the angel said, "There is a child born today in the city of Bethlehem near here. He will grow up and teach men to love one another, and not to quarrel and hurt one another; and His name will be Jesus Christ." And then the angel told the shepherds to go to that stable, and look at that little child in the manger. Which they did; and they kneeled down by Him in His sleep, and said "God bless this child."[32]

The Trouble with Presents

What do you want
    On Christmas morning
What do you look forward to
    On Christmas day?
I don't care what I find
    In my Christmas stocking
So long as it's a game
    That only one can play.

I'm tired of always getting
    On Christmas morning
To keep me amused through
    The whole of Christmas day
Boxes of cards
    Or Snakes and ladders
And games that only *two*
    Or *more* can play.

No wonder King John
    Was always furious
No wonder he ranted
    On Christmas day,
And craved for and *craved* for
    A red rubber ball*
For a ball is a present
With which *one* can play.

Though I'm not so sure
    Now I think about it!

Have you ever tried to play
    With a ball indoors?
It's sure to smash all
    The ornaments and vases
Or get stuck out of reach
    Behind a chest of drawers.

And you can't go outside
    Because it's snowing like fury
Or the rain's tipping down
    In buckets from the sky;
And the temperature's dropped
    With a thud below zero
And if you step out in that
    You're sure to freeze and die!

There's a box of candy
    That will "spoil" my dinner
Or worse is sure to make me
    Feel "frightfully sick"
And there's no point in learning
    My new conjuring game
If there's nobody available
    To enjoy the trick.

What's the point of having
    On Christmas morning
A present that requires
    A horde of other folks;

Even a fun book's
> Not very funny
If you can't discover anyone
> To laugh at the jokes.

I'm fed up with Shepherds
> On Christmas morning
They had each other
> To share in their fun;
Even those globe trotting
> Kings make me furious
As *they'd* have been furious
> If they'd been just *one*!

What about a book
> On Christmas morning?
Who wants to settle
> In a corner *alone*
Reading Milton's *Ode*
> *On Christ's Nativity!*

Every time I wake up
> On Christmas morning
I know what's going to happen
> As the day wears on;
Every time I ask my parents
> To play with me
They're going to say "O
> *Not now*. Later, son!"

For Mother's all snarled up
> Cooking the turkey;
"Now I'm sure you wouldn't want
> To eat it all raw!
Can't you go and play
> By yourself for a moment!
Where are all those super
> New toys I saw?"

But I can't blow my whistle
> Or thump my tin drum,
Or Dad who's feeling "fragile"
> Will blow a fuse!
Though why they gave them to me
> In the first place, beats me,
Out of all the other
> Presents they could choose!

Well, the train looks wizard
> But I daren't lay down the tracks,
For they take up so much space
> That they'll get in the way.

Oh why can't some genius
> Invent for Christmas morning
A really super game
> That only *one* can play.[33]

JOHN SMITH

Little Jesus

Little Jesus, wast Thou shy
Once, and just as small as I?
And what did it feel like to be
Out of Heaven, and just like me?
Didst Thou sometimes think of *there*,
And ask where all the angels were?

I should think that I would cry
For my house all made of sky;
I would look about the air,
And wonder where my angels were;
And at waking 'twould distress me—
Not an angel there to dress me!

Hadst Thou ever any toys,
Like us little girls and boys?
And didst Thou play in Heaven with all
The angels that were not too tall,
With stars for marbles? Did the things
Play *Can you see me?* through their wings?

And did Thy mother let Thee spoil
Thy robes with playing on *our* soil?
How nice to have them always new
In Heaven, because 'twas quite clean blue!

Didst Thou kneel at night to pray,
And didst Thou join Thy hands, this way?
And did they tire sometimes, being young,

And make the prayer seem very long?
And dost Thou like it best that we
Should join our hands to pray to Thee?
I used to think, before I knew,
The prayer not said unless we do.
And did Thy mother at the night
Kiss Thee and fold the clothes in right?
And didst Thou feel quite good in bed,
Kiss'd, and sweet, and Thy prayers said?

Thou canst not have forgotten all
That it feels like to be small:
And Thou know'st I cannot pray
To Thee in my father's way—
When Thou was so little, say,
Couldst Thou talk Thy Father's way?

So, a little Child, come down
And hear a child's tongue like Thy own;
Take me by the hand and walk,
And listen to my baby-talk.
To Thy Father show my prayer
(He will look, Thou art so fair),
And say; "O Father, I, Thy Son,
Bring the prayer of a little one."

And He will smile, that children's tongue
Has not changed since Thou wast young!

FRANCIS THOMPSON

Christmas Tree

little tree
little silent Christmas tree
you are so little
you are more like a flower

who found you in the green forest
and were you very sorry to come away?
see I will comfort you
because you smell so sweetly

I will kiss your cool bark
and hug you safe and tight
just as your mother would
only don't be afraid

look the spangles
that sleep all the year in a dark box
dreaming of being taken out and allowed to shine,
the balls the chains red and gold the fluffy threads,

little tree

Christmas tree

put up your little arms
and I'll give them all to you to hold
every finger shall have its ring
and there won't be a single place dark or unhappy

then when you're quite dressed
you'll stand in the window for everyone to see
and how they'll stare!
oh but you'll be very proud

and my little sister and I will take hands
and looking up at our beautiful tree
we'll dance and sing
"Noel Noel!"[34]
E. E. CUMMINGS

rms

all to you to hold

the Word

"Only five more shopping days"

"Be the first in your neighborhood"

"And what do you want for Christmas, little girl?"

"Ho, ho, ho!"

"Only four more shopping days"

"'Twas the night before Christmas"

"And a partridge in a pear tree"

"Only three more shopping days"

"Only two more"

"Only one"

"Merry Christmas!"

Christmas words are joyful words. Many of them are tinselly and jolly. All of them warm as a Yuletide fireplace. But most of these words are only the temporal glitz on the enduring meaning of Christmas.

Perhaps the true meaning can best be understood in the symbolic words of John: "The Word was made flesh and dwelt among us" (John 1:14).

All my heart

this night rejoices as I hear,

far and near, Sweetest angel

voices. "Christ is born" their

choirs are singing, till the air

everywhere now with joy

is ringing.

PAUL GERHARDT

The Word Became Flesh

In the beginning was the Word, and the Word was with God, and the Word was God. He was with God in the beginning.

Through him all things were made; without him nothing was made that has been made. In him was life, and that life was the light of men. The light shines in the darkness, but the darkness has not understood it.

The Word became flesh and made his dwelling among us. We have seen his glory, the glory of the One and Only, who came from the Father, full of grace and truth.

JOHN 1:1-5, 14 NIV

The Christmas Story

ACCORDING TO ST. MATTHEW AND ST. LUKE

AND EXPRESSED IN THE FAMILIAR KING JAMES VERSION

OF THE SCRIPTURE

It came to pass in those days, that there went out a decree from Caesar Augustus, that all the world should be taxed. (And this taxing was first made when Cyrenius was governor of Syria.) And all went to be taxed, every one into his own city.

And Joseph also went up from Galilee, out of the city of Nazareth, into Judaea, unto the city of David, which is call Bethlehem; (because he was of the house and lineage of David) to be taxed with Mary his espoused wife, being great with child.

And so it was, that while they were there, the days were accomplished that she should be delivered. And she brought forth her firstborn son, and wrapped him in swaddling clothes, and laid him in a manger; because there was room for them in the inn.

And there were in the same country shepherds abiding in the field, keeping watch over their flock by night. And, lo, the angel of the Lord came upon them, and the glory of the Lord shone round about them; and they were sore afraid.

And the angel said unto them, "Fear not: for behold, I bring you good tidings of great joy, which shall be to all people. For unto you is born this day in the city of David a Saviour, which is Christ the Lord.

"And this shall be a sign unto you; ye shall find the babe wrapped in swaddling clothes, lying in a manger.

And suddenly there was with the angel a multitude of the heavenly host praising God, and saying, "Glory to God in the highest, and on earth peace, goodwill toward men."

And it came to pass, as the angels were gone away from them into heaven, the shepherds said one to another, "Let us now go even unto Bethlehem, and see this thing which is come to pass, which the Lord hath made known unto us."

And they came with haste, and found Mary, and Joseph, and the babe lying in a manger. (Luke 2:8-16)

Now when Jesus was born in Bethlehem of Judaea in the days of Herod the king, behold, there came wise men from the east to Jerusalem, saying "Where is he that is born King of the Jews? For we have seen his star in the east, and are come to worship him."

When Herod the king heard these things, he was troubled, and all Jerusalem with him. And when he had gathered all the chief priests and scribes of the people together, he demanded of them where Christ should be born.

And they said unto him, "In Bethlehem of Judaea: for thus it is written by the prophet, 'And thou Bethlehem, in the land of Juda, art not least among the princes of Juda: for out of thee shall come a Governor, that shall rule my people Israel.'"

Then Herod, when he had privily called the wise men, enquired of them diligently what time the star appeared. And he sent them to Bethlehem, and said, "Go and search diligently for the young child; and when ye have found him, bring me word again, that I may come and worship him also" (Matthew 2:1-8).

When they had heard the king, they departed; and, lo, the star, which they saw in the east, went before them, till it came and stood over where the young child was. When they saw the star, they rejoiced with exceeding great joy.

And when they were come into the house, they saw the young child with Mary his mother, and fell down, and worshipped him: and when they had opened their treasures, they presented unto him gifts; gold, and frankincense, and myrrh.

And being warned of God in a dream that they should not return to Herod, they departed into their own country another way (Matthew 2:9-12).

And when they were departed, behold, the angel of the Lord appeareth to Joseph in a dream, saying, Arise, and take the young child and his mother, and flee into Egypt, and be thou there until I bring thee word: for Herod will seek the young child to destroy him.

When he arose, he took the young child and his mother by night, and departed into Egypt. And was there until the death of Herod: that it might be fulfilled which was spoken of the Lord by the prophet, saying, "Out of Egypt have I called my son" (Matthew 2:13-15).

But when Herod was dead, behold, and angel of the Lord appeareth in a dream to Joseph in Egypt, saying "Arise, and take the young child and his mother, and go into the land of Israel: for they are dead which sought the young child's life."

And he arose, and took the young child and his mother, and came into the land of Israel. But when he heard that Archelaus did not reign in Judaea in the room of his father Herod, he was afraid to go thither: notwithstanding, being warned of God in a dream, he turned aside into the parts of Galilee: and he came and dwelt in a city called Nazareth: that it might be fulfilled which was spoken by the prophets, "He shall be called a Nazarene" (Matthew 2:19-23).

The Mystery of the Incarnation

A tired old doctor died today, and a baby boy was born—
A little new soul that was pink and frail,
    and a soul that was gray and worn.
And—halfway here and halfway there
On a white, high hill of shining air—
They met and passed and paused to speak
    in the flushed and hearty dawn.

The man looked down at the soft, small thing,
    with wise and weary eyes;
And the little chap stared back at him,
    with startled, scared surmise,
And then he shook his downy head—
"I think I won't be born," he said;
"You are too gray and sad!" And he shrank
    from the pathway down the skies.

But the tired old doctor roused once more
    at the battle cry of birth,
And there was memory in his look, of grief
    and toil and mirth.
"Go on!" he said. "It's good—and bad:
It's hard! *Go on!* It's ours, my lad."
And he stood and urged him out of sight,
    down to the waiting earth.[35]

HAROLD FRANCIS BRANCH

The Magnificat
MARY'S SONG

Mary [after the heavenly messenger's announcement that she would give birth to Jesus] said:

"My soul glorifies the Lord
   and my spirit rejoices in God my Savior,
for he has been mindful
   of the humble state of his servant.
From now on all generations will call me blessed,
   for the Mighty One has done great things for me—
   holy is his name.
His mercy extends to those who fear him,
   from generation to generation.
He has performed mighty deeds with his arm;
   he has scattered those who are proud in their inmost thoughts.
He has filled the hungry with good things
   but has sent the rich away empty.
He has helped his servant Israel,
   remembering to be merciful
to Abraham and his descendants forever.
   even as he said to our fathers."

LUKE 1:46-55 NIV

The Benedictus

ZECHARIAH'S SONG

Zechariah [at the birth of his son, John the Baptist] was filled with
the Holy Spirit and prophesied:

"Praise be to the Lord, the God of Israel,
>   because he has come and has redeemed his people.
He has raised up a horn of salvation for us
>   in the house of his servant David
(as he said through his holy prophets of long ago),
salvation from our enemies
>   and from the hand of all who hate us—
to show mercy to our fathers
>   and to remember his holy covenant,
>   the oath he swore to our father Abraham:
to rescue us from the hand of our enemies,
>   and to enable us to serve him without fear
>   in holiness and righteousness before him all of our days.

And you, my child, will be called a prophet of the Most High;
>   for you will go on before the Lord to prepare the way for him,
to give his people the knowledge of salvation
>   through the forgiveness of their sins,
because of the tender mercy of our God,
>   by which the rising sun will come to us from heaven
to shine on those living in darkness
>   and in the shadow of death,
to guide our feet into the path of peace."

LUKE 1:68-79 NIV

That Holy Thing

They all were looking for a king
    To slay their foes and lift them high:
Thou cam'st a little baby thing
    That made a woman cry.

O Son of man, to right my lot
Nought but thy presence can avail;
Yet on the road thy wheels are not,
    Nor on the sea thy sail!

My fancied ways why shouldst thou heed?
    Thou com'st down thine own secret stair;
Com'st down to answer all my need,
    Yea, every bygone prayer!

GEORGE MACDONALD

Originally written in French,

the words of this prayer express village life

village life

in the provinces—the kind of life

the boy Jesus understood.

The Prayer of the
Children of Provence

Little Jesus of the Crib,

Give us the virtues of those who surround you.

Make us philosophical as the fisherman,

Carefree as the drummer,

Merry in exploring the world as the troubadour

Eager for work as the bugler,

Patient as the spinner,

Kind as the ass,

Strong as the ox which keeps you warm.

Give us the sacred leisure of the hunter.

Give us also the desire of the shepherd for earthly things,

The pride of the trade of the knife grinder and the weaver,

The song of the miller.

Grant us the knowledge of the Magi,

The cheerfulness of the pigeon,

The impulsiveness of the cock,

The discretion of the snail,

The meekness of the lamb.

Give us the goodness of bread,

The tenderness of the wild boar,

The salt of the haddock,

The good humor of old wine,

The ardor of the candle,

The purity of the star.[36]

Christmas Is a Book

BY MARGARET COUSINS

From my earliest memories, Christmas has always been the climax of the year . . . full of secrets and surprises, tumult and shouting, comings and goings.

The smell of spruce and cedar vied with the benign odors of elaborate cooking in our house . . . serried ranks of pies, mince apple, and butterscotch; the noble cakes, swooning in snowfalls of fresh coconuts or drifted fudge or Lady Baltimore icing; the pink hams sizzling in sweet pickle juice; the lordly turkey turning brown in the oven; the cookies, the hot breads, the home produced candy spiky with walnuts and pecans.

And then there was the tree, adorned in its freight of spun glass and tinsel, cherishing the battered old ornaments (the one the puppy licked the paint off of and the angel with the splinted wing) along with the new, piled round with lovely loot.

It was such a day . . . Christmas . . . with all the aunts and uncles and cousins driving up rosy cheeked from the cold and swamped with packages. Divested of wraps, the ladies swarmed on the kitchen, chattering like a flight of sparrows as they scraped the celery, basted the bird, or unmolded the cranberry sauce . . . who married whom since last year, who begat whom, who was in love and who was out of love. The men sat around the fire, talking about crops and government.

The children plied between, round-eyed, mesmerized, sodden with happiness at the prospect of the feast and the good temper of the elders, frenetic with the thoughts of what the tree might eventually disclose.

Besides these memories, Christmas to me has always meant a book. From the first limp leather copy of Robert Louis Stevenson's *A Child's Garden of Verses*, now missing its back completely and dog-eared by time and circumstance, all the Christmases of my life continue to line up on bookshelves. When I look at them, even in the dead of summer, they summon the recollection of happy days.

Consider the Christmas I received *The Jungle Book* ("A brave heart and a courteous tongue, manling, will carry thee far in the jungle that is the world"). For the first time I looked at my aunt and saw beyond the grown-up state to the little girl she must have been. My aunt made me a present of Kipling and of herself. She ceased to be an aunt and became a friend.

I suppose I must have wanted the things most girls want for Christmas . . . bangles and bracelets and sealskin muffs and French perfume . . . and I must have got them, too, though they have now gone the way of all trinkets. But I counted on a book. I waited for the oblong package that lay heavy in my hand, full of the mystery of another mind, as well as being a special communication from the donor.

After the book was handed down from the Christmas tree, I was never completely sociable. I had to keep peering at it and was unable to keep my mind on the conversation. It was the book I took off to bed when the last candle was guttered.

Well, those books are with me still. When it comes time to ballast possessions, I cannot persuade myself to give away *The Little Colonel's House Party* or the volume of Browning's poems, so sentimentally inscribed by one who thinks of me sentimentally no longer, or *The Magic Mountain*, which I had such a struggle to finish. I cannot give them away though I have outgrown them or never grown up to them.

The whole perfume of Christmas emanates from their well-worn pages and the people who made the mine rise before me in a succession of happy poses.

Christmas is a book.[37]

*The true narrative of Jesus' first coming
has its roots in the prophetic words
of the Old Testament.*

✳ ✳ ✳

The Gospel According to the Old Testament

GOD WITH US

You who bring good tidings to Zion,
go up on a high mountain.
You who bring good tidings to Jerusalem,
lift up your voice with a shout,
lift it up, do not be afraid;
say to the towns of Judah.
"Here is your God!"

ISAIAH 40:9 NIV

SHEPHERD OF PEACE

But you, Bethlehem . . . out of you will come for me one who will be ruler over Israel. He will stand and shepherd his flock in the strength of the LORD, in the majesty of the name of the LORD his God. And they will live securely, for then his greatness will reach to the ends of the earth. And he will be their peace.

MICAH 5:2, 4-5

KING OF KINGS

The royal son . . . will rule from sea to sea and from the River to the ends of the earth. All kings will bow down to him and all nations will serve him. May his name endure forever; may it continue as long as the sun. All nations will be blessed through him, and they will call him blessed.

PSALM 72:8, 11, 17

✳ ✳ ✳

Literary critics have judged

"Ode on the Morning of Christ's Nativity"

to be some of the most sublime words in the

a family

English language, and some Christian believers

tradition

have made it a practice to read these lines

to the family every Christmas morning.

Although some lines will need to be interpreted

to youngsters, consider making this a family tradition.

✳ ✳ ✳

Ode on the Morning of Christ's Nativity

BY JOHN MILTON

(ABRIDGED)

I

This is the month, and this the happy morn,

Wherein the Son of Heaven's eternal King,

Of wedded maid and virgin mother born,

Our great redemption from above did bring;

For so the holy sages once did sing,

That he our deadly forfeit should release,

And with his father work us a perpetual peace.

III

Say, Heavenly Muse, shall not thy sacred vein

Afford a present to the infant God?

Hast thou no verse, no hymn, or solemn strain,

To welcome him to this his new abode,

Now while the Heaven, by the sun's team untrod,

Hath took no print of the approaching light,

And all the spangled host keep watch in squadrons bright?

IV

See how from far, upon the eastern road,

The star-led wizards haste with odours sweet:

O run, prevent them with humble ode,

And lay it lowly at his blessed feet!

Have thou the honour first thy Lord to greet,

And join thy voice unto the Angel Quire,

From out his secret altar touched with hallowed fire.

THE HYMN

I

It was the winter wild,

While the Heaven-born Child

    All meanly wrapt in the rude manger lies;

Nature, in awe to him,

Had doffed her gaudy trim,

    With her great Master so to sympathize. . . .

V

But peaceful was the night

Wherein the Prince of Light

    His reign of peace upon the earth began;

The winds, with wonder whist,

Smoothly the waters kist,

    Whispering new joys to the mild Ocean,

Who now hath quite forgotten to rave,

While birds of calm sit brooding on the charmed wave.

VI

The stars, with deep amaze,

Stand fixed in steadfast gaze,

    Bending one way their precious influence,

And will not take their flight,

For all the morning light,

    Or Lucifer that often warned them thence;

But in their glimmering orbs did glow,

Until their Lord himself bespake, and bid them go.

VII

     And though the shady gloom

     Had given day her room,

        The sun himself withheld his wonted speed,

     And hid his head for shame,

     As his inferior flame,

        The new-enlightened world no more should need;

     He saw the greater Sun appear

     Than his bright throne or burning axletree could bear.

VIII

     The shepherds on the lawn,

     Or ere the point of dawn,

        Sat simply chatting in a rustic row;

     Full little thought they then

     That the mighty Pan

        Was kindly come to live with them below;

     Perhaps their loves, or else their sheep,

     Was all that did their silly thoughts so busy keep.

IX

     When such music sweet

     Their hearts and ears did greet,

        As never was by mortal finger strook,

     Divinely-warbled voice

     Answering the stringed noise

        As all their souls in blissful rapture took;

     The air, such pleasure loath to lose,

     With thousand echoes still prolongs each Heavenly close.

XIV

    For if such holy song

    Enrap our fancy long,

        Time will run back and fetch the age of gold;

    And speckled Vanity

    Will sicken soon and die,

        And leprous Sin will melt from earthly mould;

    And Hell itself will pass away,

    And leave her dolorous mansions to the peering day.

XV

    Yea, Truth and Justice then

    Will down return to men,

    Orbed in a rainbow; and, like glories wearing,

    Mercy will sit between,

    Throned in celestial sheen,

        With radiant feet the tissued clouds down steering;

    And Heaven, as at some festival.

    Will open wide the gates of her high palace-hall.

XXVII

    But see! the Virgin blest

    Hath laid her Babe to rest;

        Time is our tedious song should here have ending:

    Heaven's youngest-teemed star

    Hath fixed her polished car,

    Her sleeping Lord with handmaid lamp attending;

    And all about the courtly stable

    Bright-harnessed angels sit in order serviceable.

*The written word, even if it's so small as a
note, has the power to change a life.*

❋　❋　❋

Snow for Christmas
BY VINCENT STARRETT

Fears had been expressed that there would be no snow
for Christmas, but three days before the world's holiday it
began to fall. Quietly it came, like a thief in the night, and
in the morning it lay thickly in the streets, soft, feathery
and glistening. During the day it fell again, and by night-
fall it covered everything within view. The roofs and gables
of the neighborhood were heavy with snow, and the bare
branches of the trees seemed to droop with its weight.

To David Thursk, for all the white loveliness of the
scene, it brought its inevitable sorrow. Standing at the
upstairs front windows of his home, as evening set in, he
watched the street lamps become globes of pale light in
the chill dusk, and his heart was heavy with the thought of
his father. The old-fashioned stone block beside the curb
across the way was suddenly a grave of ice; the ancient
dwelling at which he gazed seemed to lean and totter
toward some dreadful revelation.

Tomorrow marked an anniversary, the first anniversary
of his father's death. It would be a year on Christmas
morning since John Thursk had come down those steps for
the last time on the shoulders of his friends. He had loved
the Christmas season. On a Christmas morning he had
first seen the dawn make ribbons of light through those
shutters, now closed perhaps forever; and on a Christmas
morning he had been laid away beneath his final coverlet
of earth. He had earned his repose, the good, kindly man.

But David Thursk still mourned for his dead father. The pride had been great. No tears had run from David's eyes the day his father died. A man's tears are like diamonds at the core of a mountain. But in his heart a poignant hurt still throbbed and ached.

There had been nights when his agony had seemed more than he could bear. There came to him moments of seeming revelation when the full horror of what had happened brought him to a sitting position in his bed; when a sense of the finality of the separation was stark upon him. The terror and the mystery of death! Never again to see and know the man whose understanding had filled his heart, in whom he had seen himself ennobled and glorified. At such times he grasped desperately at the straws of religion that swam about him on the dark stream that was his mind. Alternately they tortured and comforted him. At other times he was rebellious at the injustice of death, the injustice of the shrouding mystery; times when, in a frenzy of hate, he wanted to tear the skies apart to unveil the sham and cruelty of whatever lay behind. It would be an act of defiance, of obscene insolence, an insult so gigantic as perhaps to lay the world in ruins.

What he really wished was simply proof of all that early he had been taught to believe; some shining presence with valiant voice unanswerably to declare the best news true; a miracle of comfort and illusion. For there had never been anyone quite like John Thursk, not even David's mother, long dead, a placid and peaceful memory.

Darkness had fallen over the city. A red glow, square and warm, sprang out of a neighboring window, and was reflected upon the snow field beneath. A second followed, and then a third. The shadows of the trees wavered in the oblique planes of light. With a sigh, David turned from his window. Below stairs sounded a medley of pleasant noises; a rattle of pans and dishes, the closing of an oven door, and in the intervals a warming gust of voices in happy altercation. The evening meal was preparing, and the younger John was keeping persistently underfoot. Something of the heartiness of the occasion came to the lonely man on the stairs, and with a little smile he finished the descent and stood briskly rubbing his hands before the open fireplace.

"Dear old Dad!" he murmured, as happier memories began to crowd his mind. "How he would have loved to be with us tonight!"

When the dinner dishes had been cleared away, and his wife had gone upstairs with the younger John, he smoked a pipe before the fire, and the thought of his father no longer disturbed him. It was pleasant now to think of the fine old fellow. Not that he had been really old. Sixties! That was part of the tragedy and injustice of it. David could almost hear that deep, remembered laugh from the big chair on the other side of the grate. The flames danced fantastically on the hearth, unchanged as always, and by a little stretch of fancy David could see his father leaning forward to poke at the truant sparks and fags that endeavored to escape the holocaust.

His stick was there in the corner, where it had stood since his death; the stout staff he had cut and trimmed and varnished himself, companion of his strolls about the neighborhood. He had been a famous walker. How the squirrels had run to him at the familiar rattle of that old stick on the pavement! His books too were there, in the old bookcase that had been brought across the street with the books. Gallant stories of highhearted ladies and gentlemen of another day, punctuated at intervals by sober history and old-fashioned poetry. There was never such another man as John Thursk. There never could be such another.

"John Thursk just missed being a great man, by inches," somebody had said of him, after his death. When the compliment had been relayed to his son, David had smiled and replied: "He was something better than that; he was a great human being. It is the hardest of all things to be. Great men are relatively common."

Now Christmas was at hand, and everything was going forward as in other years. Only John Thursk was absent from the familiar scene. For years he had been there, and now he was not there. He would never be there again. Everything else was as it had been, yet nothing was the same.

David Thursk heard his wife's step upon the stairs, and put aside his dreaming. She entered the room and placed a letter in his hand.

"I've been wild to give you this all evening," she told him, "but I was afraid John would catch me at it, and think I didn't understand. You mustn't let him know you have read it."

Her husband received the letter with a smile, which altered as he glanced at the superscription.

"Poor little chap!" he said quaintly and turned the envelope in his hands. Hideously smeared with ink as it was, and more than a little dirty, it was addressed quite plainly, albeit tortuously, to "Santa Claus, North Pole, Norway."

"Read it," said his wife, still proudly smiling; and awkwardly he inserted his fingers beneath the flap.

"It's almost a betrayal," he protested. "I really feel guilty, Nora!"

"Skittles!" she deprecated. "He'd be proud as a peacock if he thought you liked it. There's a clause in it relating to you; that's why he asked me not to show it to you."

With sensitive fingers David unfolded the paper and read his son's communication, a not particularly remarkable document filled with solemn injunctions and ecstatic promises. His eyes blurred for an instant, and were turned upon the leaping flames as he handed it back.

"Poor little chap!" he said again. "We must get him everything he wants, within reason. But, do you know, Nora, I seriously question the wisdom of allowing such letters to be written. They serve no purpose other than to disappoint the child, in some particular, and to perpetuate a lying legend that, later, if he has sense, he will not thank us for putting into his head."

He spoke with more vigor than he had intended and his wife was shocked.

"Why, David!" she cried. "I thought you loved that old legend. You've always been so happy at Christmas—except, of course—last Christmas. I've heard you tell John about Santa Claus, yourself, and answer his questions about him. Your father loved it too. I remember you and your father helping John to write a letter to—"

She broke off suddenly, and her voice was anxious. "David, are you ill?"

He shook his head impatiently. "I know," he said, "I do love it, or I always thought I loved it. I loved it as a boy—although I still remember the agony I suffered when my mother told me it wasn't so. I believed for a long time," he added wistfully. "I must have been a pretty big boy when she told me; too old to be believing that sort of thing."

He stared hard into the flames.

"The fact is, Nora, we believe too many things. We're taught things that aren't so, because they are pleasant things to believe. And because they are pleasant, we go on believing them long after we ought to know better. We know they're not so, and still we go on believing them. We won't give them up. Life would be too terrible without them. We'd go crazy if we didn't believe something. And we clutch at straws to make things seem true that we know are only lies, told us by our parents to make us happy. Happy! We'd be happier if we were told nothing, and grew up believing nothing. Then we wouldn't expect things to happen that can't happen. It wouldn't hurt us so much when the unhappy things came. We'd have learned to expect them, and not to cry afterward."

He realized that he was becoming incoherent.

"I'm sorry, Nora, if I seemed to speak hotly. I didn't mean it that way. I do love it all—the whole Christmas season; everything it stands for. I only wish to God that I could believe it all again!

That's what I meant. If I hadn't been taught all this—about Santa Claus—about God and heaven—"

He stopped again, and she laid a hand on his shoulder and another on his bent head. His body shook so that she was alarmed; but she concealed her apprehension and spoke without nervousness.

"You've been thinking about your father," she said slowly. "I know how you feel, and I'm sorrier than I can tell you. You know, I went through it all with you, and I miss him almost as much as you do. I've been thinking about him a lot today," she concluded on a note intended to comfort him. Immediately, she added more brightly: "I asked John today if he remembered how his grandfather used to help him write his letters to Santa Claus, and he said he wished Grandfather were here to help him, now."

Understanding the kindly intent of the anecdote, David smiled up at her. "Did he? Good little chap! It was nice of him to ask for a new desk for me, at the office. He must have heard me say I needed one."

Late that night, as he sat alone before the fire, David again noticed his son's letter. It lay face upward on the table, close to his hand, where his wife had dropped it. He took it up idly and began to finger it. Poor little chap! What disillusionments, he wondered, were ahead for John? What disappointments, and what overwhelming sorrows? And what a dreadful responsibility one undertook who brought children into the world!

And yet how jolly it had been in the old days. When his father had been with them, he—David—had been happy without believing, as had John Thursk. They had been happy in another's belief. Happy in encouraging that belief. Was it a vicious thing that they had done? They had sought to make John happy. Was it so evil a thing to make a child happy? Surely happiness was a thing to be taken wherever found. The trouble was, he—David—had been too happy—too happy all along the line. He had believed in everything too hard. Whatever was blissful and soothing, he had been taught, he had accepted without question, and he had fervently believed, until with mounting years and some modicum of intelligence, had come the doubts natural to all who think. Even then he had fought them back—or had put them out of his mind. His naive agnosticism had been overwhelmed by avalanches of proof and reproach, and new delights had been added to the legend. Still the doubts had persisted, until alternately he had been torn between belief and unbelief, between bitter atheism and ardent acceptance of everything that was fantastic and comforting. In the end he had adopted the easy attitude of the many; perhaps it was so, perhaps it was not so; at any rate, there was nothing that he could do about it, nothing he could ascertain beyond question; and the happiest solution of the difficulty was not to think of it at all. And so he had not thought of it at all.

Now the death of his father had brought it all back with new and more terrible tortures for his soul. Now he had a profound and ghastly interest in the problem, a personal interest that, curiously, he had not felt when his mother died. For a time David believed, desperately, knowing that he was afraid not to, and knowing, deep underneath, that he did not believe.

To make a child happy! To make a man happy! To make a soul happy! And how jolly it all had been in the old days. If only he could believe again! That was what he wanted, and it could never be. He knew it. He knew that he could not even pretend any more.

He turned the letter over and over in his hands, while he stared into the fire. Yes, he would like to go back and believe it all again. The straggling characters on the envelope caught his eye, and he smiled. To write a letter to Santa Claus again! And believe that it would be answered! However, that was past—and rapidly, he thought, he was becoming a raving lunatic. Dear old Dad! Had he ever had doubts? Had he ever been tormented in this way? How quiet had been his philosophy! How fine his tolerance!

David's heart overflowed. He turned his chair to the table. Slowly he drew a sheet of paper toward him, and reached for a pen. The ink bottle was handy. One thing, at least, he could do with entire sincerity. He could set down his love for his father. Not that his father had not known; but no words had been spoken. Of course his father had known. But it would be a relief and a happiness to write it down; to say the foolish, sentimental, loving words that had lain so long unsaid in his heart.

A quaint idea came to him, sitting there; it had been with him, subconsciously, for some moments. He would write a letter to his father! Just as if he were still living and could read it. In it he would say all of the things that his reserve would never have permitted him to say aloud to his father's face, and that the reserve of John Thursk would never have permitted him to hear without embarrassment.

The idea pleased David enormously. He dipped his pen into the bottle. It was an idiotic thing, of course, although no more ridiculous than that in which he had encouraged his son. Self-consciousness began to steal over him, but he held fast to his idea and recaptured the mood. He would even seal the letter in an envelope, and address it, as the younger John had done.

But where?

He smiled happily. "John Thursk—Address Unknown." He would write the words on an envelope, and Dad—wherever he might be—would understand and know, at last. The younger John's letter would be dropped into the postbox tomorrow; but his own would be—Why, yes! it too would be mailed. It would be dropped into the fire. In a swift moment of fancy he saw the letter lying in the deep glow, at first white, then rapidly becoming a dull brown. The edges were curling, his father's name seemed to stand forth in letters of fire; the envelope was opening; then a little burst of flame, a heap of crumbling black, and the message was a red spark whirling up the chimney and into the outer air. Up . . . up . . . and out . . . a red spark mounting higher and higher into the night, toward . . . ?

"Dear old Dad," David wrote, and paused. Once more he dipped his pen into the ink bottle; and then his heart began to pour itself out across the sheet.

II

ON Christmas Eve, the barometer dropped starkly and an arctic storm broke over the city. The snow, which had fallen all day long, vanished on the wings of an icy blast out of the north. The wind roared in the streets and whined dismally in the chimneys. It plucked great armfuls of snow from the drifts and flung them across the night in swirling clouds and columns. The cold was bitter, and as the night advanced the cry of the storm rose higher. Few persons were abroad in the streets. The lights gleamed ghostily through the driving spray of ice and snow.

David Thursk sat before the open fire in the living room of his home and listened to the fury of the storm. The hour was late, and he was alone. An hour before, his wife had placed her final gift on the glittering tree, and climbed the stairs to her room. For a time he had heard her stirring in the room above; then silence had fallen on the place, a silence of which the background of storm had become a part. For many minutes he had not moved in his chair. He was thinking again of his dead father, and of a wind-swept grave. It was cold tonight out there on the hillside. John Thursk had loved a roaring fire on an open hearth. He had disliked the cold.

As they were affected by the gusts outside, the blue and yellow flames alternately flickered with low hissing and tongued roaring up the chimney. Leaning forward to apply another log, David fancied that again he saw his letter lying upon the fire, a square of white that swiftly became a black wafer, stamped with a glowing spark of red; and again he saw it swiftly mounting to the eternities, a valiant gleam lost in the dark immensity of space.

It had been a childish fancy and a childish performance, but it had been good to be a child again. Many times, in moments of cynical sanity, he had blushed about his folly; had seen in that leaping scarlet flame the counterfeit of his own illusions. For it is in the nature of fire and flame, he told himself, to turn to smoke and ashes. He rationalized his folly and again found comfort, only again to find himself floundering in the labyrinths of theology. Dimly he felt that it was all madness. Madness to believe, madness not to believe, madness to attempt to understand or explain. The greatest minds were as helpless before the mystery as his own. "To be or not to be" was not the question posited by death. The question had never been put. It was not as simple as that, and it had not only two horns. Yet he must accept wholly or wholly reject. He might not pick and choose. A religion subsisted by its dogmas only. Men did not become martyrs to a code of ethics, to that which was comprehensible and involved no passion. But his own emotion, he realized, was for his father; it had little to do with religious ecstasy.

Times without number he reproached himself for the pride that had sealed within his lips the expressions of affection that now lay so heavily on his heart. And times without number he comforted himself with the thought that all was well, that somewhere—somehow—his father knew. And yet—were it only possible to call back a single day, an hour, five minutes of that other time that now seemed to have been so incredibly happy, how he would employ the moments to make clear the deeps of his heart! Every syllable he had poured from the silences of his soul into that letter, gone forth into mystery, would find its duplicate on his tongue. Not the windy sentiment of rhetoric, but the simple story of a boy's long love for his father, in such words as he might have uttered in childhood.

Exactly a year ago this dreadful night, John Thursk lay dying in the old home across the street. Only by the pressure of his hand in David's hand, and of David's hand in his, had father and son spoken. Only a few hours now, and the clock hands would mark the moment of the solemn anniversary.

David's eyes were turned upon the clock. Midnight had struck some minutes before. The fire was falling into ash. Half-heartedly he stirred to replenish it. Outside, the storm had not abated; if anything, its fury had increased. At intervals a white smother flung itself against the panes, beyond the drawn blinds, and the cold fingers of a cedar tapped urgently against the wall of the house, beside the steps. A grim and deadly night, he thought. . . . Then heavy feet crunched upward on the steps, and David Thursk came upright from his chair as the shrill alarm of the doorbell sounded through the house.

With a curious feeling of apprehension he glanced again at the clock. Then his mind functioned automatically, and his lips formed the words, "A telegram!"

But from whom? And with what conceivable message on this night of riot?

For an instant his heart seemed to stop beating; then his feet moved of their own volition and he walked quickly into the corridor and opened the inner door. In the passage between door and door he wrestled for an instant with the latch. And then the storm whirled past him with savage eyes, and seemed to fill the entry.

On the porch, against the doorstep, stood a tall stranger wrapped in an overcoat. His great collar was turned up against the gale, and a huge muffler swathed his face almost to the eyes, which were protected by the peak of a high cap that descended at the sides and back.

"Special delivery," said the man gruffly, as the dim light from inside fell outward across the doorsill. "For David Thursk," he added.

"I am David Thursk," said David, accepting the envelope from the gloved fingers. "A bad night to be out," he continued with a little shiver. "Do you want me to sign for it? You'd better step inside for a minute. It will give you a chance to get warm." He drew his smoking jacket more closely around him.

The messenger hesitated; he had been groping in his pocket as if for a pencil. His eyes smiled and seemed to blur. Their gleam and the droop of his shoulders called sharply on David's sympathies.

"You are older than is usual with messengers," he added kindly, noting the man's hesitation. "If you care to come inside while I open this, I'll make some tea for us both. We might even have a pipe together, eh? You must be cold, and there is a good fire inside."

What strange vicissitudes, he wondered, had brought his visitor to such a pass. The man appeared to be quite elderly; not at all the sort of brisk lad ordinarily employed by the post office for such errands. A queer sense of the unreality of the episode came suddenly to David, even as his heart warmed to the derelict on his doorstep. His prompt hospitality, although born of an emotion not unusual in a lonely man, seemed all at once to be charged with a disturbing significance. For a moment even the midnight letter had been forgotten in an unexplainable desire to make this cheerless stranger happy before a fire, to ply him with tea and tobacco, and warm his heart with conversation.

A thin white avalanche flung itself up the steps with a roar; for an instant it filled the entry and obliterated the figure on the doorstep. Choking and coughing, brushing the snow from his garments, David turned his back and shoulders to the assault. When it had cleared the messenger had moved back from the door; he stood now at the head of the descending flight. His voice when David heard it again was low and gruff.

"Thank you, Mr. Thursk, but I guess not. I'd like to, very much—but not tonight. I must get back."

And suddenly the man's figure seemed to droop. He stood with tilted head, one shoulder lifted slightly above the level of the other; a peculiar mannerism. The gruff voice cleared.

"It's good of you to ask me. I'd like to have tea with you sometime— yes, and smoke a pipe, too. Most of all, I'd like to talk with you. That would be great happiness for me. You asked me in because you thought I was cold and unhappy; but I'm not. You've warmed me and made me very happy. I'll see you again sometime, you know; when I have another message—out this way. You are very like your father, David Thursk!"

Then David's heart skipped a beat, and instantly ran faster than ever. Out of a little empty silence, he heard his voice whispering: "You knew my father?"

The storm-clad figure turned its eyes; and suddenly, in a blinding flash of revelation, David knew what manner of stranger this was that he had invited to enter his home. Shuddering, he shrank back into the doorway.

"You took my father!" he cried. "I know you now. You are . . ." But the stranger smiled so kindly that there was no room for fear, and his voice, clear and high, struck through David's heart like a flight of bird notes.

"Thank you, David, for your invitation," he said. "When I come again, don't fear that I shall not accept. I shall be glad to warm myself before your fire. It was a kindly thought. And perhaps you will care to go with me for a distance, when I leave. I could ask no better company. . . . Good night, David!"

"Now!" cried David Thursk, eagerly. "Let me go with you now!"

But the messenger had turned away and was stamping down the steps through the long snow drifts. His deep laugh seemed to echo against the night.

"When I come again," called the memorable voice. "Farewell!"

His feet crunched on the walk; the tall figure straightened until it seemed to obscure the light, until it seemed to fill the street and the sky, until . . .

Somewhere above and behind a voice was calling anxiously, and David knew it was his wife's voice. "David!" she called; and vaguely he knew that in a minute she would come down to join him. Slowly he began to close the door.

Something inside was trying to tell him something; his mind was shredding itself against barricades of intervening bewilderment. Desperately he fought back toward comprehension. The messenger! That stranger at the door! What was it that was clamoring at his heart? A revelation was impending that would shake his reason. The droop of those familiar shoulders, the poise and tilt of that familiar head; the eyes that had compelled him to ask a midnight stranger to sit beside him at the fire. Even the voice, at first gruff and harsh, which at the last had struck through him like the sound of a distant bell. That final laugh, deep as an organ note. How could he have forgotten it!

He had almost closed the door, but suddenly he wrenched it open so that it crashed against the wall and splintered at the comer.

"Dad!"

His cry of anguish rang above the storm. He flung himself down the steps and into the deserted street, calling the name. He screamed and sobbed; and the wind seized his words and flung them across the night, and up into the skies, and over the empty spaces of the world. He ran up and down the sidewalk in the deep snow, calling. He found the trail of footprints leading away from the steps, and saw them vanish into unbroken drifts before they reached the walk. From end to end the street lay bare and white under the lights, under the stars—and there was no footfall in all creation.

III

DAVID THURSK came back to consciousness slowly. Even when it was certain that he would recover, he asked no questions for some days, but lay quietly and thoughtfully in his bed, thinking thoughts as long and slow as had been his return to life. Then, very quietly, one day he turned to his wife and asked for the letter.

She was very much surprised, but she rose instantly from her chair.

"What letter do you mean, dear?" she asked brightly, preparing to seek out anything that he might care to see.

But when he had told her, her face was grave and her eyes became a little frightened. There was no one near, however, on whom she might call for advice, and so she answered as best she was able.

"David," she said, "you must try to understand what happened to you that night. I was asleep upstairs, with John, and I thought I heard the front door open. Then for a little while I heard nothing at all. I called to you, but you didn't answer. And then I heard you throw open the door and run out into the storm. I heard you calling. I found you out there in the snow. One of the neighbors helped me to get you into the house, and I telephoned for the doctor. You have been very ill ever since. There wasn't any letter, David. You frighten me when you tell me you had a letter from your father."

"I wrote to him," he replied gravely, "the night you showed me John's foolish, pathetic letter to the North Pole. I posted my letter in the fire. It sounds like madness, doesn't it? But you would think me madder still if I told you what occurred on Christmas Eve—and so I shall not tell you, Nora darling, and I shall never speak of it again."

When she had gone away he lay back gently on his pillow and watched the winter sunlight on the windowpane.

"Dear old Dad!" he said, half aloud, half smiling. "Shall I recognize you when you come again? And is it until next year, or for fifty years, that you would have me wait for you? No matter, I shall be ready when you ring; you shall not go away alone. We know each other now, you and I. I have been close to mystery, and I think that also I have been close to madness. It is not well to inquire too closely even into oneself. But I have understood your message. It is just to love—and to tell others that you love. You will come again in a solemn hour. If there be an awakening beyond that hour, it is because of love. And if there shall be no awakening, that too, I think, will be because of love."

He smiled.

"Meanwhile, it is well to live, and to find happiness in love. I have much to do."

For some minutes he lay thinking, then quietly dropped off to sleep. His wife, entering the room an instant later, listened for a moment to his peaceful breathing and tiptoed to her chair.[38]   ✳

According to the Word:
Every Day Is Christmas

Christmas is not a day or a season, but a condition of heart and mind. If we love our neighbors as ourselves; if in our riches we are poor in spirit and in our poverty we are rich in grace; if our charity vaunteth not itself, but suffereth long and is kind; if when our brother asks for a loaf we give ourselves instead; if each day dawns in opportunity and sets in achievement, however small; then every day is Christ's day and Christmas is always near.

JAMES WALLINGFORD

of *Music*

Perhaps of all the arts, music has the greatest power to transport the listener to other days and other places. Do you remember the first time you heard one of the great choruses from Handel's *Messiah*, or a symphony orchestra play a suite from Tchaikovsky's *Nutcracker*, or a recording of Bing Crosby singing "White Christmas?"

The only background music shepherds heard in that Judean pasture some 2,000 years ago was the monotonous chirp of crickets and the bored conversation of "baaas" by a flock of sheep close by. But all of that humdrum changed when the creative finger of God pushed the play button and a heavenly host broke through the night with the original oratorio anthem, "Glory to God in the highest, and peace to His people on earth."

From all that dwell
below the skies
Let the Creator's praise arise;
Let the Redeemer's name
be sung Through every land,
by every tongue.

Eternal are thy mercies,
Lord, Eternal truth attends thy
word; Thy praise shall sound
from shore to shore,
Till suns shall rise and
set no more.

ISAAC WATTS

Silent Night, Holy Night

The organ of the little church Arndorf near Salzburg, Austria, had in the last days before Christmas became unfit for further use. Mice had eaten at the bellows, and this seriously troubled the parish priest, Father Josef Mohr. He went to the church organist and school master Franz Gruber and voiced his concern, "We must have something special for midnight mass."

On the day before Christmas Eve Father Mohr was called to administer last rites to a dying woman. It was late when he returned to his village. Pausing on a high spot overlooking the town, he observed the snowy mountains that loomed above him. Below him in the valley the dark outline of the village could be seen. Here and there a faint light glimmered in the dark, and over all was that vast stillness so particular to the panorama of nature. Suddenly, the cleric murmured, "It must have been something like this—that silent holy night in Bethlehem."

Powerfully affected, Mohr hurried home, sat at his desk, and began to write. Late that night he paused, read over what he had written, then read it again [early translation from the German];

Silent night, Holy night,

All is dark, save the light,

Yonder where they sweet vigil keep,

O'er the Babe, who in silent sleep,

Rests in heavenly peace,

Rests in heavenly peace.

Silent night, peaceful night,

Darkness flies, all is light;

Shepherds hear the angels sing,

Alleluia! Hail the King,

Christ the Saviour is born,

Christ the Saviour is born.

Silent night, Holy night,

Child of heaven, Oh how bright,

Was Thy smile, when Thou wast born,

Blest indeed that happy morn,

Full of heavenly joy,

Full of heavenly joy.

The lyrics pleased him and he retired with satisfaction. Arising the next morning, the priest took up his manuscript, reread it, hastened to his friend Franz Gruber and read it to him. As soon as Gruber read the lovely words inner voices seemed to fill his humble quarters with an angelic chorus. Indeed, he caught the true spirit of the hymn. He sang it to his wife, and in the hushed silence that followed she mused, "We will die—you and I—but this song will live."

At Christmas Eve midnight the organ was still silent in the church at Arnsdorf. The console and great pipes were gathering dust. When the congregation gathered in the sanctuary people commented on how they missed the great hymns played by Mr. Gruber. There was a quiet hush when Gruber stepped into the choir stall and pick out the melody of "Silent Night, Holy Night" on his guitar. In a second Josef Mohr stood beside him and began to sing the everlasting words of the new Christmas hymn. The congregation was stunned by the music's simplicity. Some of them tried to hum the new melody along with Gruber's guitar. They sang it once, then twice, and then a third time. By the last singing, the whole congregation had learned the medley and were humming along with their pastor and music director.

As was the custom of that parish, each worshiper had brought a candle from home and before leaving the building he or she lit it from the paschal candle at the altar. Down the hillside from the church, and into the valley the string of worshipers held their candles high and quietly sang their new Christmas hymn that just suited the quiet night and starry sky.[39]   ✳

The Miracle of Silent Night

Silent Night, Holy Night

A starlit night of holiness and awe.

A glimmer of eternal love

Offering a timeless, infinite gift

Of supreme hallowed grace.

All is Calm, All Is Bright

Prayer is a sea of tranquility,

A tide of serenity that brings forth

An everlasting calm into our lives.

Holy Infant So Tender and Mild

Our thoughts, words, and deeds

Must be gentle and loving

And if we were thinking of, talking to,

And caring for the Infant Jesus.

Round Yon Virgin Mother and Child

Let us bring our fears, sorrows,

Joys and prayers of gratitude

As we kneel before Mary's infant Son

In the chapel of our hearts.

Sleep in Heavenly Peace,

Sleep in Heavenly Peace.

The peace of the sleeping Infant

Prevails, in holiness and grace,

Remaining with us always

As we live in heavenly peace.

Silent Night, Holy Night

Holiness is a flower
Born of silent courage—
Courage inspired by prayer
And the love of our Heavenly Father.

Shepherds Quake at Thy Sight

A sight to behold! Fear not!
Embrace God's messenger,
The angel of the Lord,
With love, humility and trust.

Glories Stream from Heaven Afar

The glory of God shines
All about us, wherever we may be,
His illustrious light constantly projected
Upon the screen of life.

Heavenly Hosts Sing Alleluia

Let us sing Alleluia
With the heavenly hierarchy;
Let our joyful voices be heard
By all people of all nations.

Christ the Savior Is Born,
Christ the Savior is born.

The redeemer of all God's people,
The Christ Child is born not only
In the town of Bethlehem
But in each of us.

Silent Night, Holy Night

The glorious brilliance of God's love
Glitters and gleams upon us
Like the star of Bethlehem
On that holy night of old.

Son of God, Love's Pure Light

What greater gift could God send us
Than His Infant Son wrapped
Not only in swaddling clothes,
But in purity, love, and truth?

Radiant Beams from Thy Holy Face

The sacred smile radiating
From the Infant's venerable face
Enlightens our faith with divine love.

With the Dawn of Redeeming Grace

Children of light, awake each dawn
In the splendor of God's Holy love
And His sanctifying grace.

Jesus Lord, at Thy Birth,
Jesus, Lord at Thy Birth.

Each Christmas, we rejoice
For the infant Jesus is born.
Each new day, we rejoice
For the Christ Child grows
In wisdom, age, and grace within us.[40]

DOROTHY TRAVERS ZISA

* * *

A few hymnals contain this lovely

Christmas hymn. Many of us are familiar

with the last stanza, but the lines that come

before have all the power, atmosphere,

and deep feeling as have any

Christina Rosetti poem. As a hymn,

the musical setting is by Gustav Holst,

composer of the well-known "The Planets."

* * *

In the Bleak Mid-winter

In the bleak mid-winter
    Frosty wind made moan,
Earth stood hard as iron,
    Water like a stone;
Snow had fallen, snow on snow,
    Snow on snow,
In the bleak mid-winter
    Long ago.

Our God in heaven cannot hold him,
    Nor earth sustain;
Heaven and earth shall flee away
    When he comes to reign:
In the bleak midwinter a
    Stable place sufficed
The Lord God incarnate,
    Jesus Christ.

Angels and archangels
    May have gathered there,
Cherubim and seraphim
    Thronged the air;
But his mother only,
    In her maiden bliss,
Worshiped the beloved
    With a kiss.
What can I give him,
    Poor as I am?
If I were a shepherd,
    I would bring a lamb;
If I were a wise man,
    I would do my part;
Yet what I can I give him—
    Give my heart.[41]

CHRISTINA ROSETTI

Songs of Christmas

Carolers singing as of yore,
Holly bedecking every door,
Red woolen stockings hung up with glee,
Icicles draped on a Christmas tree,
Santa coming on Christmas Eve,
Toys left so wee ones may believe,
Mistletoe slyly hung here and there,
And, filling the cold, clear winter air,
Songs of "Merry Christmas" everywhere.

May the sights and sounds of Christmas
And the joy each does impart
Cause a special warmth and glow to
Long remain within your heart.[42]

PEGGY MILCUCH

Here We Come A-Caroling

Here we come a-caroling
Among the leaves so green;
Here we come a-wand'ring,
So fair to be seen.
Love and joy come to you,
And to you glad Christmas too;
And God bless you and send you
A happy New Year,
And God send you a happy New Year.

We are not daily beggars
That beg from door to door;
But we are neighbors' children,
Whom you have seen before.
Love and joy come to you,
And to you glad Christmas too;
And God bless you and send you
A happy New Year,
And God send you a happy New Year.

Good master and mistress,
As you sit by the fire,
Pray think of us poor children,
Who wander in the mire.
Love and joy come to you,
And to you glad Christmas too;
And God bless you and send you
A happy New Year,
And God send you a happy New Year.

God bless the master of this house,
Likewise the mistress too,
And all the little children,
That round the table go.
Love and joy come to you,
And to you glad Christmas too;
And God bless you and send you
A happy New Year,
And God send you a happy New Year.

TRADITIONAL

The Friendly Beasts

Jesus, our brother, kind and good,
Was humbly born in a stable rude,
And the friendly beasts around Him stood,
Jesus, our brother, kind and good.

"I," said the donkey, shaggy and brown,
"I carried His mother uphill and down;
I carried her safely to Bethlehem town;
I," said the donkey shaggy and brown.

"I," said the cow all white and red,
"I gave Him my manger for His bed;
I gave Him my hay to pillow His head;
I," said the cow all white and red.

"I," said the sheep with the curly horn,
"I gave Him my wool for His blanket warm;
He wore my coat on Christmas morn;
I," said the sheep with the curly horn.

"I," said the dove from the rafters high,
"Cooed Him to sleep, my mate and I;
We cooed Him to sleep my mate and I;
I," said the dove from the rafters high.

And every beast by some good spell
In the stable dark was glad to tell
Of the gift he gave Immanuel,
The gift he gave Immanuel.

12TH CENTURY CAROL

What Child Is This?

What Child is this who, laid to rest,

on Mary's lap is sleeping?

Whom angels greet with anthems sweet,

while shepherds watch are keeping?

(Refrain)

This, this is Christ the King,

whom shepherds guard and angels sing.

Haste, haste to bring Him laud,

the Babe, the Son of Mary.

Why lies He in such mean estate

where ox and ass are feeding?

Good Christians fear; for sinners here

the silent Word is pleading.

(Refrain)

So bring Him incense, gold, and myrrh;

come, peasant, king to own Him.

The King of Kings salvation brings;

let loving hearts enthrone Him.

(Refrain)[43]

RICHARD DIX
(SUNG TO "GREENSLEEVES")

＊　＊　＊

Henry Wadsworth Longfellow is not best known

as a hymn writer, but this carol was written

by him at a time when the thought of peace

weighed heavily upon his mind. Turning to history,

we discover that Longfellow wrote these lines

in 1863, when the Civil War was at its climax.

They still have power for the twenty-first century.

＊　＊　＊

I Heard the Bells on Christmas Day

I heard the bells on Christmas Day
their old familiar carols play,
And wild and sweet the words repeat
of peace on earth, good will to men.

I tho't how, as the day had come, the
belfries of all Christendom
Had rolled along th'unbroken song of
peace on earth goodwill to men.

And in despair I bowed my head.
"There is no peace on earth," I said,
"For hate is strong, and mocks the
song of peace on earth, goodwill to men."

Then peeled the bells more loud and
deep" "God is not dead, nor doth He sleep;
The wrong shall fail, the right prevail,
with peace on earth goodwill to men.

Till ringing, singing on its way, the
were revolved from night to day—
A voice, a chime, chant sublime, of
peace on earth goodwill to men.[44]

HENRY WADSWORTH LONGFELLOW

O Little Town of Bethlehem

O little town of Bethlehem, how still we see thee lie!
Above thy deep and dreamless sleep the silent stars go by.
Yet in thy dark streets shineth the everlasting light;
The hopes and fears of all the years are met in thee tonight.

For Christ is born of Mary; and gathered all above,
While mortals sleep, the angels keep their watch of wond'ring love.
O morning stars together proclaim the holy birth;
And praises sing to God, the King, and peace to men on earth.

How silently, how silently the wondrous gift is giv'n!
So God imparts to human hearts the blessings of His heav'n.
No ear may hear His coming; but in this world of sin,
Where meek souls will receive Him still, the dear Christ enters in.

O holy Child of Bethlehem, descend on us, we pray.
Cast out our sin, and enter in; be born in us today.
We hear the Christmas angels their great glad tidings tell.
O come to us; abide with us, our Lord Emmanuel.[45]

PHILLIPS BROOKS

A Christmas Hymn

Tell me what is this innumerable throng
    Singing in the heavens a loud angelic song?
These are they who come with swift and shining feet
    From round about the throne of God the Lord of Light to greet.

O, who are these that hasten beneath the starry sky,
    As if with joyful tidings that through the world shall fly?
The faithful shepherds these, who greatly were afeared
    When, as they watched their flocks by night,
the heavenly hosts appeared.

Who are these that follow across hills of night
    A star that westward hurries along the fields of light?
Three wise men from the east who myrrh and treasures bring
    To lay them at the feet of him, their Lord and Christ and King.

What babe new-born is this that in a manger cries?
    Near on her bed of pain his happy mother lies.
O, see! the air is shaken with white and heavenly wings—
    This is the Lord of all the earth, this is the King of Kings.

Tell me, how may I join in, this holy feast
    With all the kneeling world, and I of all the least?
Fear not, O faithful heart, but bring what most is meet;
    Bring love alone, true love alone, and lay it at his feet.[46]

RICHARD WATSON GILDER

There's a Song in the Air!

There's a song in the air!
There's a star in the sky!
There's a mother's deep prayer
And a baby's low cry!
And the star rains its fire with the beautiful sing,
For the manger of Bethlehem cradles a King!

There's a tumult of joy
O'er the wonderful birth,
For the Virgin's sweet boy
Is the Lord of the earth.
Ay! the star rains its fire while the beautiful sing,
For the manger of Bethlehem cradles a King!

In the light of that star
Lie the ages impearled;
And that song from afar
Has swept over the world.
Every hearth is aflame, and the beautiful sing
In the homes of the nations that Jesus is King!

We rejoice in the light And we echo the song
That comes down thro' the night
From the heavenly throng.
Ay! we shout to the lovely evangel they bring,
And we greet in His cradle our Saviour and King!

JOSIAH GILBERT HOLLAND

✳ ✳ ✳

This ancient carol is in the form

an

of an imaginary conversation between

imaginary

Joseph, Mary, and the hostess of the

conversation

Bethlehem inn that turned

the couple away on the night

Jesus was born.

✳ ✳ ✳

Another Street

St. Joseph:

"Another street we'll try,
A courtyard there may be
Here, before mine eye
Is this grand hostelrie."

Mary, The Virgin:

"Prithee, of your grace,
No further can I go.
Alone seek you a place;
My strength it faileth so."

St. Joseph:

"Hostess dear and kind,
Pray, of your great pitie,
Some little corner find,
To lodge my faint ladie!"

The Hostess:

"Common folks and poor
In here we never keep
Try that other door;
'Tis there such people sleep."

TRADITIONAL

Christmas Caroling

The winter night was cold and crisp,
  And stars were in the sky,
But as the wind would sometimes mount,
  We turned our collars high.
'Twas worth a shiver now and then
  To hear the songs ring out,
And though some snowflakes drifted down
  A crowd soon stood about.

"O Little Town of Bethlehem"
  And "Silent Night" were heard,
"Joy to the World" and "Deck the Halls,"
  Proclaiming God's great word.
The hymn books trembled in our hands
  As by the street lamp's glow
We sang our very hearts away
  That Christmas long ago.

Hot chocolate waited at the church
  And cookies Mom had made
For all the carolers returned,
  Whose songs would never fade;
For in a book called memory,
  Which keeps each Christmas Day,
The friendships and the songs are found
  Deep in the heart to stay.[47]

ALICE KENNELLY ROBERTS

Carol of the Brown King

Of the three Wise Men
Who came to the king,
One was a brown man,
So they sing.

Of the three Wise Men
Who followed the star,
One was a brown king
From afar.

They brought fine gifts
Of spices and gold
In jeweled boxes
Of beauty untold.

Unto His humble
Manger they came
And bowed their heads
In Jesus' name.

Three Wise Men,
One dark like me—
Part of His
Nativity.[48]

LANGSTON HUGHES

The Joy
Laughter

# of Laughter

Christmas laughter comes from many sources—from the remembrance of gifts that were just not quite right (like the hand-knit sweater with arms that would have been too long on King Kong) or miscues in Sunday School pageants (like the shepherd in a short robe who wouldn't go on unless he was allowed to wear tube socks and red high tops) or the year someone forgot to take the bag of giblets out of the turkey.

The Bethlehem event was certainly not a laughing matter, but when one reads between the lines it's easy to be amused by the image of the rag-tag band of shepherds on the streets of Bethlehem looking for a baby; how some over-worked innkeepers responded to small-town Mary and Joseph; what a paranoid King Herod said to his wife after the Magi left; what one cow mooed to the other when the Nazareth couple took over their stall in the barn.

Enjoy this joy of Christmas—the light-hearted laughter that springs from familiar and loving relationships.

This 15th-century English carol is full

of beautiful pictures and illusions to Jesus' adult life.

The Holly and the Ivy

The Holly and the Ivy,
 When they are both full grown
Of all the trees are in the wood,
 The Holly bears the crown.

O the rising of the sun,
 And the running of the deer,
The playing of the merry organ,
 Sweet singing in the choir.

The Holly bears a blossom
 As white as any flower;
And Mary bore sweet Jesus Christ
 To do poor sinners good.

The Holly bears a prickle
As sharp as any thorn;
And Mary bore sweet Jesus Christ
 On Christmas in the morn.

The Holly bears a back
 As bitter as any gall;
And Mary bore sweet Jesus Christ
 For to redeem us all.

The Holly and the Ivy
 Now both are full well grown:
Of all the trees are in the wood
 The Holly bears the crown.

TRADITIONAL

The Computer's First Christmas Card

BY EDWIN MORGAN

jollymerry
hollyberry
jollyberry
merryholly
happyjolly
jollyjelly
jellybelly
bellymerry
hollyheppy
jollyMolly
marryJerry
merryHarry
hoppyBarry
heppyJarry
boppyheppy
berryjorry
jorryjolly
moppyjelly
Mollymerry
Jerryjolly
bellyboppy
jorryhoppy
hollymoppy
Barrymerry
Jerryhappy
happyboppy
boppyjolly
jollymerry
merrymerry
merrymerry
merryChris
ammerryasa
Chrismerry

asMERRYCHRYSANTHEMUM[49]

* * *

The annual family Christmas form letter

that has become quite popular in recent

years has rubbed Elizabeth Mooney the

wrong way. This Opposite Editorial piece

by Miss Mooney appeared in the

December 25, 1983 Washington Post.

* * *

And May All Your Christmas Be Blight

BY ELIZABETH C. MOONEY

*D*ear Alice and Bud:

Got your wonderful, warm Xeroxed letter in lieu of a Christmas card and just loved getting caught up on your family doings. Your annual letter is always a bright spot among the usual Christmas cards, and you needn't apologize that you have so many friends it seems the only way. We just adore knowing we're on that list of dear friends.

I was sorry to hear that the appliances weren't working well and that the cat had been sick. Bud's operation sounds grim, but I'm glad he's up on crutches. Harry says it's lucky the back didn't act up until you got back from Mexico. I was sorry to hear Alice didn't find the shopping opportunities up to her hopes, but I'm sure glad Bud found rum there at $2 a quart. And of course it always makes Christmas a little cheerier to hear your lifestyle continues to be busy and happy. I'm sure Bud never has an idle moment, what with all that barbecue cooking and the lawn work.

Harry and I were sorry to hear your nephew's wife, Dodie had a miscarriage and that Allen—of course I remember his skin problems—has quit his job in the arts and crafts department of the senior citizens hall. But I know he'll enjoy white water rafting while he sorts out his priorities. I always say what's money for if you can't support your children. Tell Allen Happy New Year for us.

I was astounded to hear Bud found vanilla for only $1 a pint across the border in Nogales. One does use up vanilla so fast, and it's handy to be able to lay in a supply. The devaluation of the peso must have been a real boon when you stumbled on that bargain.

Bud's high school reunion in June sounds like a real blast. Too bad he had laryngitis and couldn't tell them about some of the unique experiences you include in your Christmas letter every year. I know they would have loved hearing about the new way you have of keeping your pool clean. We couldn't tell, by the way, which one of you it was who fell in fully clothed at your Thanksgiving party. Sometimes the "we" you use in your letters get confusing.

We have been thinking for years that we should pop in on you out there in sunny Arizona. Every Christmas when you invite us in your letter, we tell ourselves we should go. You sound so cordial and your life sounds so much fun. Would it be okay if we brought the kids and Harry's mother? And maybe the dog? I'll give you a day or two notice.

Well, I guess I'd better sign off, but I just felt I had to sit right down and write to you when your letter came. And the handwritten note at the end made us feel so special.

A Merry Christmas and Happy New Year to you, too.

Love

Elizabeth and Harry

On Christmas Cards

BY PAUL M. MILLER

I do not receive many Christmas cards anymore. This is not surprising, as I never remember to send any out. The most I have ever done, when feeling most strenuous, was to scramble out a few New Year's cards to people who had sent me Christmas cards, and whose remembrance of me stirred my gratitude. But I do always receive some, and I got a few this year.

I have been looking at them all before cremating them. Those which come from the more intellectual of my friends have no longer anything particularly Christmas-cardy about them. They are in good taste, designed by or for the senders, admirably printed, and in point of language ready for the scrutiny of the most fastidious critic of style.

Nothing could be more refined. There are no sprigs of holly on these, no claspings of amputated hands, no villages amid snowy landscapes. They have pictures of the sender's dogs, house, vacation site, or favourite charity. Each card looks like a silent protest against the old kind of card. As I look at them I hear them say, "What an improvement we are! How clearly we demonstrate that Christmas greetings can be conveyed with sophistication and lack of vulgarity." They have found ways of circumventing any credal problems; omit the word *Christmas*. Find euphemisms the will not offend the non-religious. Wish them: *Season Greetings, Happy Holiday, Winter Solstice,* etc. All are very chaste, and very few of them contain a single line of verse, even mediocre verse.

Yet from the more old fashioned and less aspiring remnant of my acquaintance there still come a few tokens of the more Christmassy variety. Some even boast an acknowledgement of Christ's birthday in verse. It was one of these quatrains that checked me in the middle of my cremation ceremonies. It ran as follows:

> "A Happy, Blessed Christmas to you" we say,
> May the Christ Child ever find you,
> Walking in His Sonlight through every day
> And cast all shadows behind you.

Well, you will say, there is nothing very odd about that verse; not so good, but not very odd. Wait a moment. The odd thing is that under those four lines is printed the name "Browning."

I stand open to correction. But I must warn you, I was an English literature major and thoroughly studied the Victorian poets. I really cannot suppose that Robert Browning wrote those lines. Nor can I believe that his wife Elizabeth Barrett wrote them. There have been, no doubt, other Brownings. Henry Browning or Nicodemus Browning or George Bernard Browning or any of a zillion other Brownings. But if Robert Browning was really the author he must certainly have had a bad off-day, when his style was indistinguishable from that of any other Christmas card poet. (Perhaps this is why sentiments have become rather banal in recent years.)

As my pile of greetings go up in smoke, I can't help but surmise the Christmas message brought by an angel two thousand years ago. "Peace on earth, goodwill toward men." Why? Because to us was born a Savior. His are words that no Hallmark sentiment writer could ever create. He cared enough to send us the very best.   ✳

A PC Christmas Message

POSTED BY SIMPSONS ON DECEMBER 22, 1998 AT 06:23:02:

POLITICAL CORRECTNESS, HAS IT GONE TOO FAR . . .

*D*ear "Whoever,"

Please accept with no obligation, implied or implicit, our best wishes for an environmentally conscious, socially responsible, low stress, non-addictive, gender neutral, celebration of the winter solstice holiday, practiced within the most enjoyable traditions of the religious persuasion of your choice, or secular practices of your choice, with respect for the religious/secular persuasions and/or traditions, or their choice not to practice religious or secular traditions at all.

And a fiscally successful, personally fulfilling, and medically uncomplicated recognition of the onset of the generally accepted calendar year 1999, but not without due respect for the calendars of choice of other cultures whose contributions to society have helped make Britain great (not to imply that Britain is necessarily greater than any other country), and without regard to the race, creed, colour, age, physical ability, religious faith, choice of computer platform, or sexual preference of the wishee.

(By accepting this greeting you are accepting these terms. This greeting is subject to clarification or withdrawal. It is freely transferable with no alteration to the original greeting. It implies no promise by the wisher to actually implement any of the wishes for her, himself, or others, and is void where prohibited by law, and is revocable at the sole discretion of the wisher. This wish is warranted to perform as expected within the usual application of good tidings for a period of one year, or until the issuance of a subsequent holiday greeting, whichever comes first, and warranty is limited to replacement of this wish or issuance of a new wish at the sole discretion of the wisher.)

Happy politically correct holidays!

A Carol for Children

God rest you, merry Innocents,
    Let nothing you dismay,
Let nothing wound an eager heart
    Upon this Christmas Day.

Yours be the genial holly wreaths,
    The stockings and the tree;
An aged world to you bequeaths
    Its own forgotten glee.

Soon, soon enough come crueler gifts,
    The anger and the tears;
Between you now there sparsely drifts
    A handful yet of years.

Oh dimly, dimly glows the star
    Through the electric throng;
The bidding in temple and bazaar
    Drowns out the silver song.

The ancient altars smoke afresh,
    The ancient idols stir;
Faint in the reek of burning flesh
    Sink frankincense and myrrh.

Gasper, Balthazar, Melchior!
    Where are your offerings now?
What greetings to the Prince of War,
    His darkly branded brow?

Two ultimate laws alone we know,
    The ledger and the sword—
So far away, so long ago,
    We lost the infant Lord.

Only the children clasp his hand:
    His voice speaks low to them,
And still for them the shining band
    Wings over Bethlehem.

God rest you, merry Innocents,
    While innocence endures.
A sweeter Christmas than we to ours
    May you bequeath to yours.[50]

OGDEN NASH

A Miserable Merry Christmas

BY LINCOLN STEFFENS

Christmas was coming, but Christmas was always coming and grownups were always talking about it, asking you what you wanted and then giving you what they wanted you to have. Though everybody knew what I wanted, I told them all again. My mother knew that I told God, too, every night. I wanted a pony, and to make sure that they understood, I declared that I wanted nothing else.

"Nothing but a pony?" my father asked.

"Nothing," I said.

"Not even a pair of high boots?"

That was hard. I did want boots, but I stuck to the pony. "No, not even boots."

"Nor candy? There ought to be something to fill your stocking with, and Santa can't put a pony into a stocking."

That was true, and he couldn't lead a pony down the chimney either. But no. "All I want is a pony," I said. "If I can't have a pony, give me nothing, nothing."

Now I had been looking myself for the pony I wanted, going to sales stables, inquiring of horsemen, and I had seen several that would do. My father let me "try" them. I tried so many ponies that I was learning fast to sit on a horse. I chose several, but my father always found some fault with them. I was in despair. When Christmas was at hand, I had given up all hope of a pony, and on Christmas Eve I hung my stocking along with my sisters'. I speculated on what I'd get; I hung up the biggest stocking I had, and we all went reluctantly to bed to wait till morning. Not to sleep; not right away. We were told that we must not only sleep promptly, we must not wake up till seven-thirty the next morning—or if we did, we must not go to the fireplace for our Christmas. Impossible.

We did sleep that night, but we woke up at six A.M. We lay in our beds and debated through the open doors whether to obey till, say, half-past six. Then we bolted. I don't know who started it, but there was a rush. We all disobeyed; we raced to disobey and get first to the fireplace in the front room downstairs. And there they were, the gifts, all sorts of wonderful things, mixed up piles of presents; only, as I disentangled the mess, could I see that my stocking was empty; it hung limp; not a thing in it; and under and around it—nothing. My sisters had knelt down each by her pile of gifts; they were squealing with delight, till they looked up and saw me standing there in my nightgown with nothing. They left their piles to come to me and look with me at my empty place. Nothing. They felt my stocking: nothing.

I don't remember whether I cried at that moment, but my sisters did. They ran with me back to my bed, and there we all cried till I became indignant. That helped some. I got up, dressed, and driving my sisters away, I went alone out into the yard, down to the stable, and there, all by myself, I wept. My mother came out to me by and by; she found me in my pony stall, sobbing on the floor, and she tried to comfort me. But I heard my father outside; he had come part of the way with her, and she was having some sort of angry quarrel with him. She tried to comfort me; besought me to come to breakfast. I could not; I wanted no comfort and no breakfast. She left me and went on into the house with sharp words for my father.

I don't know what kind of breakfast the family had. My sisters said it was "awful." They were ashamed to enjoy their own toys. They came to me, and I was rude. I ran away from them. I went around to the front of the house, sat down on the steps, and, the crying over, I ached. I was wronged, I was hurt—I can feel now what I felt then, and I am sure that if one could see the wounds upon our hearts, there would be found still upon mine a scar from that terrible Christmas morning. And my father, the practical joker, he must have been hurt, too, a little. I saw him looking out of the window. He was watching me or something for an hour or two, drawing back the curtain ever so little lest I catch him, but I saw his face, and I think I can see now the anxiety upon it, the worried impatience.

After—I don't know how long—surely an hour or two—I was brought to the climax of my agony by the sight of a man riding a pony down the street, a pony and a brand-new saddle; the most beautiful saddle I ever saw, and it was a boy's saddle; the man's feet were not in the stirrups; his legs were too long. The outfit was perfect; it was the realization of all my dreams, the answer to all my prayers. A fine new bridle, with a light curb bit. And the pony! As he drew near, I saw the pony was really a small horse, what we call an Indian pony, a bay, with black mane and tail, and one white foot and a white star on his forehead. For such a horse as that I would have given, I could have forgiven, anything.

But the man, a disheveled fellow with a blackened eye and a fresh-cut face, came along, reading the numbers on the houses, and, as my hopes—my impossible hopes—rose, he looked at our door and passed by, he and my pony, and the saddle and the bridle. Too much. I fell upon the steps, and having wept before, I broke now into such a flood of tears that I was a floating wreck when I heard a voice.

"Say kid," it said, "do you know a boy name Lennie Steffins?"

I looked up. It was the man on the pony, back again, at our house.

"Yes," I spluttered through my tears. "That's me."

"Well," he said, "then this is your horse. I've been looking all over for you and your house. Why don't you put your number where it can be seen?"

"Get down," I said.

He got down, and boosted me up to the saddle. He offered to fit the stirrups to me, but I didn't want him to. I wanted to ride.

"What's the matter with you?" he asked angrily. "What you crying for? Don't you like the horse? He's a dandy, this horse. I know him of old. He's fine."

I hardly heard. I could scarcely wait, but he persisted. He adjusted the stirrups and then, finally, off I rode, slowly, at a walk, so happy, so thrilled, that I did not know what I was doing. I did not look back at the house or the man, I rode off up the street, taking note of everything—of the reins, of the pony's long mane, of the carved leather saddle. I had never seen anything so beautiful. And mine! I was going to ride up past Miss Kay's house. But I noticed on the horn of the saddle some stains like raindrops, so I turned and trotted home, not to the house but to the stable. There was the family, father, mother, sisters, all working for me, all happy. They had been putting in place the tools of my new business: blankets, curry comb, brush, pitchfork—everything, and there was hay in the loft.

"What did you come back so soon for?" somebody asked. "Why didn't you go on riding?"

I pointed to the stains. "I wasn't going to get my new saddle rained on," I said. And my father laughed. "It isn't raining," he said. "Those are not raindrops."

"They are tears," my mother gasped, and she gave my father a look which sent him into the house. Worse still, my mother offered to wipe away the tears still running out of my eyes. I gave her such a look as she had given him, and she went off after my father, drying her own tears.

My sisters remained and we all unsaddled the pony, put on his halter, led him to his stall, tied and fed him. It began really to rain; so all the rest of that memorable day we curried and combed that pony. The girls plaited his mane, forelock, and tail, while I pitchforked hay to him and curried and brushed, curried and brushed. For a change we brought him out to drink; we led him up and down, blanketed like a race horse; we took turns at that. But the best, the most inexhaustible fun, was to clean him.

When we went reluctantly to our midday Christmas dinner, we smelt of horse, and my sisters had to wash their faces and hands. I was asked to, but I wouldn't, till my mother bade me look in the mirror. Then I washed up—quick. My face was caked with muddy lines of tears that had coursed over my cheeks to my mouth. Having washed away that shame, I ate my dinner, and as I ate I grew hungrier and hungrier.

It was my first meal that day, and as I filled up on the turkey and the stuffing, the cranberries and the pies, the fruit and the nuts—as I swelled, I could laugh. My mother said I still choked and sobbed now and then, but I laughed, too; I saw and enjoyed my sisters' presents till—I had to go out and attend to my pony, who was there, really and truly there, and the promise, the beginning of a happy double life. And—I went and looked to make sure—there was the saddle, too, and the bridle.

But that Christmas, which my father had planned so carefully, was it the best or the worst I ever knew? He often asked me that; I never could answer as a boy. I think now that it was both. It covered the whole distance from broken-hearted misery to bursting happiness—too fast. A grownup could hardly have stood it.[51]   ✳

Trouble at the Inn

BY DINA DONOHUE

For years now whenever Christmas pageants are talked about in a certain little town in the Midwest, someone is sure to mention the name of Wallace Purling. Wally's performance in one annual production of the Nativity play has slipped into the realm of legend. But the old-timers who were in the audience that night never tire of recalling exactly what happened.

Wally was nine that year and in the second grade, though he should have been in the fourth. Most people in town knew that he had difficulty in keeping up. He was big and clumsy, slow in movement and mind. Still, Wally was well liked by the other children in his class, all of whom were smaller than he, though the boys had trouble hiding their irritation when the uncoordinated Wally would ask to play ball with them.

Most often they'd find a way to keep him off the field, but Wally would hang around anyway—not sulking, just hoping. He was always a helpful boy, a willing and smiling one, and the natural protector, paradoxically, of the underdog. Sometimes if the older boys chased the younger ones away, it would always be Wally who'd say, "Can't they stay? They're no bother."

Wally fancied the idea of being a shepherd with a flute in the Christmas pageant that year, but the play's director, Miss Lombard, assigned him to a more important role. After all, she reasoned, the Innkeeper did not have too many lines, and Wally's size would make his refusal of lodging to Joseph more forceful.

And so it happened that the usual large, partisan audience gathered for the town's Yuletide extravaganza of the crooks and crèches, of beards, crowns, halos, and a whole stageful of squeaky voices. No one on stage or off was more caught up in the magic of the night than Wallace Purling. They said later that he stood in the wings and watched the performance with such fascination that from time to time Miss Lombard had to make sure he didn't wander onstage before his cue.

Then the time came when Joseph appeared, slowly, tenderly guiding Mary to the door of the inn. Joseph knocked hard on the wooden door set into the painted backdrop. Wally the Innkeeper was there waiting.

"What do you want?" Wally said, swinging the door open with a brusque gesture.

"We seek lodging."

"Seek it elsewhere." Wally looked straight ahead but spoke vigorously. "The inn is filled."

"Sir, we have asked everywhere in vain. We have traveled far and are very weary."

"There is no room in the inn for you." Wally looked properly stern.

"Please, good innkeeper, this is my wife, Mary. She is heavy with child and needs a place to rest. Surely you must have some small corner for her. She is so tired."

Now for the first time, the Innkeeper relaxed his stiff stance and looked down at Mary. With that, there was a long pause, long enough to make the audience a bit tense with embarrassment.

"No! Be gone!" the prompter whispered from the wings.

"No!" Wally repeated automatically. "Be gone!"

Joseph sadly placed his arm around Mary, and the two of them started to move away. The Innkeeper did not return inside his inn, however, Wally stood there in the doorway, watching the forlorn couple. His mouth was open, his brow creased with concern, his eyes filling unmistakably with tears.

And suddenly this Christmas pageant became different from all others.

"Don't go, Joseph," Wally called out. "Bring Mary back." And Wallace Purling's face grew into a bright smile. "You can have my room."

Some people in town thought that the pageant had been ruined. Yet there were others—many, many others—who considered it the most Christmassy of all Christmas pageants they had ever seen.[52]   ✳

Jest 'Fore Christmas

Father calls me William, sister calls me Will,
    Mother calls me Willie, but the fellers call me Bill!
Mighty glad I ain't a girl—ruther be a boy,
    Without them sashes, curls, and things that's worn by Fauntleroy!
Love to chaw green apples an' go swimmin' in the lake—
    Hate to take the castor oil they give for belly-ache!
'Most of the time, the whole year round, there ain't no flies on me,
    But jest 'fore Christmas I'm good as I kin be!

Got a yeller dog named Sport, sic him on the cat;
    First thing she knows she doesn't know where she is at!
Got a clipper sled, an' when us kids go out to slide,
    'Long comes the grocery cart, an' we all hook a ride!
But sometimes when the grocery man is worried an' cross,
    He reaches at us with his whips, an' larrup up his hoss,
And then I laff and' holler, "Oh, ya never teched me!"
    But jest 'fore Christmas I'm good as I kin be!

Gran'ma says she hopes that when I become a man,
    I'll be a missionary like her oldest brother, Dan,
As was et up by the Cannibuls that lives in Ceylon's Isle,
    Where every prospeck pleases, an' only man is vile!
But gran'ma she has never been to see a Wild West show,
    Nor read the Life of Daniel Boone, or else I guess she'd know
That, Buff'lo Bill and cowboys is good enough 'for me!
    Except, jest 'for Christmas, when I'm good as I can be!

And when old Sport he hangs around, so solemn-like an' still,

His eyes they keep a-sayin': "What's the matter, little Bill?"

The old cat sneaks down off her perch an' wonders what's become

Of them two enemies of hern that used to make things hum!

But I am so perlite an' tend so earnestly to biz,

That mother says to father: "How improved our Willy is!"

But father, havin' been a boy hisself, suspicions me

When jest 'fore Christmas, I'm as good as I kin be!

For Christmas, with its lots an' lots of candies, cakes, an' toys,

Was made, they say, for proper kids and' not for naughty boys;

So wash your face an' bresh yer hair, an' mind yer p's and q's,

An' don't but out your pantaloons, and don't wear out yer shoes;

Say "Yessum" to the ladies, an' "Yessur" to the men,

An' when they's company, don't pass your plate for pie again;

But, thinking of the things yer'd like to see upun that tree,

Jest 'fore Christmas be as good as yer kin be![53]

BY EUGENE FIELD

Fruitcake Is Forever

BY RUSSELL BAKER

Thirty-four years ago, I inherited the family fruitcake. Fruitcake is the only food durable enough to become a family heirloom. It had been in my grandmother's possession since 1880, and she passed it on to a niece in 1933.

Surprisingly, the niece, who had always seemed to detest me, left it to me in her will. There was the usual family backbiting when the will was read. Relatives grumbled that I had no right to the family fruitcake. Some whispered that I had "got to" the dying woman when she was *in extremis* and guided her hand while she altered her will.

Nothing could be more absurd, since my dislike of fruit cake is notorious throughout the family. This distaste dates from a Christmas dinner when, at the age of 15, I dropped a small piece of fruitcake and shattered every bone in my right foot.

I would have renounced my inheritance except for the sentiment of the thing, for the family fruitcake was the symbol of our family's roots. When my grandmother inherited it, it was already eighty-six years old, having been baked by her great-grandfather in 1794 as a Christmas gift for President George Washington.

Washington, with his high-flown view of ethical standards for government workers, sent it back with thanks, explaining that he thought it was unseemly for Presidents to accept gifts weighing more than eighty pounds. This, at any rate, is the family story, and you can take it for what it's worth, which probably isn't much.

There is no doubt, though, about the fruitcake's great age. Sawing into it six Christmases ago, I came across a fragment of a 1794 newspaper with an account of the lynching of a real estate speculator in New York City.

Thinking the thing was a valuable antique, I rented bank storage space and hired Brinks guards every Christmas to bring it out, carry it to the table, and return it to the vault after dinner. The whole family, of course, now felt entitled to come for Christmas dinner.

People who have never eaten fruitcake may think that after thirty-four years of being gnawed at by assemblages of twenty-five to thirty diners my inheritance would have vanished. People who have eaten fruitcake will realize that it was still almost as intact as on the day George Washington first saw it. While an eon, as someone has observed, may be two people and a ham, a fruitcake is forever.

It was an antique dealer who revealed this truth to me. The children had reached college age, the age of parental bankruptcy, and I decided to put the family fruitcake in the antique market.

"Over 200 years old?" the dealer sneered. "I've got one at home that's over 300," he said. "If you come across a fruitcake that Julius Caesar brought back from Gaul, look me up. I'll give you ten dollars for it.[54]

*   *   *

A Christmas Eve story written

in quaint nineteenth century English,

and set in Thomas Hardy's apocryphal

Wessex County in southwestern England.

*   *   *

The Thieves Who Couldn't Help Sneezing

By Thomas Hardy
Author of *Far from the Madding Crowd*
and *The Return of the Native*

Many years ago, when oak-trees now past their prime were about as large as an elderly gentleman's walking stick, there lived in Wessex a yeoman's son, whose name was Hubert. He was about fourteen years of age, and was as remarkable for his candor and lightness of heart as for his physical courage, of which he was a little vain.

One cold Christmas Eve his father sent him on an important errand to a small town several miles from home. He traveled on horseback, and was detained by the business till a late hour of the evening. At last, however, it was completed; he returned to the inn, the horse was saddled, and he started on his way. His journey homeward lay through the Vale of Blackmore, a fertile but somewhat lonely district, with heavy clay roads and crooked lanes. In those days, too, a great part of it was thickly wooded.

It must have been about nine o'clock when, riding along amid the overhanging trees upon his stout-legged nag, Jerry, and singing a Christmas carol at the top of his lungs, Hubert fancied that he heard a strange noise among the boughs. This brought to his mind that the spot he was traversing bore an evil name. Men had been waylaid there. He looked at Jerry, and wished the horse had been of any other color than light gray; for the docile animal's form was visible even here in the dense shade. "What do I care?" he said aloud, after a few minutes of reflection. "Jerry's legs are too nimble to allow any highwayman to come near me."

"Ha! ha! indeed," was said in a deep voice; and the next moment a man darted from the thicket on his right hand, another man from the thicket on his left hand, and another from a tree trunk a few yards ahead. Hubert's bridle was seized, he was pulled from his horse, and although he struck out with all his might, as a brave boy would naturally do, he was overpowered. His arms were tied behind him, his legs bound tightly together, and he was thrown into the ditch. The robbers whose faces he could now dimly perceive to be artificially blackened, at once departed, leading off the horse.

As soon as Hubert had a little recovered himself, he found that by great exertion he was able to extricate his legs from the cord; but, in spite of every endeavor, his arms remained bound as fast as before. All, therefore, that he could do was to rise to his feet and proceed on his way with his arms behind him, and trust to chance for getting then unfastened. He knew that it would be impossible to reach home on foot that night, and in such a condition; but he walked on. Owing to the confusion which this attack caused in his brain, he lost his way, and would have been inclined to lie down and rest till morning among the dead leaves had he not known the danger of sleeping without covers in a frost so severe. So he wandered further onwards, his arms wrung and numbed by the cord which pinioned him, and his heart aching for the loss of poor Jerry, who never had been known to kick, or bite, or show a single vicious habit. He was not a little glad when he discerned through the trees a distant light. Towards this he made his way, and presently found himself in front of a large mansion with flanking wings, gables, and towers, the battlements and chimneys showing their shapes against the stars.

All was silent; but the door stood wide open, it being from this door that the light shone which had attracted him. On entering he found himself in a vast apartment arranged as a dining-hall, and brilliantly illuminated. The walls were covered with a great deal of dark paneling, formed into molded panels, carvings, closet doors, and the usual fittings of a house of that kind. But what drew his attention most was the large table in the midst of the hall, upon which was spread a sumptuous supper, as yet untouched. Chairs were placed around, and appeared as if something had occurred to interrupt the meal just at the time when all were ready to begin.

Even had Hubert been so inclined, he could not have eaten in his helpless state, unless by dipping his mouth into the dishes, like a pig or cow. He wished first to obtain assistance; and was about to penetrate further into the house for that purpose when he heard hasty footsteps in the porch and the words, "Be quick!" uttered in the deep voice which he heard when he was dragged from the horse. There was only just time for him to dart under the table before three men entered the dining hall. Peeping from beneath the hanging edges of the tablecloth, he perceived that their faces, too, were blackened, which at once removed any remaining doubts he may have felt that these were the same thieves.

"Now, then," said the first—the man with the deep voice—"Let us hide ourselves. They will be back again in a minute. That was a good trick to get them out of the house—eh?"

"Yes. You well imitated the cries of a man in distress," said the second.

"Excellently," said the third.

"But they will soon find out that it was a false alarm. Come, where shall we hide? It must be some place we can stay in for two or three hours, till all are in bed and asleep. Ah! I have it. Come this way! I have learnt that the further closet is not opened once in a twelve-month; it will serve our purpose exactly."

The speaker advanced into the corridor which led from the hall. Creeping a little further forward, Hubert could discern that the closet stood at the end, facing the dining-hall. The thieves entered it, and closed the door. Hardly breathing, Hubert glided forward, to learn a little more of their intention, if possible; and coming close, he could hear the robbers whispering about the different rooms where the jewels, silver plates, and other valuables of the house were kept, which they plainly meant to steal.

They had not been long in hiding when a gay chattering of ladies and gentlemen was audible outside on the terrace. Hubert felt that it would not do to be caught prowling about the house, unless he wished to be taken for a robber himself; and he slipped softly back to the hall, out at the door, and stood in a dark corner of the porch, where he could see everything without being seen himself. In a moment or two a whole troop of people came gliding past him and into the house. There were an elderly gentleman and a lady, eight or nine young ladies, as many young men, besides half-a-dozen men-servants and maids. The mansion had apparently been quite emptied of its occupants.

"Now, children and young people, we will resume our meal," said the old gentleman. "What the noise could have been I cannot understand. I never felt so certain in my life that there was a person being murdered outside my door."

The ladies began saying how frightened they had been, and how they had expected an adventure, and how it had ended in nothing after all.

"Wait a while," Hubert said to himself. "You'll have adventure enough by-and-by, ladies."

It appeared that the young men and women were married sons and daughters of the old couple, who had come that day to spend Christmas with their parents.

The door was then closed, Hubert being left outside on the porch. He thought this a proper moment for asking their assistance; and, since he was unable to knock with his hands, began boldly to kick the door.

"Hullo! What disturbance are you making here?" said a footman who opened it; and seizing Hubert by the shoulder, he pulled him into the dining-hall. "Here's a strange boy I have found making a noise in the porch, Sir Simon."

Everybody turned.

"Bring him forward," said Sir Simon, the old gentleman before mentioned. "What were you doing there my boy?"

"Why his arms are tied!" said one of the ladies.

"Poor fellow!" said another.

Hubert at once began to explain that he had been waylaid on his journey home, robbed of his horse, and mercilessly left in this condition by the thieves.

"Only to think of it!" exclaimed Sir Simon.

"That's a likely story," said one of the gentlemen guests, incredulously.

"Doubtful, hey?" asked Sir Simon.

"Perhaps he's a robber himself," suggested a lady.

"There is curiously wild wicked look about him, certainly, now that I examine him closely," said the old mother.

Hubert blushed with shame; and instead of continuing his story, and relating that robbers were concealed in the house, he doggedly held his tongue, and half resolved to let them find out their danger for themselves.

"Well, untie him," said Sir Simon. "Come, since it is Christmas Eve, we'll treat him well. Here, my lad; sit down in that empty seat at the bottom of the table, and make as good a meal as you can. When you have had your fill we will listen to more particulars of your story.

The feast then proceeded; and Hubert, now at liberty, was not at all sorry to join in. The more they ate and drank the merrier did the company become. All went as noisily and as happily as a Christmas gathering in old times possibly could do.

Hubert, in spite of his hurt feelings at their doubts of his honesty, could not help being warmed both in mind by the good cheer, the scene and the example of hilarity set by his neighbors. At last he laughed as heartily at their stories and repartees as the Baronet, Sir Simon, himself. When the meal was almost over one of the sons said to Hubert, "Well, my boy, how are you? Can you take a pinch of snuff?" He held out one of the snuff boxes which were becoming common among young and old throughout the country.

"Thank you," said Hubert, accepting a pinch.

"Tell the ladies who you are, what you are made of, and what you can do," the young man continued, slapping Hubert upon the back.

"Certainly," said our hero, drawing himself up, and thinking it best to put a bold face on the matter. "I am a travelling magician."

"Indeed!"

"What shall we hear next?"

"I can conjure up a tempest in a cupboard," Hubert replied.

"Ha-ha!" said the old Baronet, pleasantly rubbing his hands. "We must see this performance. Girls, don't go away: here's something to be seen."

"Not dangerous, I hope?" said the old lady.

Hubert rose from the table. "Hand me your snuff box, please," he said to young man who had offered it to him. "And now," he continued, "without the least noise, follow me. If any of you speak the spell will be broken."

They promised obedience. He entered the corridor, and, taking off his shoes, went on tiptoe to the closet door, the guests advanced in a silent group at a little distance behind him. Hubert next placed a stool in front of the door, and, by standing upon it was tall enough to reach the top. He then, just as noiselessly, poured all the snuff from the box along the upper edge of the door, and, with a few short puffs of breath, blew the snuff through the open space above the door into the interior of the closet. He held his finger to his lips to the assembly, warning them to be silent.

"Dear me, what's that?" said the old lady, after a minute or two had elapsed.

A suppressed sneeze had come from inside the closet.

Hubert pressed his finger against his lips again.

"How very singular," whispered Sir Simon. "This is most interesting."

Hubert took advantage of the moment to gently slide the bolt of the closet door into place. "More snuff," he said, calmly.

"More snuff," said Sir Simon. Two or three gentlemen passed their boxes, and the contents were blown in at the top of the closet. Another sneeze, not quite so well suppressed as the first was heard: then another, which seemed to say that it would not be suppressed under any circumstance whatever. At length there arose a perfect storm of sneezes.

"Excellent, excellent conjuring for one so young!" said Sir Simon. "I am much interested in this trick of throwing the voice—called ventriloquism, I believe."

"More snuff," said Hubert.

"More snuff," said Sir Simon. Sir Simon's man brought a large jar of the best scented.

Hubert once more charged the upper crack of the closet, and blew the snuff unto the interior, as before. Again he charged the closet, emptying the whole contents of the jar. The tumult of sneezes became really extraordinary to hear—there was no stopping them. It was like wind, rain, and sea battling in a hurricane.

"I believe there are men inside, and that it is no trick at all!" exclaimed Sir Simon, the truth flashing on him.

"There are," said Hubert. "They are come to rob your house this Christmas Eve; and they are the same who stole my horse."

The sneezes changed to spasmodic groans. One of the thieves, hearing Hubert's voice, cried, "Oh! mercy! mercy! let us out of this closet!"

"Where's my horse?" called out Hubert.

"Tied to the tree in the hollow behind Short's store. Mercy! mercy! let us out, or we shall die of suffocation!"

All the Christmas guests now perceived that this was no longer sport, but serious business. Guns and cudgels were procured; all the men-servants were called in, and arranged in position outside the closet. At a signal Hubert withdrew the bolt, and stood on the defensive. But the three robbers, far from attacking them, were found crouching in the corner, gasping for breath. They made no resistance; and, being pinioned, were placed in an outhouse till the morning.

Hubert now gave the remainder of his story to the assembled company, and was profusely thanked for the services he had rendered. Sir

Simon pressed him to stay over the night, and accept the use of the best bedroom the house afforded, which had been occupied by Queen Elizabeth and King Charles successively when on their visits to this part of the country. But Hubert declined, being anxious to find his horse Jerry.

Several of the guests accompanied Hubert to the spot behind the store, alluded to by the thieves, and there the horse stood, uninjured, and quite unconcerned. At sight of Hubert he neighed joyfully; and nothing could exceed Hubert's gladness at finding him. He mounted, wished his friends "Happy Christmas!" and cantered off, reaching home safely about four o'clock in the morning.[55] ✳

The Stock Exchange Carol

Swift we be come on joyful feet,
Through wind and snow from Lombard Street,
To tell glad tidings far and wide
Of Patagonian Allied.
> Noel, Noel, Noel, Noel!
> Sing jolly men, buy and sell,
> For Trans Rhd. Corp. (ex bonus) Tea
> Has risen again to 93.

Lo! Far and near we hear the call,
And Belgian Zinc's begun to fall,
Sing we and tell with joyous tongue
How badly old Tom George was stung.
> Noel, Noel, etc.

• Bright is the light, and wild, and strange,
That shines above the Stock Exchange;
Contentment crowns the happy scene—
There is a boom in Margarine.
> Noel, Noel, etc.

High over all a Voice is heard—
"Lord Funck is buying Tin Preferred!"
Thus chants th'angelic syndicate,
"Sell out, sell out at 48!"
> Noel, Noel, etc.[56]

J. B. MORTON

Screenwriter Larry Enscoe has created the

town of Warmwater, Illinois, "That blessed

town where all people live in one accord and

where there hasn't been a major sin for over

thirty years." Here is how some of the citizens

of Warmwater observe Christmas.

Christmas Scenes from Warmwater, Illinois

By Lawrence G. Enscoe

SCENE ONE

Myrtle Fetschwanger and the Church Mice Boutique Pep Rally

(The LIGHTS come up on a church "Fireside Room." We hear the drone of many voices in the background. MYRTLE FETSCHWANGER, MARTHA LONGACRE, and GRACE ALBRITTON sit around a long table, center. Metal chairs face them. The table is festooned with Christmas decorations and several boutique gift items: quilts, wreaths, ornaments etc. The Pianist plays background carols. After a moment, MYRTLE begins tapping her coffee cup with a spoon.)

MYRTLE: Ladies, ladies . . . LADIES! Thank you. Oh, you're all just so excited tonight, aren't you? Well, Merry Christmas to all of you. *(A chorus of "Merry Christmases.")* Thank you. All right, down to business. As you know, ladies, my name is Myrtle Fetschwanger, and I'm the . . . Queen Mouse for this year's Church Mice boutique. And as you also know, tomorrow morning is Saturday, the day we've been waiting for all year! That's right, it's our "He's the Reason for the Season" Smart Shopper Boutique and Luncheon. Tomorrow morning our fellowship hall will be filled with smiling shoppers just waiting to reward you for all the hard work you've done. Hundreds will pass through our church doors to look at your gift items. Oh, we're going to make a killing! Though, as we all know, the money all goes to the parking lot renovation fund.

(Applause.)

And, ladies, as you well know, too, this is Friday night, the night we always get together to enjoy one another's labors of love and to have . . . shall we say, our little Church Mice pep rally and cheese feed.

(More applause.)

Well, this is it, isn't it, gals. What we've been working for all year. But it has been worth it; so many wonderful gift items! True, it *has* been a struggle making time to come down to the boutique work-shops every Monday night since Easter. *(Smiles.)* Long hours, stiff fingers, glue in our eyebrows. *(They laugh.)* Remember that, Doris! Oh, what a kick that was! Anyway, I must say that some of us have worked extra hard this year, and you know who you are, ladies! But there's one among us who has made that extra effort. She has really made the sacrifices, gone the extra mile, as it were, to make our bou-tique extra special this year. Ladies, I give you Grace Albritton, winner of this year's "Little Elf Mouse" award!

(Applause. GRACE stands, dazed. MYRTLE pins a huge, garish, pine needled award with a picture of a mouse in a Santa's hat on her. They continue clapping. GRACE faces forward.)

GRACE: I don't know what to . . . I can't think of any . . . I haven't had any sleep for six days. I'm . . . I . . . haven't seen my husband since Tuesday. Not since I tried to shoot him with my glue gun for eating the walnuts I was trying to shellac—

MYRTLE *(standing)*: Ah, thank you, Dear—

GRACE: Has anyone seen Henry? About this tall. Always wears plaid.

MYRTLE *(taking GRACE'S shoulders)*: Thank you, Grace.

GRACE *(turning to MYRTLE)*: Is the boutique over yet, Myrtle? Is it over?

MYRTLE *(pushing her down into her seat)*: It is for you, Dear.

GRACE: Oh, thank you.

MYRTLE: Doris, get Grace here another cup of coffee, hmmmm? Some of Pastor Dorcas's double strength blend. Thanks, Hon. *(Turns back.)* All right, Church Mice! We have a little bit of business to attend to before we can get to Bab Miller's delicious manger-shaped pastries and tea.

(Applause.)

First off, a little . . . unpleasant business. This morning someone dropped off a box of these for the boutique. (*She holds up a brown bottle with felt antlers.*) It's a "Christmoose" made from a . . . well, a bottle of Miller Lite with little felt antlers. Now, albeit, it has a certain . . . charm, but we on the Church Mice Boutique Board do not feel it is appropriate for a church-sponsored event. I won't say any names, now, but there'll be a herd of "Christmoose" in a box in the foyer after the fellowship tonight. (*Pause. She shuffles some papers.*) Now for the second matter. And this is . . . a little difficult. I don't quite know how to go about this . . . but . . . (*She turns to MARTHA.*) All right, cough 'em up, Martha.

MARTHA (*aghast*): What?

MYRTLE: Now, don't make me say it, Dear.

MARTHA: Myrtle, what are you—?

MYRTLE: Tickets.

MARTHA: Tickets?

MYRTLE: Boutique tickets.

> (*A gasp all around. MARTHA stares, open-mouthed.*)

MYRTLE: We're waiting, Dear.

> (*MARTHA swallows hard and slowly pulls a huge stack of tickets out of her purse.*)

MARTHA: I . . . I'm sorry. I couldn't sell them all. I . . . I tried, but I—

MYRTLE: Hand them over, Martha.

MARTHA (*doing so*): I really . . . I really tried—

MYRTLE: My, they are heavy, aren't they?

MARTHA: I was so busy. The choir cantata and the women's Bible Study and . . . and the Church Mice Saturday morning fellowships . . . and, and—

MYRTLE: My, you asked for so many, didn't you? I wonder how many tables at the boutique luncheon won't be filled now.

MARTHA: And Alan! You know Alan had that terrible flu that was going around. He was sicker than a—

MYRTLE: I suppose we could get Mr. Rodrigues to set up a few less tables tomorrow so the room won't look so . . . empty.

MARTHA: All right! I'll sell 'em! *(She grabs the stack.)* I promise! I'll go door-to-door tonight! I won't even stay for Bab Miller's manger pastries! I'll sell 'em!

MYRTLE: Well, fine, Dear. No pressure. *(Turns back to the others)* Well, ladies. I want you to know how proud I am of each and every one of you for your unselfish, hard work. Pastor Dorcas has asked me to tell you how much he appreciates all your efforts. Now, remember, no . . . how shall I say . . . hard sells tomorrow. Just sit behind your tables and smile, OK? Sandy, I don't want you to cry this year if someone stops at your table but doesn't buy anything. And Dorothy, I think the glue and glitter on your fingers was a bit much, hmmmm? Let's let the Lord move people to purchase, shall we? *(Looks up.)* All right, Babs, are you ready back there? Oh, fine. Ladies, let's get out there and win one for the pastor, hmmm? Team spirit. Let's make the day special for everyone. Winona? Will you ask God's blessing on the boutique and the pastries?

> *(They start to bow their heads.)*

MYRTLE: Oh, and ladies, remember we're all going to rendezvous in the Fireside Room after the Christmas Eve service, right? We'll choose a new chairperson for next year's boutique then. All right, Church Mice? Let's see if we can't get a real headstart on next year's boutique, hmmmm?

> *(She drops her head to pray as the LIGHTS go to blackout. After a moment, the LIGHTS at a table with a lamp, an open Bible, come up on HELEN LINGERFIELD sitting with a notebook. She is working feverishly. "Silent Night" is playing in the background.)*

HELEN: That's right, I need a Gabriel! And *three* shepherds. That makes nine kids so far. Oh, great. Three wise men. I forgot about the three . . . maybe I could get Big Bobby Brunstein for the wise men. Maybe Ill have just one . . . really *big* wise man.

(*MYRON LINGERFIELD comes in and watches her. He has a string of blinking lights in his hand and a fistful of tinsel in the other.*)

HELEN: Do I need sheep? Can I get by with Mary Eckleston bleating offstage? I know they're going to want sheep. They'll probably want cattle lowing, too. Cecil B. DeMille, I could just wring your—(*She spins around.*) Whadd'you want!

MYRON (*jumping*): Ah! Oh, honey. I didn't want to disturb what you—

HELEN: Well, you did, Buster.

MYRON: I . . . I . . .

HELEN: Spill it! I've got the Lord's work here!

MYRON: Well, shoot, honey. It's just that we're all trimming the tree in here, and . . . and, well the kids look just so cute!

HELEN (*uninspired*): Yeah?

MYRON: Well, little Janny has tinsel all in her hair, it's the cutest thing. And Baby Woochers has the little treetop angel and he's making it fly around—

HELEN: Uh huh.

MYRON: Dear, these years never come back to us—

HELEN: So make it a Kodak moment!

MYRON: Honey!

HELEN: Get out! I've got sheep on my hands here!

MYRON: Honey bumpkins—

HELEN: OUT!

(*MYRON stumbles back and out.*)

HELEN (*flips through the Bible*): Let me see. Heavenly host! Great, just . . . just—(*looking up*). You have to make such a big production out of everything? All right . . . How about a heavenly solo?

(*Blackout.*)

ANNOUNCER: Every day the excitement is mounting as each moment takes us closer to the day of wonder. Why, look! Here's John and Larry out for their Christmas tradition of buying a tree. John and Larry are just so excited. Doesn't Christmas bring out the child in all of us?

SCENE TWO

JOHN AND LARRY

(A Christmas lot. One scrawny tree. JOHN and LARRY enter from opposite sides in heavy coats, hats and mittens. They are talking to their children, offstage.)

JOHN: It's OK, son. Honey, Daddy was only kidding about sending you out into the woods alone to find your own tree. I know how much you love this tree here—

LARRY *(same time)*: Stop crying, now. I heard you. You want this scrawny old thing. It does not remind you of Mommy. You want me to tell her you said that?

(They reach out for the tree, still looking offstage.)

JOHN/LARRY: Look, I said I'm getting the stupid—!

(They have grabbed each other's hand. Pause. They slowly turn to see each other. They quickly pull their hands back.)

JOHN: Oh, hey, Larry. How are you?

LARRY: Just fine, John. And yourself?

JOHN: Great . . . just great. Uh, Merry Christmas to you.

LARRY: The same to you.

(Pause.)

LARRY: Got all your shopping done?

JOHN: Not quite. You?

LARRY: Well, just a few things I need to pick up.

(Pause.)

JOHN: Hey, isn't that funny we both ended up on the missions committee at church?

LARRY: That was something, boy. Didn't know you even wanted to be on the committee.

JOHN: Yeah, well. I was surprised to see you on the committee, too. Oh, not that you're not missions minded or anything.

LARRY: Oh, sure. Really think it's important to reach out to those . . . heathen around the world.

JOHN: Yep. (*Pause.*) So what brings you here?

LARRY: Well, rushing to get a tree. We got a late start this year. You know how busy things can get at work this time o' year. Especially in sales.

JOHN: Tell me about it. You know, Larry, I saw some real gorgeous trees over on the Gilman Avenue side of the lot. Real beauties. Thought I'd tell you about 'em.

LARRY: Well, you know I saw some wonderful trees over by the register there. They're straight as an arrow. All perfect sides. Not one've 'em has a side you'd have to turn toward a wall, you know what I mean?

JOHN: Well, that's just great. Thanks for the tip.

LARRY: And thank you. I'll just mosey over and check out those trees you told me about.

> (*They don't move.*)

JOHN (*pointing offstage*): Oh, wow! Look at those trees they're setting up over there. Looks like a new shipment in.

> (*LARRY looks offstage. JOHN grabs the tree and starts to hightail it. LARRY spins back and grabs a handful of trunk. They begin one-upping on the trunk until they've got nowhere to go.*)

JOHN: Look, Appleton, my little Joanie wants this tree and this tree only, catch my drift? There's plenty of other piney wonders in this lot.

LARRY: No, you look, Miller. Little Lawrence has his heart set on this tree. At Christmas he always gets whatever he wants, got it? He loves this tree.

JOHN: The kid loves this tree? This scrawny old thing? Limbs half hanging off.

LARRY: Half bald—

JOHN: Couldn't hang a bulb on it—

LARRY: Garland would slip off.

JOHN: A sad excuse for a Christmas tree—

> (*They grab the tree.*)

JOHN/LARRY: BUT IT'S MINE!!

> (*They start pulling, then look offstage.*)

JOHN: Oh, it's OK, honey. Daddy's just pretending—

LARRY: Don't cry, Lawrence. Daddy and his friend are just playing "Pin the Price Tag on the Tree." (*Spinning back.*) All right, Miller, how much you want for the tree?

JOHN: Not a cent, Appleton. This tree is mine, got it? I'm telling you, back off. I dibbed this tree.

LARRY (*laughing*): *You* what?

JOHN: When I walked in the place, I dibbed the tree.

LARRY: Look, *I'm* the one who called it.

JOHN: I called it, from the entrance.

LARRY: I called it from the parking lot.

JOHN: When?

LARRY: Ten minutes ago.

JOHN: I dibbed it this morning, OK? I drove by and saw it from Gilman Avenue and I dibbed it.

LARRY: You did not!

JOHN: I did so!

LARRY: Nu huh. Prove it!

> (*They glare at one another and lunge for the tree, pulling it like a tug-of-war rope.*)

LARRY: It's mine, Bonehead! This tree has my name written all over it!

JOHN: Leggo of it, Appleton! Leggo before I flock your face!

> (*They stop and look offstage*)

LARRY: Both kids're crying!

JOHN: What's their problem?

LARRY/JOHN: YOU WANT THE TREE OR NOT!

LARRY: What do you mean "no"?

JOHN: Now, Joanie, that's not what you told Daddy before, Honey?

LARRY: What do you mean it's not a Christmas tree anymore?

JOHN: You know Daddy only wants to get you what'll make you happy.

LARRY: Kids. Huh! Go figure 'em.

JOHN: Well, they don't think like us, that's for sure.

(They put the tree down.)

LARRY: Well, I'm glad you've finally opened your eyes, Lawrence. This tree would've looked horrible in the front room.

JOHN: The little treetop angel would have flown away from this one, Joanie.

LARRY: Well. (Chuckles.) Kids sure know how to embarrass their parents sometimes, huh?

JOHN: Yeah, and all we're trying to do is give 'em a happy holiday.

LARRY: Well, it is all for them, isn't it?

JOHN: That's right. Christmas is for the kids. They're the ones who seem to . . . get caught up in the whole thing.

LARRY: Right you are. Where'd you say those trees were, John?

JOHN: On the Gilman Avenue side. Over there.

LARRY: Great. Thanks a lot. And Merry Christmas.

JOHN: Same to you. (They head.)

JOHN: Daddy's sorry, Honey. He didn't mean to upset you.

LARRY: No, Son. That was Daddy's friend. I wasn't really angry at him. It's Christmas, remember?

JOHN: I was just playacting, sweetheart. Daddy wouldn't really get that mad.

JOHN/LARRY: It was only a tree.

(The lights go to blackout. The PIANIST plays a few measures of "I'll be Home for Christmas," then "O Come All Ye Faithful.")

ANNOUNCER: Christmas in Warmwater. A time when all thoughts turn to home and family. A time when sweet memories drift through the mind, reminding one of those happy days of youth and those who made Christmases past something to remember. All over the city doors are swinging wide open, and mothers and fathers are throwing out their arms and wiping wet eyes, as families are reunited in the warmth and joy that is Christmas.

Margaret's Christmas Memories

(LIGHTS up, a little dim. MARGARET, wrapped in a white blanket and wearing slippers, is sitting in a chair. An easel and canvas stand before her. A small table with some paints, a withered poinsettia, and a radio. A stack of six completed paintings or so stand against the table. MARGARET talks to an empty chair opposite her. The radio is playing "O Come, All Ye Faithful." MARGARET is humming along)

MARGARET: I just love carols, don't you, honey? They never seem to grow old, do they? Or . . . out of date. And nobody ever seems to forget one once it's learned. Carols are like a sweet memory, huh? Always there in the back of your mind when you want to bring them out and play them again. *(She daubs at the painting.)* Oh, I'm working on this year's Christmas painting. You didn't know about them? Every year . . . well, in the last few years anyway, I always do a Christmas painting. Memories . . . or scenes from when I was growing up. Christmas when I was child. Christmas was very special then. Very different. I don't want anyone to forget, especially not me, so I pick out a little . . . what's that word? Vignette. A little vignette and I paint it. It's funny, though. I remember colors mostly. I can remember a picture, sure, but the emotion is always a color to me. I can remember the print on my mother's dress, or the design and hue of the wallpaper in the kitchen. It's strange the kind of things you remember. Things . . . details that rush back at the oddest moments, blotting out big pictures and . . . emotions. *(Daubs. Looks and wrinkles her nose.)* The wallpaper in the front room that year was red, yellow, and orange. Little ducks and flowers. I remember I hated it. Christmas was sure sweet then. Oh, but my mother and father had to squeeze pennies until they turned their fingers copper. That's how copper wire was invented, did you know that? My mother and father pulling on a penny! Never had a red cent, it seems, but they always made Christmas magic out of thin air. Really something. They filled it up with hot cocoa and laughter and singing. It felt like there was enough light and heat to keep you warm through the rest of the winter. Of course, we didn't get much on Christmas morning. But I didn't mind. You know, I never bothered asking the other kids in school what they got. I didn't care. What my parents gave me wrapped in gold or green packages didn't matter. It's funny because now I can't remember what most of the toys were. They're like baby teeth. One day they're gone and you don't remember the last day you had them.

(Pause. She daubs for a moment.) What I remember most was Mother and Dad's face when I opened my package. I always made a big show about how much I loved what they got me, just so I could see 'em smile over and over again. To this day I make a fuss over presents, even if I don't like them, because the greatest gift is someone thinking about you, isn't it? (She shuffles around the stack of pictures.) Hmmmm . . . I think I've got something that'll just . . . here it is. (Shows the painting to the chair.) That's my mother and father there. Sitting on that really old divan. It was pale green. My dad, see right there? My dad's poking my mother in the rib with his elbow. He's winking and saying, "See, I knew she'd love it." Mother'd just nod like she'd always do. Beaming. That was the best. That's me dancing around in my new nightgown. We always got a new nightgown at Christmas. Lasted all year. Had to. (Phone rings off. MARGARET looks up.) Is that for me? Hello? Is that—? (Phone stops. Pause. MARGARET starts looking through the paintings. She finds one and holds it up.) I have a fun one here. That's my sister. She's standing at the bottom of the stairs looking into the dark front room while my parents were busy wrapping presents in the kitchen with my Uncle Buster. He always used to spend Christmas with us. Y'see, I wanted to find out what we got for Christmas. I couldn't wait until the morning for some reason I can't remember now, so I paid my sister, Lucy, a nickel to go down and sneak a look-see. Well, that was the last year I did that. I could always act pleased no matter what I got, but I could never act surprised. (*Finds another painting and shows it to the empty chair.*) Oh! (*Laughs.*) I love this one. This is a sweet one. This is Christmas morning. I was . . . 11? Oh, I don't know. Anyways, y'see our robes are over the chairs in front of the furnace. Mother put them there so they'd be toasty when we went into the cold front room to open the gifts. She's back there making hot chocolate. One of three times we had hot chocolate all year. At the table, Dad's got his big, black Bible open there. The big one with important papers and dried flowers stuck inside that always fell out when he opened it. He's getting ready to read about the shepherds and the angels. And the wise men, of course. Father always read us about the wise men before we opened any of the gifts. He didn't want us to forget why we gave gifts to one another.

(*Small pause.*) See that wallpaper there. I hated that color. (*A phone rings, offstage. MARGARET sets the painting down and spins around, looking offstage.*) Is that for me? Is that for me? Is that Kate? Hello? Is anyone out there? Will someone tell me if she calls? Hello? (*Turns back; looks at the paintings.*) Oh! This one is me. (*Laughs.*) I'm seven. I know that for sure. I'm pointing up at the Christmas Star on Christmas Eve. Well, I thought it was the Christmas Star. See it way up there? Oh, it was probably the North Star or something, but I always thought it was the Bethlehem Star shining down, leading everyone who could see it to Jesus. (*Pause. She puts the painting down.*) I wish I could see that star. It's too cloudy now to see anything. (*MICHAEL, a young man, pops his head into the room.*)

MICHAEL: Hiya, Margaret. Ten minutes till lights out, OK? (*He starts to go.*)

MARGARET: Michael? (*MICHAEL comes back in. We see he's wearing a white coat with the emblem of a convalescent hospital on it. MICHAEL is a little slow.*) Michael, was that phone call for me?

MICHAEL (*a bad liar*): What phone call?

MARGARET: Just a second ago. I heard the phone ring.

MICHAEL: Oh, yeah. No, that was for Mr. Mednick down the hall. It was his son.

MARGARET: Oh, I see. Well, I'm expecting a call from Kate. That's my—

MICHAEL: Your daughter, right? Yeah, I've been keepin' an ear peeled for her call, Margaret. Just like every Christmastime. No go yet, ma'am.

MARGARET: Sure nothing came for me this afternoon? I was asleep for a couple of hours after lunch and I'm afraid someone might not have wanted to wake me, and so left it at the front desk. A package? Something like that?

MICHAEL: Well, I don't think so. I didn't see nothin'.

MARGARET (*quietly*): Oh, I see. (*Long pause.*)

MICHAEL: Maybe your daughter's real busy. People get real busy just before Christmas, y'know, with work 'n all. Especially if they like, work in a store or somethin'. She work in a store, Margaret?

MARGARET: What? Oh . . . no. She's a writer for a newspaper.

MICHAEL: Well, that's it. Lotta stories before Christmas, y'know. Human interest stuff. Firemen givin' toys to poor kids and that sort o' stuff. She's probably swamped up to her eyeballs. (*Pause.*) S'what I think.

MARGARET (*not looking at him*): Seems like she was always swamped up to her eyeballs.

MICHAEL: That so? Busy kid, huh? Better than getting' all underfoot and such like. I guess. (*MARGARET starts to cry, softly.*) Oh . . . ah, no, hey, Margaret. Don't do that. (*Comes to her.*) You know she's going to call, or come by, or something, huh? There's still a couple've days till Christmas and all.

MARGARET: What did I do, Michael? What did I do that was so wrong? (*Holds up a painting.*) See? I put her robe by the heater so it'd be warm for Christmas morning. I read about the shepherds and the angels. I used the same big, black Bible with all the flowers inside.

MICHAEL: Hey, that picture's somethin', Margaret.

MARGARET: I made her hot chocolate. She's my heart, Michael. Why can't Christmas even bring her here? Why does she turn my favorite holiday into such pain? What did I do to deserve to be so lonely?

MICHAEL: You didn't do nothin', Margaret. I know that. (*Points at the painting.*) Hey, I wish I had a Christmas like this. She was lucky.

MARGARET: I bought her a nightgown. See? It's on the bed. Would you take it out to the front desk in case she comes while I'm asleep? She'll need it by now.

MICHAEL: Sure can, Margaret. (*Stops.*) Oh, man! I almost forgot. There was somethin' at the front desk.

MARGARET: What?

MICHAEL: Somethin' at the front desk.

MARGARET: What is it?

MICHAEL: I dunno. I'll go get it.

> (*He darts out. MARGARET daubs at the painting, but can't concentrate and puts the brush down. MICHAEL comes back in with a gaudy, cellophane-wrapped basket of fruit and nuts.*)

MICHAEL: Here it is.

MARGARET: That's for me?

MICHAEL: Sure is.

MARGARET: From Kate?

MICHAEL: Yes, ma'am.

MARGARET (*takes it*): Where's the card? Is there any card? A note somewhere.

MICHAEL (*uncomfortable*): Well, no . . . nothin' like that—

MARGARET: Then how do you know it's for—(*She catches on.*) Oh, Michael! It's lovely. I just adore fruit. I never seem to get enough fresh fruit in here, y'know? She's so thoughtful, Kate is.

MICHAEL: Yes, ma'am. I gotta finish makin' the rounds, so, ah . . . Merry Christmas, Margaret.

MARGARET: Merry Christmas, Michael.

(He ducks out. MARGARET sets the basket down. She cries for a moment, then wipes her face and looks at the painting She daubs at it.)

MARGARET *(to the chair)*: This one I'm doing now? It shows my father coming home from work on Christmas Eve. See, he's holding his hat on against the wind. Lucy and I are rushing out to meet him. We both wanted to get the first kiss from him. The first kiss on Christmas Eve was the best. "First kiss, Daddy!" I'm yelling out. "Give me the first kiss!" *(She laughs. (Pause.) She turns up the radio.)* I love the carols, don't you? They never grow old. And no one ever forgets 'em.

(The LIGHTS fade to blackout. In the darkness the PIANIST begins to play "O Come, O Come, Emmanuel.")

ANNOUNCER: Well, closer and closer. The days just seem to fly by here in Warmwater. In fact, it's already the Sunday before the Big Day. And as Christmas nears, the church becomes a buzz of activity as folks can't wait to be a part of every program, every possible chance to participate in the joy that is Christmas.

(LIGHTS on PASTOR DORCAS and HELEN LINGERFIELD sitting on an altar pew. A pulpit stands center. Organ music finishes the last of a hymn. DORCAS takes the pulpit.)

DORCAS: Brethren, as you know Christmas is quickly closing in on us—anyone finished their shopping? *(Laughs.)* Well, I take a medium size, 15 and-a-half neck, and my favorite color is green! *(Laughs. HELEN modestly so.)* As you know, it's also time for the Christmas pageant, which will be held on Christmas Eve at 7:30 PM. Helen Lingerfield has so graciously volunteered to head up the . . . shall we say, production—

HELEN: It's certainly becoming one.

DORCAS: Now, I encourage all of you to lend a hand to Helen, and you children . . . I want you to take part in this rich and rewarding experience. I myself played Gabriel once in my church Christmas pageant when I was kid. And I was a donkey three times.

HELEN: I won't touch that one.

DORCAS: So, Helen, come on up here and tell the folks what you need.

HELEN *(as she passes)*: How about two more weeks.

DORCAS: Now, Helen, the Lord's timing is perfect.

HELEN *(taking the pulpit)*: Hello, everyone. As Pastor Dorcas has told you, I'm heading up the Christmas pageant this year. Now, I need every boy and girl to participate, and all the parents to help whip up a few costumes and props. Rehearsals will start directly after the late service this morning, with practices on Monday night, Tuesday afternoon and night, Wednesday night, Thursday night, and on Christmas Eve afternoon for several hours. If we need extra rehearsals, we'll schedule them later. Lines have to be memorized by tomorrow night and the children's costumes have to be ready in two days. Well, that's the challenge before us. Now, can I see a show of hands of how many kids want to get involved in the pageant? Anyone? Anyone? *(Looking back.)* Pastor, why are all the mothers holding their kids' hands down?

PASTOR *(looking out)*: I think they're just checking their nails. *(Standing.)* I see that hand!

WOMAN'S VOICE *(offstage)*: No you don't!

PASTOR: Oh, sorry. *(Sits.)*

HELEN: Well. I'll be in the foyer if anyone wants to come and sign up. *(As PASTOR DORCAS passes her going to the pulpit.)* I hope the donkey costume still fits.

PASTOR *(clearing his throat)*: Ah . . . Hymn number 233—"Almost Persuaded."

(The PIANIST begins to play the hymn as the LIGHTS go to blackout.)

ANNOUNCER: We shall return to spirited, sacrificing, supportive Warmwater in just a moment, but first . . . *(Blackout.)*[57]

# of Family

There's a wonderful scene in Mennotti's Christmas opera *Amahl and the Night Visitors*, where a crippled boy and his mother are housing the three kings on the quest for the Christ child. While they are sleeping, the mother is tempted to take some of the gold destined for Bethlehem or beyond. In her heartbreaking aria Mother sings that she knows a child who is lowly and poor; who could be destined something better than goats and gruel—it's her son, her darling, her Amahl.

But families everywhere know that the Babe born in Bethlehem was not a shepherd boy for whom gold coins would bring happiness. The child born in Bethlehem was the Word—and God the Father was in Him, in order to reconcile the world to Himself.

Draw close together at Christmas. Read the stories of the season, memorize the second chapter of Luke, love each other, and invite Jesus into your family circle as you celebrate His birth.

It is Christmas in the mansion,
Yule-log fires and silken frocks;
It is Christmas in the cottage,
Mother's filling little socks.

* * *

It is Christmas on the highway,
In the thronging, busy mart;
But the dearest, truest Christmas
Is the Christmas in the heart.

* * *

So remember while December
Brings the only Christmas Day,
In the year let there be Christmas
In the things you do and say;

* * *

Wouldn't life be worth the living
Wouldn't dreams be coming true
If we kept the Christmas spirit
All the whole year through?

UNKNOWN

*　*　*

The next two selections are from

the classic writer of family values,

Louisa May Alcott. It is about the March family

and their adventures during the Civil War,

when father and husband was serving as

an army chaplain. If they are anything,

the March sisters are ingenious,

as these two pieces bear witness.

*　*　*

Christmas at Orchard House

BY LOUISA MAY ALCOTT

"Christmas won't be Christmas without any presents," grumbled Jo, lying on the rug.

"It's so dreadful to be poor!" sighed Meg, looking down at her old dress.

"I don't think it's fair for some girls to have plenty of pretty things, and other girls nothing at all," added little Amy, with an injured sniff.

"We've got father and mother and each other," said Beth contentedly, from her corner.

The four young faces on which the firelight shone brightened at the cheerful words, but darkened again as Jo said sadly,—

"We haven't got father, and shall not have him for a long time."

She didn't say "perhaps never," but each silently added it, thinking of father far away, where the fighting was.

Nobody spoke for a minute; then Meg said in an altered tone, "You know the reason mother proposed not having any presents this Christmas was because it is going to be a hard winter for everyone; and she thinks we ought not to spend money for pleasure, when our men are suffering so in the army. We can't do much, but we can make our little sacrifices, and ought to do it gladly. But I am afraid I don't."

And Meg shook her head, as she thought regretfully of all the pretty things she wanted.

"But I don't think the little we should spend would do any good. We've each got a dollar, and the army wouldn't be much helped by our giving that. I agree not to expect anything from mother or you, but I do want to buy the book *Undine and Sintram* for myself; I've wanted to so long," said Jo, who was a bookworm.

"I planned to spend mine in new music," said Beth, with a little sigh, which no one heard but the hearth brush and kettle holder.

"I shall get a nice box of Faber's drawing pencils; I really need them," said Amy decidedly.

"Mother didn't say anything about our money, and she won't wish us to give up everything. Let's each buy what we want, and have a little fun; I'm sure we work hard enough to earn it," cried Jo, examining the heels of her shoes in a gentlemanly manner.

"I know I do—teaching those tiresome children nearly all day, when I'm longing to enjoy myself at home," began Meg, in the complaining tone again.

"You don't have half such a hard time as I do," said Jo. "How would you like to be shut up for hours with a nervous, fussy old lady, who keeps you trotting, is never satisfied, and worries you till you're ready to fly out of the window or cry?"

"It's naughty to fret; but I do think washing dishes and keeping things tidy is the worst work in the world. It makes me cross; and my hands get so stiff, I can't practice well at all," and Beth looked at her rough hands with a sigh that anyone could hear that time.

"I don't believe any of you suffer as I do," cried Amy, "for you don't have to go to school with impertinent girls, who plague you if you don't know your lessons, and laugh at your dresses, and label your father if he isn't rich, and insult you when your nose isn't nice."

"If you mean libel, I'd say so, and not talk about labels, as if papa was a pickle bottle," advised Jo, laughing.

"I know what I mean, and you needn't be satirical about it. It's proper to use good words, and improve your vocabulary," returned Amy, with dignity.

"Don't peck at one another, children. Don't you wish we had the money papa lost when we were little, Jo? Dear me! how happy and good we'd be, if we had no worries!" said Meg, who could remember better times.

"You said, the other day, you thought we were a deal happier than the King children, for they were fighting and fretting all the time, in spite of their money."

"So I did, Beth. Well, I think we are; for, though we do have to work, we make fun for ourselves, and are a pretty jolly set, as Jo would say."

"Jo does use such slang words!" observed Amy, with a reproving look at the long figure stretched on the rug. Jo immediately sat up, put her hands in her pockets, and began to whistle.

"Don't, Jo; it's so boyish!"

"That's why I do it."

"I detest rude, unladylike girls!"

"I hate affected, niminy-piminy chits!"

"'Birds in their little nests agree,'" sang Beth, the peacemaker, with such a funny face that both sharp voices softened to a laugh, and the "pecking" ended for that time.

"Really, girls, you are both to be blamed," said Meg, beginning to lecture in her elder-sisterly fashion. "You are old enough to leave off boyish tricks, and to behave better, Josephine. It didn't matter so much when you were a little girl; but now you are so tall, and turn up your hair, you should remember that you are a young lady."

"I'm not! and if turning up my hair makes me one, I'll wear it in two tails till I'm twenty," cried Jo, pulling off her net, and shaking down a chestnut mane. "I hate to think I've got to grow up, and be Miss March, and wear long gowns, and look prim. It's bad enough to be a girl, anyway, when I like boys' games and work and manners! I can't get over my disappointment in not being a boy; and it's worse than ever now, for I'm dying to go and fight with papa, and I can only stay at home and knit, like a poky old woman!" Jo shook the blue army sock she was knitting till the needles rattled like castanets, and her ball bounded across the room.

"Poor Jo! It's too bad, but it can't be helped; so you must try to be contented with making your name boyish, and playing brother to us girls," said Beth, stroking the rough head at her knee with a hand that all the dishwashing and dusting in the world could not make ungentle in its touch.

"As for you, Amy," continued Meg, "you are altogether too particular and prim. Your airs are funny now; but you'll grow up an affected little goose, if you don't take care. I like your nice manners and refined ways of speaking, when you don't try to be elegant; but your absurd words are as bad as Jo's slang."

"If Jo is a tomboy and Amy a goose, what am I, please?" asked Beth, ready to share the lecture.

"You're a dear, and nothing else," answered Meg warmly; and no one contradicted her, for the "Mouse" was the pet of the family.

The room in which the girls sat was a comfortable old room, though the carpet was faded and the furniture very plain for a good picture or two hung on the walls, books filled the recesses, chrysanthemums and Christmas roses bloomed in the windows, and a pleasant atmosphere of homepeace pervaded it.

Margaret, the eldest of the four, was sixteen, and very pretty, with large eyes, plenty of soft, brown hair, a sweet mouth, and white hands; Fifteen-year-old Jo was very tall, thin, and brown, and reminded one of a colt. Her long, thick hair was her one beauty; Round shoulders had Jo, big hands and feet, a flyaway look to her clothes, and the uncomfortable appearance of a girl who was rapidly shooting up into a woman, and didn't like it. Elizabeth—or Beth, as everyone called her—was a rosy, smooth haired, brighteyed girl of thirteen, with a shy manner, a timid voice, and a peaceful expression, which was seldom disturbed. Her father called her "Little Tranquillity"; Amy, though the youngest, was a most important person—in her own opinion at least. A regular snowmaiden, with blue eyes, and yellow hair, curling on her shoulders, pale and slender, and always carrying herself like a young lady mindful of her manners.

The clock struck six; and, having swept up the hearth, Beth put a pair of slippers down to warm. Somehow the sight of the old shoes had a good effect upon the girls; for mother was coming, and everyone brightened to welcome her. Meg stopped lecturing, and lighted the lamp. Amy got out of the easy chair without being asked, and Jo forgot how tired she was as she sat up to hold the slippers nearer to the blaze.

"They are quite worn out; Marmee must have a new pair."

"I thought I'd get her some with my dollar," said Beth.

"No, I shall!" cried Amy.

"I'm the oldest," began Meg, but Jo cut in with a decided—"I'm the man of the family now papa is away, and I shall provide the slippers, for he told me to take special care of mother while he was gone."

"I'll tell you what we'll do," said Beth; "let's each get her something for Christmas, and not get anything for ourselves."

"That's like you, dear! What will we get?" exclaimed Jo.

Everyone thought soberly for a minute; then Meg announced, as if the idea was suggested by the sight of her own pretty hands, "I shall give her a nice pair of gloves."

"Army shoes, best to be had," cried Jo.

"Some handkerchiefs, all hemmed," said Beth.

"I'll get a little bottle of cologne; she likes it, and it won't cost much, so I'll have some left to buy my pencils," added Amy.

"How will we give the things?" asked Meg.

"Put them on the table, and bring her in and see her open the bundles. Don't you remember how we used to do on our birthdays?" answered Jo.

"Let Marmee think we are getting things for ourselves, and then surprise her. We must go shopping tomorrow afternoon, Meg; there is so much to do about the play for Christmas night," said Jo, marching up and down, with her hands behind her back and her nose in the air.

"I don't mean to act any more after this time; I'm getting too old for such things," observed Meg, who was as much a child as ever about "dressing up" frolics.

"You won't stop, I know, as long as you can trail round in a white gown with your hair down, and wear goldpaper jewelry. You are the best actress we've got, and there'll be an end of everything if you quit the boards," said Jo. "We ought to rehearse tonight. Come here, Amy, and do the fainting scene, for you are as stiff as a poker in that."

"I can't help it; I never saw anyone faint, and I don't choose to make myself all black and blue, tumbling flat as you do. If I can go down easily, I'll drop; if I can't, I shall fall into a chair and be graceful." Amy was not gifted with dramatic power, but was chosen because she was small enough to be borne out shrieking by the villain of the piece.

"Do it this way; clasp your hands so, and stagger across the room, crying frantically, 'Roderigo! Save me! Save me!'" and away went Jo, with a melodramatic scream which was truly thrilling.

Amy followed, but she poked her hands out stiffly before her, and jerked herself along as if she went by machinery; and her "Ow!" was more suggestive of pins being run into her than of fear and anguish. Jo gave a despairing groan, and Meg laughed outright, while Beth let her bread burn as she watched the fun, with interest.

"It's no use! Do the best you can when the time comes, and if the audience laughs, don't blame me. Come on," cried Meg, and the rehearsal ended in a general burst of laughter.

II

Jo was the first to wake in the gray dawn of Christmas morning. No stockings hung at the fireplace, and for a moment she felt as much disappointed as she did long ago, when her little sock fell down because it was so crammed with goodies. Then she remembered her mother's promise, and, slipping her hand under her pillow, drew out a little crimson-covered book. She knew it very well, for it was that beautiful old story of the best life ever lived, and Jo felt that it was a true guidebook for any pilgrim going the long journey. She woke Meg with a "Merry Christmas," and bade her see what was under her pillow. A green-covered book appeared, with the same picture inside, and a few words written by their mother, which made their one present very precious in their eyes. Presently Beth and Amy woke, to rummage and find their little books also—one dove-colored, the other blue; and all sat looking at and talking about them, while the east grew rosy with the coming day. In spite of her small vanities, Margaret had a sweet and pious nature, which unconsciously influenced her sisters, especially Jo, who loved her very tenderly, and obeyed her because her advice was so gently given.

"Girls," said Meg seriously, looking from the tumbled head beside her to the two little nightcapped ones in the room beyond, "mother wants us to read and love and mind these books, and we must begin at once. We used to be faithful about it; but since father went away, and all this war trouble unsettled us, we have neglected many things. You can do as you please; but I shall keep my book on the table here, and read a little every morning as soon as I wake, for I know it will do me good, and help me through the day."

Then she opened her new book and began to read. Jo put her arm round her, and, leaning cheek to cheek, read also, with the quiet expression so seldom seen on her restless face.

"How good Meg is! Come, Amy, let's do as they do. I'll help you with the hard words, and they'll explain things if we don't understand," whispered Beth, very much impressed by the pretty books and her sisters' example.

"I'm glad mine is blue," said Amy; and then the rooms were very still while the pages were softly turned, and the winter sunshine crept in to touch the bright heads and serious faces with a Christmas greeting.

"Where is mother?" asked Meg, as she and Jo ran down to thank her for their gifts, half an hour later.

"Goodness only knows. Some poor creeter come abeggin', and your ma went straight off to see what was needed. There never was such a woman for givin' away vittles and drink, clothes," replied Hannah, who had lived with the family since Meg was born, and was considered by them all more as a friend than a servant.

"She will be back soon, I think; so fry your cakes, and have everything ready," said Meg, looking over the presents which were collected in a basket and kept under the sofa, ready to be produced at the proper time. "Why, where is Amy's bottle of cologne?" she added, as the little flask did not appear.

"She took it out a minute ago, and went off with it to put a ribbon on it, or some such notion," replied Jo, dancing about the room to take the first stiffness off the new army slippers.

"How nice my handkerchiefs look, don't they? Hannah washed and ironed them for me, and I marked them all myself," said Beth, looking proudly at the somewhat uneven letters which had cost her such labor.

"Bless the child! She's gone and put 'Mother' on them instead of 'M. March.' How funny!" cried Jo, taking up one.

"Isn't it right? I thought it was better to do it so, because Meg's initials are 'M.M.,' and I don't want anyone to use these but Marmee," said Beth, looking troubled.

"It's all right, dear, and a very pretty idea—quite sensible, too, for no one can ever mistake it now. It will please her very much, I know," said Meg, with a frown for Jo and a smile for Beth.

"There's mother. Hide the basket, quick!" cried Jo, as a door slammed, and steps sounded in the hall.

Amy came in hastily, and looked rather abashed when she saw her sisters all waiting for her. "Where have you been, and what are you hiding behind you?" asked Meg, surprised to see, by her hood and cloak, that lazy Amy had been out so early.

"Don't laugh at me, Jo! I didn't mean anyone should know till the time came. I only meant to change the little bottle for a big one, and I gave all my money to get it, and I'm truly trying not to be selfish anymore."

As she spoke, Amy showed the handsome flask which replaced the cheap one; and looked so earnest and humble in her little effort to forget herself that Meg hugged her on the spot, and Jo pronounced her "a trump," while Beth ran to the window, and picked her finest rose to ornament the stately bottle.

"You see I felt ashamed of my present, after reading and talking about being good this morning, so I ran round the corner and changed it the minute I was up: and I'm so glad, for mine is the handsomest now."

Another bang of the street door sent the basket under the sofa, and the girls to the table, eager for breakfast.

"Merry Christmas, Marmee! Many of them! Thank you for our books; we read some, and mean to every day," they cried, in chorus.

"Merry Christmas, little daughters! I'm glad you began at once, and hope you will keep on. But I want to say one word before we sit down. Not far away from here lies a poor woman with a little newborn baby. Six children are huddled into one bed to keep from freezing, for they have no fire. There is nothing to eat over there; and the oldest boy came to tell me they were suffering hunger and cold. My girls, will you give them your breakfast as a Christmas present?"

They were all unusually hungry, having waited nearly an hour, and for a minute no one spoke; only a minute, for Jo exclaimed impetuously, "I'm so glad you came before we began!"

"May I go and help carry the things to the poor little children?" asked Beth eagerly.

"I shall take the cream and the muffins," added Amy, heroically giving up the articles she most liked.

Meg was already covering the buckwheats, and piling the bread into one big plate.

"I thought you'd do it," said Mrs. March, smiling as if satisfied. "You shall all go and help me, and when we come back we will have bread and milk for breakfast, and make it up at dinnertime."

They were soon ready, and the procession set out. Fortunately it was early, and they went through back streets, so few people saw them, and no one laughed at the queer party.

A poor, bare, miserable room it was, with broken windows, no fire, ragged bedclothes, a sick mother, wailing baby, and a group of pale, hungry children cuddled under one old quilt, trying to keep warm.

How the big eyes stared and the blue lips smiled as the girls went in.

"Ach, mein Gott! It is good angels come to us!" said the poor woman, crying for joy.

"Funny angels in hoods and mittens," said Jo, and set them laughing.

In a few minutes it really did seem as if kind spirits had been at work there. Hannah, who had carried wood, made a fire. Mrs. March gave the mother tea and gruel, and comforted her with promises of help, while she dressed the little baby as tenderly as if it had been her own. The girls, meantime, spread the table, set the children round the fire, and fed them like so many hungry birds—laughing, talking, and trying to understand the funny broken English.

"Des ist gut!" "Die Engelkinder!" cried the poor things, as they ate, and warmed their purple hands at the comfortable blaze.

The girls had never been called angel children before, and thought it very agreeable, especially Jo, who had been considered a "Sancho" ever since she was born.

That was a very happy breakfast, though they didn't get any of it; and when they went away, leaving comfort behind, I think there were not in all the city four merrier people than the hungry little girls who gave away their breakfasts and contented themselves with bread and milk on Christmas morning.

"That's loving our neighbor better than ourselves, and I like it," said Meg, as they set out their presents, while their mother was upstairs collecting clothes for the poor Hummels.

Not a very splendid show, but there was a great deal of love done up in the few little bundles; and the tall vase of red roses, white chrysanthemums, and trailing vines, which stood in the middle, gave quite an elegant air to the table.

"She's coming! Strike up, Beth! Open the door, Amy! Three cheers for Marmee!" cried Jo, prancing about, while Meg went to conduct mother to the seat of honor.

Beth played her gayest march, Amy threw open the door, and Meg enacted escort with great dignity. Mrs. March was both surprised and touched; and smiled with her eyes full as she examined her presents, and read the little notes which accompanied them. The slippers went on at once, a new handkerchief was slipped into her pocket, well scented with Amy's cologne, the rose was fastened in her bosom, and the nice gloves were pronounced a "perfect fit."

There was a good deal of laughing and kissing and explaining, in the simple, loving fashion which makes these home festivals so pleasant at the time, so sweet to remember long afterward, and then all fell to work.[58]

The Christmas Play

BY LOUISA MAY ALCOTT

THE CHRISTMAS PLAY

On Christmas night a dozen girls piled on to the bed, which was the dress circle, and sat before the blue and yellow chintz curtains in a most flattering state of expectancy. There was a good deal of rustling and whispering behind the curtain, a trifle of lamp-smoke, and an occasional giggle from Amy, who was apt to get hysterical in the excitement of the moment. Presently a bell sounded, the curtains flew apart, and the Operatic Tragedy began.

"A gloomy wood," according to the one play-bill, was represented by a few shrubs in pots, green baize on the floor, and a cave in the distance. This cave was made with a clothes-horse for a roof, bureaus for walls; and in it was a small furnace in full blast, with a black pot on it and an old witch bending over it. The stage was dark, and the glow of the furnace had a fine effect, especially as real steam issued from the kettle when the witch took off the cover. A moment was allowed for the first thrill to subside; then Hugo, the villain, stalked in with a sword at his side, a slouched hat, black beard, mysterious cloak and boots.

After pacing to and fro in much agitation, he struck his forehead, and burst out in a wild strain, singing of his hatred of Roderigo, his love for Zara, and his pleasing resolution to kill the one and win the other. The gruff tones of Hugo's voice, with an occasional shout when his feelings overcame him, were very impressive, and the audience applauded the moment he paused for breath. Bowing with the air of one accustomed to public praise, he stole to the cavern, and ordered Hagar to come forth with a commanding, "What ho! minion! I need thee!"

Out came Meg, with grey horse-hair hanging about her face, a red and black robe, a staff, and cabalistic signs upon her cloak. Hugo demanded a potion to make Zara adore him, and one to destroy Roderigo. Hagar, in fine dramatic melody, promised both, and proceeded to call up the spirit who would bring the love philtre—

"Hither, hither, from thy home,
Airy sprite, I bid thee come!
Born of roses, fed on dew,
Charms and potions canst thou brew?

Bring me here, with elfin speed,
The fragrant philtre which I need;
Make it sweet and swift and strong.
Spirit, answer now my song!

A soft strain of music sounded, and then at the back of the cave appeared a little figure in cloudy white, with glittering wings, golden hair, and a garland of roses on its head. Waving a wand, it sang—

"Hither I come,
From my airy home,
Afar in the silver moon.
Take this magic spell,
And use it well,
Or its power will vanish soon!"

And, dropping a small, gilded bottle at the witch's feet, the spirit vanished. Another chant from Hagar produced another apparition, not a lovely one; for with a bang an ugly black imp appeared, and, having croaked a reply, tossed a dark bottle at Hugo, and disappeared with a mocking laugh. Having warbled his thanks and put the potions in his boots, Hugo departed; and Hagar informed the audience that, as he had killed a few of her friends in times past, she has cursed him, and intends to thwart his plans and be revenged on him. Then the curtain fell, and the audience reposed and ate candy while discussing the merits of the play.

A good deal of hammering went on before the curtain rose again; but when it became evident what a master-piece of stage-carpentering had been got up no one murmured at the delay. It was truly superb! A tower rose to the ceiling; half-way up appeared a window, with a lamp burning at it, and behind the white curtain appeared Zara in a lovely blue and silver dress, waiting for Roderigo. He came in gorgeous array, with plumed cap, red cloak, chestnut love-locks, a guitar, and the boots, of course.

Kneeling at the foot of the tower, he sang a serenade in melting tones. Zara replied, and, after a musical dialogue, consented to fly. Then came the grand effect of the play. Roderigo produced a rope ladder, with five steps to it, threw one end up, and invited Zara to descend. Timidly she crept from her lattice, put her hand on Roderigo's shoulder, and was about to leap gracefully down when (Alas! alas for Zara) she forgot her train—it caught in the window— the tower tottered, leant forward, fell with a crash, and buried the unhappy lovers in the ruins!

A universal shriek arose as the russet boots waved wildly from the wreck, and a golden head emerged, exclaiming, "I told you so! I told you so!" With wonderful presence of mind, Don Pedro, the cruel sire, rushed in, dragged out his daughter with a hasty aside—"Don't laugh! Act as if it was all right!"—and, ordering Roderigo up, banished him from the kingdom with wrath and scorn.

Though decidedly shaken by the fall of the tower upon him, Roderigo defied the old gentleman, and refused to stir. This dauntless example fired Zara; she also defied her sire, and he ordered them both to the deepest dungeons of his castle. A stout little retainer came in with chains, and led them away, looking very much frightened and evidently forgetting the speech he ought to have made.

Act 3 was the castle hall; and here Hagar appeared, having come to free the lovers and finish Hugo. She hears him coming, and hides; sees him put the potions into two cups of wine and bid the timid little servant: "Bear them to the captives in their cells, and tell them I shall come anon." The servant takes Hugo aside to tell him something, and Hagar changes the cups for two others which are harmless. Ferdinando, the minion, carries them away, and Hagar puts back the cup which holds the poison meant for Roderigo.

Hugo, getting thirsty after a long warble, drinks it, loses his wits, and, after a good deal of clutching and stamping, falls flat and dies; while Hagar informs him what she has done in a song of exquisite power and melody.

This was a truly thrilling scene, though some persons might have thought that the sudden tumbling down of a quantity of long hair rather marred the effect of the villain's death. He was called before the curtain, and with great propriety appeared leading Hagar, whose singing was considered more wonderful than all the rest of the performance put together.

Act 4 displayed the despairing Roderigo on the point of stabbing himself because he has been told that Zara has deserted him. Just as the dagger is at his heart a lovely song is sung under his window, informing him that Zara is true, but in danger, and he can save her if he will. A key is thrown in, which unlocks the door, and in a spasm of rapture he tears off his chains and rushes away to find and rescue his lady-love.

Act 5 opened with a stormy scene between Zara and Don Pedro. He wishes her to go into a convent, but she won't hear of it; and, after a touching appeal, is about to faint, when Roderigo dashes in and demands her hand. Don Pedro refuses, because he is not rich. They shout and gesticulate tremendously, but cannot agree, and Roderigo is about to bear away the exhausted Zara when the timid servant enters with a letter and a bag from Hagar, who has mysteriously disappeared.

The latter informs the party that she bequeaths untold wealth to the young pair, and an awful doom to Don Pedro if he doesn't make them happy. The bag is opened, and several quarts of tin money shower down upon the stage, till it is quite glorified with the glitter. This entirely softens the "stern sire": he consents without a murmur. All join in a joyful chorus, and the curtain falls upon the lovers kneeling to receive Don Pedro's blessing in attitudes of the most romantic grace.

Tumultuous applause followed, but received an unexpected check, for the cot-bed on which the "dress-circle" was built suddenly shut up and extinguished the enthusiastic audience. Roderigo and Don Pedro flew to the rescue, and all were taken out unhurt, though many were speechless with laughter. The excitement had hardly subsided when Hannah appeared, with "Mrs. March's compliments, and would the ladies walk down to supper?"[59] ✳

Merry Christmas

By Jake Falstaff

The school was to have a Christmas tree, and Christmas doings. On the last day before the vacation there were no classes. Instead, all the scholars helped to trim the tree.

They made chains of colored paper and festoons of strung popcorn. They unpacked a big box of brittle ornaments, and hung up those that weren't broken. In the afternoon, some of the women of the neighborhood came in and helped, and later some men came in too, and built a flight of seats on the rostrum.

They left the desks to the visitors. The schoolhouse was crowded at seven o'clock when the doings began. Every desk held at least two adults, and there were dozens standing up around the sides of the room. Babies were hushed.

On the blackboard, in colored chalk, was the masterpiece of Albert Smeed, the penman. It was a very elaborate bird, drawn all in one line and over it in old English letters, "Merry Christmas."

The scholars and the grown people sang the first song together: "Silent Night, Holy Night." Then the teacher called on old Solomon Preavy, who was a Civil War veteran, a bailiff in the courthouse, and an ordained preacher. In a quaking voice, the old man asked a Christmas blessing.

The children sang: "Up on the house, no delay, no pause, clatter the steeds of Santa Claus. Down through the chimney with loads of toys. Ho for the little ones' Christmas joys!" A pale, tall, beautiful girl played "Star of the East" on a violin, and two very bashful little girls sang "Beside a Manger Lowly." A sixth-grade boy recited, "Father calls me William, sister calls me Will, mother calls me Willie, but the fellers call me Bill."

A small boy, called up to recite "'Twas the Night Before Christmas," got overcome with embarrassment along about the tenth line and ran bawling to the desk where his mother sat.

After some more speaking, the teacher began to distribute the presents which had been laid under the tree. Lemuel was astonished to hear his name called. He got five presents—one from the teacher (Pickwick Papers), and four from other scholars. One of them was a hand-painted plate from the little girl with pigtails who told him to mind his own beeswax on the first day he went to Maple Valley School.

He was terribly embarrassed because he had not brought any presents for anybody.

There was some excitement in the back of the room. Some of the big boys of the township, considering themselves too old to go to the schoolhouse doings, were trying to climb up the schoolhouse with the apparent intention of stopping the chimney.

Stern fathers went out to attend to them.

When the formal services were over, Lemuel ran to Barbara. "I never gave any of them anything," he said.

Barbara patted his head. "Yes, you did," she said. "I found out who was giving you things, and put things under the tree for them. I forged your name to the cards."

Ora and Barbara took Lemuel along over to Uncle Simon's on Christmas Eve. He supposed that it meant some kind of celebration They hadn't told him anything, but he knew that they were taking the set of puzzles and parlor tricks he was giving Clyde and that they had some other packages along.

Lemuel was in the sitting room, and had taken a good quick look into the kitchen and downstairs bedroom before he would admit to himself that Uncle Simon's didn't have a Christmas tree! He could barely conceal his surprise.

It was a fact that Clyde was nearly fifteen years old, and also that the family would be going over to Ora's (where there was a tree) for Christmas dinner. Still it seemed strange to Lemuel.

Although everybody looked a little more slicked up than usual, and Aunt Jen was wearing a gay pink apron, there was hardly any other variation from the routine. However, something smelled a good deal like newly baked cookies.

It was odd to a boy who had always spent Christmas Eve with his mother and father, the three sitting together around a brightly lighted little tree.

That was one evening when they never had any company. The ritual of present opening was always exactly the same, and even Lemuel's father, though he seemed almost as absent-minded and sober as usual, took Christmas Eve seriously.

Mrs. Hayden always passed out the gifts, calling off the name on each one with a little air of surprise. When a package was opened by one of them, the other two always watched with close attention. Lemuel's father would nod approval and nearly always comment, "Very fine; very fine indeed."

If his wife gave him a pair of black socks with a gray thread running through, Perry Hayden received them with an air of conviction from which one would have thought that he had been thinking intently of his need for black socks with a gray thread ever since July. When he got a present from Lemuel, he would nod solemnly and say, "Very thoughtful, very thoughtful."

So Lemuel felt a little chilled when he heard that the commotion out in the side yard meant that Cousin Dellie Graf and her young man, Homer Henty, had been invited over. As usual with people he had never met, he was pretty sure that he was going to feel strange.

This feeling left him as soon as Cousin Dellie came bursting in, pulling at a black curl which hung loose down on her forehead. She was a merry, curvaceous girl in an elegant stiff cocoa-taffeta dress. Her young man wore a swallow-tailed coat and a ready-made fox-in-hand tie. He was redheaded, and even more inclined to merriment than Dellie.

The young farmer started telling about the flashlight pictures he was going to take of the group.

He was on the way to being a professional photographer, it developed. He said that as soon as he sold his lower Thirty, and made some further arrangements with Old Man Snell, the photographer at Creston, he was set to take over the business there.

When Ora and Clyde asked him questions about starting out as a photographer, he maintained that it wasn't much of a chore, the way he figured it. There was a lot of business where a fellow didn't exactly have to be an expert to make good. That was because of the great numbers of new Swiss and Hungarian and Bosnian immigrants who came in for pictures as soon as they got their bearings in this country.

The newcomers would settle near Akron and work in the celery ground on farms owned by relatives who had already got a start. For their first pictures to send back to wherever they came from, they were likely to want to be rigged out in cowboy or base-ball suits or something like that, and possibly equipped with guns or fencing foils.

About six months later they were likely to go in for something more sentimental. They would sit on a big crescent moon bearing large signs such as WANT SOMEONE TO LOVE YOU? Mr. Snell even knew how to oblige with a picture taken so that a young man could seem to be pasting a soul-kiss to the lips of a gorgeous actress.

Homer said he had never realized how much trouble a man could have with the English language until he had got friendly with some of the greenhorns who came into Snell's. He had helped explain some puzzling things to them.

There was one smart young fellow, with an ambition to be a rich farmer, who wanted to know the meaning of the sign, POST NO BILLS. He thought it could mean that in this enlightened country no man might dun another by mail. Yet he thought it might also mean dollar bills or ten-dollar bills.

Then there was the young cousin of the Rahmis who couldn't understand the sign in the telegraph office at Kerriston, DON'T WRITE—TELEGRAPH. All he could get out of it was that there was something wrong with the word "telegraph." Maybe the company preferred "telegram," but it seemed senseless to spend so much effort to correct a word.

Aunt Jen brought in a plate of cookies and Uncle Simon passed around elderberry-blossom wine. This caused Homer and Dellie to do a lot of joking which sounded as if what they were about to drink was a powerful intoxicant. Homer offered her a glass with exaggerated politeness, saying, "Would you care to take your drink garbled, or do you just make it a habit to swill it down straight?"

Dellie said he shouldn't behave like that, not in the merry holiday tide. Then Dellie said that Homer ought to play or sing something, even if he didn't have the rest of his quartet with him. This was a "string quartet" composed of four young men who played at many functions. Two played potato-bug mandolins and the others played guitars. Homer said he didn't like to try alone, but if they would all sing loud enough to drown him out he would try something like "Over the Waves." He had brought his guitar along, although he said it didn't sound like much alone.

After three or four numbers, which were chiefly duets by the visitors, they insisted on everybody's really joining in for "In the Shade of the Old Apple Tree." Clyde and Homer got to letting themselves out, booming and dragging the words toward the end of each verse. When they found that this made Dellie and even Barbara giggle, they also threw in some unexpected high and low notes near the end of the refrain

About ten o'clock it seemed to be time for the flashlight pictures. Lemuel was surprised to hear that these were to be taken upstairs in the spare bedroom, which was the only place large enough to be suitable, or something.

They trooped up into the upstairs hall and then Aunt Jen flung open the door to the great spare bedroom.

"My goodness, gracious, gumption, Annabelle!" said Homer Henty. The others all cried out.

Though no lamp was lit in the room, it was gleaming brilliantly from candlelights on a great Christmas tree in one far corner, while in the opposite one the rectangle-shaped box stove shone with the coals with which it had been secretly fired until everything glowed with warmth.

For some reason the room seemed even more festive than the places where such events are customarily held. Perhaps the great four-poster bed, covered with its bright pink, lavender and white Wedding Ring quilt, and the gaudy rag rug with a Saint Bernard woven in the center (surrounded by a wreath of red roses) had something to do with the Christmasy look. The room was also festooned with brightly colored paper chains linking the tops of the ancestral pictures.

The tree was not decorated like any that Lemuel had ever seen. It had candles and popcorn and cranberry strands and gilded walnuts, but it had some stranger ornaments. The most surprising were the red-beet slices which hung on separate strings like precious tokens. He learned that this was one of the customs that had come from Switzerland with Grandpa and Grandma Nadeli, and that the beet slices would last very well for several days. There were also many fancy cookies, in shapes of everything from angels to camels. On a close inspection Lemuel saw that, though it was the prettiest tree he had ever beheld, it did not have a single store-bought trimming. At first people stood and stared, crowding at the door, until Uncle Simon had to remind them that Christmas trees don't bite. Then three huge lamps were lit and the presents were passed out.

Lemuel couldn't remember nearly all of the gifts. but he noticed that there were certain things which it was pretty much of a custom to give. From various absent female cousins and aunts to Aunt Jen and Barbara there were hand-painted dishes or handkerchiefs or corset covers. Younger people, too, seemed to give each other presents of dishes.

The dishes were usually hand-painted by the donor and might be decorated with yellow roses or enormous blackberries. The corset covers were pretty sure to have wide pink silk ribbon strung through them. Homer joked about trying one of these on, but Dellie got it away from him before he could carry out the threat.

When Aunt Jen got her present from Barbara, she looked a little tearful. It was a white hand-crocheted nightgown yoke with the word MOTHER in great solid white letters. She was also given a gold watch with a butterfly-shaped pin from Uncle Simon. Barbara received a beautiful tall glass pitcher from Clyde, and her mother had added twelve tall, heavy tumblers to match it.

Last Homer Henty took the flashlight pictures.

At first it was hard work to get started on picture taking because everybody made remarks to undo each other's composure.

Homer begged them to remember to keep their eyes wide open while the flash lasted.

For one picture he stood Clyde and Lemuel up together in front of the tree and finally got everybody so quiet that the boys felt pretty serious. In the picture that resulted they both had terribly solemn, bug-eyed expressions. As Uncle Simon expressed it, "Those boys sure stared terrible for Homer Henty's pictures."

On some of the pictures it was noted with interest later that the hour on the clock was just eleven. As such a late hour was synonymous with midnight in their minds, it became their habit, whenever they spoke of those pictures, to refer to them as the Midnight Pictures.

Grandpa Nadeli woke on Christmas morning while it was still dark. Ever since a few weeks after the stroke had paralyzed his right side, he always thought when he first woke that he was a boy.

It seemed to him that his father had called him twice, and that if he didn't hurry, his father would be coming in with a whip. So he woke scrabbling at the covers, only his right hand wouldn't scrabble. It was the realization that only the ghost of his right hand was moving that reminded Grandpa Nadeli that he was an old man.

The realization came on Christmas morning without any sting or sorrow.

"Ach, ja," Grandpa Nadeli murmured to himself. "I am an old man. Half awake and half asleep, I thought I had a whipping to eke and work to do that I hated.

"But I am safe from any man's blows, and there is no more work for me. If only for peace and ease, it is good to be an old man."

Faint light in the eastern sky made a silhouette of the wreath at the window, and he remembered that it was Christmas. A warm happiness flowed into his soul as he thought of this. It reminded him that he was a patriarch; the head of a family. He thought of the strong, stalwart comely men he had begotten and the fine women they had married; he thought of his grandchildren.

He thought of the son who had not turned out so well; the willful, errant boy who had married a woman of no account to spite his father, and had suffered the miseries of her company. Even Ben, he reflected, would be welcome today, and it might be that if he came, this would be the day on which they two could learn to see into each other's hearts, and heal what was amiss there.

He thought of his own youth; of the spring days when he went with the goats and cows, up the mountain for the long stay; of his mother leaning over a kettle in the fireplace (a picture he often remembered); of his army years, when he swaggered and drank and fought; of his courtship (mostly he remembered a hillside deep in daisies and a girl in her Old World holiday dress).

He thought of the terror-stricken weeks of the sea voyage which brought him to the New World and of the lean years that came after that. Tears rolled down his cheeks as he thought of the day he loaded his weeping children into the wagon and drove away from the farm (but it was Simon's farm now) which the sheriff had taken from him.

But these thoughts were brief, as his ill fortune was brief in the stretch of his life.

Contentment made Grandpa Nadeli stretch his good leg and his good arm. Cool, the sheets refreshed them. He groaned with the pleasure of that pain. Today he would sit at the head of a table where two generations sprung from himself ate of an abundance in which he had an interest. Gently, he began to sing a peaceful, beautiful song.

Grandma Nadeli, coming in from her chores with Schelm, heard his voice: "Stille Nacht, heilige Nacht . . ."

She stood quite still a moment in the middle of the kitchen floor, joining in the song.

About nine o'clock Grandpa and Grandma Nadeli drove in at Ora's in a cutter, covered with a black bearhide. Old Schelm was very lively. Grandma Nadeli thought it was because of the cold and the winter resting. But Grandpa Nadeli said he thought it was because of the bells that jingled on the sleds.

"He thinks he is young," Grandpa said. "If I had bells ringing beside my legs, maybe I could dance."

Because of the snow Ora carried Grandpa into the house. Grandma stomped through the drifts, and spent a great deal of time on the back porch shaking the snow out of her numerous skirts. She wiped her boots on the broom. Uncle Simons, who had kept Lemuel overnight, arrived just as she finished.

It was very gay inside. For Lemuel it was really the second half of a double Christmas. The first thing he noticed was how greatly the sitting room had been transformed since just the night before. Even the kitchen was in a decorated state.

The dainty tree was set up, and underneath it there was a tiny, elaborate farmyard that had been carved in Switzerland by Grandma's brother, the one called Uncle Geometer because of his profession. The tree was heavily covered with gauds, including a whole regiment of little toy Santa Clauses.

Lemuel was immediately invited out to peer at the browning ducks, stuffed with sauerkraut and knoepfle, and the wide dish of escalloped oysters.

When Uncle Valentine arrived it was decided that they should open all the Christmas presents which were still to be exchanged.

First were brought out the black alpaca dress goods, from Simon, for Grandma Nadeli, and the dark gray suit for Grandpa

Nadeli from Simon and Valentine. He said that now he would be fine enough to run for county recorder.

Grandma Nadeli handed to Clyde and Barbara and Lemuel the gift which she was presenting to all her grandchildren. These were quaintly bound little German Testaments.

Lemuel was amazed when Clyde began reading aloud in his Testament. His voice went up and down in deep tones, a little like Grandpa Nadeli's grace-saying voice, which still reminded the older members of the family of his pulpit days. Aunt Jen told Lemuel that Clyde's ability probably didn't indicate any natural smartness because he had had to learn the Swiss-German dialect of the Nadelis when he was younger. Uncle Simon had refused to answer their children if addressed in English, and Uncle Simon spoke to them only in Swiss, while Aunt Jen spoke only in the Pennsylvania Dutch of her people. Both the children "took the Swiss." They had to pick up their knowledge of English from hearing their parents speak to each other.

"Isn't Pennsylvania Dutch more like English than Swiss is?" asked Lemuel. Well, yes, it was closer to English, Aunt Jen admitted, but there was something about the soft Swiss dialect that was easier to catch onto.

Besides the mufflers and socks and more dishes and hankies and corset covers, and some long Amish-style aprons from Grandma Nadeli, there was a shiny new phonograph from Ora to Barbara. It did not have disks but flat records. Uncle Val had brought a new and sparkling candy jar for Grandpa Nadeli; and Ora's presented the old man with a beautiful new edition of Tolstoy's works. This made him so emotional that everybody else felt pretty much the same way. Most exciting to Lemuel were the tubular skates which Uncle Valentine's had brought for Clyde and him.

When Lemuel said, "Gee whiz, Uncle Valentine, you shouldn't give me such a wonderful pair of skates," his uncle snorted.

He said: "Oh, that's all right, boys. Of course I kind of hated to have to mortgage the farm, but still I'd do it for nephews of mine. No, I got too much pride to see a nephew of mine do without."

Murdie had taken the things out of the oven, and Aunt Jen and Barbara were fussing with other items of the coming feast.

"Yes," drawled Uncle Valentine, "I doubt anybody's eating higher this Christmas season than the Nadelis, unless maybe it was Dave Gunder."

"Why, I heard they arrested Dave for stealing a calf," Ora said.

"That's just the point," Uncle Val said. "It wasn't just any old calf he stole. I run into the sheriff last night and he told me all about it.

"When he was taking Dave into Kerriston," Uncle Val went on, "the sheriff told him that it was for stealing Lambright's prize calf and he said he guessed Dave had taken Amos Yingling's harness, too. Dave didn't deny it.

"So the sheriff asked him about the calf. 'Dave,' he said, 'what in the world did you do with Old Lambright's calf?'

"'If you want to know,' Dave said, 'I vealed it and ate it.'

"'My gravy!' the sheriff said. 'What in Sam Hill would you go to do a thing like that for?'

" 'Well,' Dave told him, 'I wanted to know what three-thousand-dollar veal tasted like.' "

Barbara had laid the table, now lengthened by the introduction of all its leaves, with the very blue dishes, from Ora's family, which had come to them at their marriage and were only for ceremonial occasions.

When they sat down to dinner Grandpa Nadeli took off his looking spectacles and put on the reading spectacles. He opened the dark book from the top of the organ and read:

"Go thy way, eat thy bread with joy, and drink thy wine with a merry heart.

"Let thy garments be always white; and let thy head lack no ointment.

"Live joyfully.

"Whatsoever thy hand findeth to do, do it with thy might; for there is no work, nor device, nor knowledge, nor wisdom in the grave, whither thou goest."

This reminder of death did not dismay them. It was like a curtain hung at the window to make the festive lamps glow brighter.

Grandpa Nadeli laid down the book and gave thanks.

He offered thanks for the joy it was to an old man to have his family at the table with him. Suddenly, in the midst of that, tears began to run down his face. He choked in the middle of a sentence, and after swallowing a few times, he said "Amen."

The rest all looked at each other with pitying and loving expressions.

From the oven Barbara and Murdie brought the duck and the two roast chickens. There were escalloped oysters, and cranberries and dried corn, and the side table was laden with salads— including a magnificent fruit salad with sections of apples and bananas and oranges and marshmallows—and all manner of cakes and pies, pumpkin, mince and Grandma Nadeli's famed onion custard.

Ora picked up the carving knife and looked at the duck. There was a knock at the door, and Clyde rose to answer it. In a moment he came back.

"It's a tramp," he said.

"Tell him to come in," Ora said. At the same time, Grandpa

Nadeli was saying, "Let him in, for he may be Jesus."

The tramp was a tall, gaunt man with deep eyes. He came in with his hat in his hand. In a voice thick with gutturals of another language he said, "God's blessing on you."

He washed his hands at the sink in the corner of the kitchen, and sat down at the place that was made for him between Clyde and Uncle Valentine. Uncle Valentine told him the names of all who were there. The wanderer said his name was Peterson.

"I am a sailor," he said, "but I was trying to get to my sister's home for Christmas. It takes me longer to go by land than I had thought."

He was very grave and silent, but after a while the rest became merry and noisy. To show that he approved of this, the man named Peterson smiled solemnly now and then, and nodded encouragingly to someone who had shouted a witticism.

When the meal was over, and they pushed back their chairs from the table and drank warm spiced wine, Peterson went to the woodbox and chose a sleek, round piece of greenish limb. With a gigantic knife he took from his pocket, he began to carve. Lemuel and Clyde went and watched him. He stood by the woodbox, being careful that the chips should fall into it. When one fell on the floor he immediately picked it up.

He carved a picture of Grandpa Nadeli, as accurate as a photograph. Everyone exclaimed over it. It became a family treasure.[60] ✳

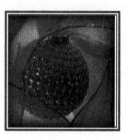

*Out upon Merry Christmas!
What's Christmas time to you but a time
for finding yourself a year older, but not
an hour richer; a time for balancing
your books and having every item in 'em
through a round-dozen of months
presented dead against you?*[61]

EBENEZER SCROOGE

Family Christmas Finances

BY KRISTIN M. TUCKER AND REBECCA LOVE WARREN

We encourage you not to become financially strapped by Christmas. Credit card payments, interest rates, and finance charges can be hazardous to our health, and end up making Scrooges of us all.

SOME SUGGESTIONS—

- Keep in mind that generosity at Christmas involves more than money. Our time, energy, enthusiasm, and caring can be thoughtful gifts as well.

- Make finances a family matter. Determine how much money is available for entertaining, giving, and decorating. Set priorities and contract to stay within these limits. If expensive gifts for relatives and friends have become a norm, feel free to break with tradition. Recipients may appreciate your creative gifts more and be inspired to follow suit. Perhaps they have wanted a change for years but lacked the courage to initiate it.

- Encourage the renovation of broken or worn-out toys as a way of sharing.

- Raise extra funds for special projects or gifts with family fundraisers: garage sales. boutiques, paper routes, etc. This money could be spent on the family or donated to a community project or special offering.

- Discuss where your family can cut corners financially.

- Avoid last-minute and impulse purchases.

- Give gifts of money for after-Christmas shopping.

- Postpone some purchases until after Christmas, when prices are reduced for toys, appliances, clothing, and bedding.

- Begin a "Christmas Fund" savings account and make regular deposits.[62]

A Christmas Carol

BY CHARLES DICKENS

(ABBREVIATED TO BE READ ALOUD AS A FAMILY)

Marley was dead, to begin with. There is no doubt whatever about that.

Old Marley was as dead as a doornail.

Scrooge never painted out old Marley's name, however, There it yet stood, years afterwards, above the warehouse door, SCROOGE and MARLEY.

Oh! But he was a tightfisted hand at the grindstone, was Scrooge! A squeezing, wrenching, grasping, scraping, clutching, covetous old sinner!

Nobody ever stopped him on the streets to say, with gladsome looks, "My dear Scrooge, how are you? When will you come to see me?" No beggars implored him to bestow a trifle, no children asked him what it was o'clock, no man or woman ever once in all his life inquired the way to such and such a place, of Scrooge.

Once upon a time of all the good days in the year, upon a Christmas eve old Scrooge sat busy in his countinghouse. It was cold, bleak, biting, foggy weather; and the city clocks had only just gone three, but it was quite dark already.

The door of Scrooge's countinghouse was open, that he might keep his eye upon his clerk, who in a dismal little cell beyond, a sort of tank, was copying letters. Scrooge had a very small fire, but the clerk's fire was so very much smaller that it looked like one coal.

"A merry Christmas, Uncle!" cried a cheerful voice. It was the voice of Scrooge's nephew.

"Bah! Humbug!"

"Christmas a humbug, Uncle! You don't mean that, I am sure!"

"I do."

"Don't be angry, Uncle. Come! Dine with us tomorrow."

"Good afternoon!"

The hour of shutting up the countinghouse had arrived. With an ill-will Scrooge, dismounting from his stool, tacitly admitted the fact to the expectant clerk in the tank, who instantly snuffed his candle out and put on his hat.

"You'll want all day tomorrow, I suppose?"

"If quite convenient, sir."

"It's not convenient, and it's not fair. If I was to stop half a crown for it, you'd think yourself mightily ill-used, I'll be bound?"

"Yes, sir."

"And yet you don't think me ill-used, when I pay a day's wages for no work."

"It's only once a year, sir!"

"A poor excuse for picking a man's pocket every twenty-fifth of December! But I suppose you must have the whole day. Be here all the earlier next morning."

Scrooge took his melancholy dinner in his usual melancholy tavern; then went home to bed. He lived in chambers that had once belonged to his deceased partner. They were a gloomy suite of rooms.

Scrooge put on his dressing gown and slippers and his nightcap and sat down before the very low fire. As he threw his head back in the chair, his glance happened to rest upon a bell, that hung in the room. It was with great astonishment, and with a strange inexplicable dread, that he saw this bell begin to ring. Soon it rang out loudly, and so did every bell in the house.

This was succeeded by a clanking noise, deep down below. Then he heard the noise much louder, on the floors below; then coming up the stairs; then coming straight towards his door.

It came on through the heavy door, and a spectre passed into the room before his eyes. And upon its coming in, the dying flame leaped up, as though it cried out, "I know him! Marley's ghost!"

"How now!" said Scrooge, caustic and cold as ever. "What do you want with me? Why do spirits walk the earth, and why do they come to me?"

"It is required of every man that the spirit within him should walk abroad among his fellowmen and travel far and wide; and if that spirit goes not forth in life, it is condemned to do so after death. My spirit—mark me!—in life my spirit never roved beyond the narrow limits of our money-changing hole; and weary journeys lie before me!"

"Seven years dead. And traveling all the time? You travel fast?"

"On the wings of the wind."

"You might have got over a great quantity of ground in seven years."

"O blind man, blind man! Not to know that no space of regret can make amends for one life's opportunities misused! Yet I was like this man!"

"But you were always a good man of business, Jacob."

"Business! Mankind was my business. I am here to warn you that you have yet a chance to escape my fate. You will be haunted by three spirits."

It walked backward from him; and every step it took, the window raised itself a little, so that when the apparition reached it, it was wide open; and the spirit floated out upon the air and disappeared.

When Scrooge awoke, it was so dark that he could scarcely distinguish the transparent window from the opaque walls of his chamber, until suddenly the church clock tolled a deep, dull, hollow, melancholy ONE.

Light flashed up in the room upon the instant, and the curtains of the bed were drawn aside by a strange figure.

"Are you the spirit, sir, whose coming was foretold to me?"

"I am!"

"Who and what are you?"

"I am the ghost of Christmas past."

"Long past?"

"No. Your past."

"What brings you here?"

"Your welfare. Rise and walk with me."

They passed through the wall, and stood in the busy thoroughfares of the city. It was made plain enough by the dressing of the shops that here, too, it was Christmastime.

The ghost stopped at a certain warehouse door, and asked Scrooge if he knew it.

"Know it! I was apprenticed here!"

They went in. At sight of an old gentleman in a Welsh wig, Scrooge cried in great excitement, "Why, it's old Fezziwig! Bless his heart, it's Fezziwig, alive again!"

Old Fezziwig laid down his pen and called out in a comfortable, oily, rich, fat, jovial voice: "Yoho, there! Ebenezer! Dick!"

A living picture of Scrooge's former self, a young man, came briskly in, accompanied by his fellow 'prentice.

"Yoho, my boys!" said Fezziwig. "No more work tonight. Christmas eve, Dick. Christmas, Ebenezer! Let's have the shutters up, before a man can say Jack Robinson! Clear away, my lads, and let's have lots of room here!"

It was done in a minute; and the warehouse was as snug and warm and dry and bright a ballroom as you would desire to see upon a winter's night.

In came a fiddler with a music book, and went up to the lofty desk, and made an orchestra of it, and tuned like fifty stomach aches. In came Mrs. Fezziwig, one vast substantial smile. In came the three Miss Fezziwigs, beaming and lovable. In came the six young followers whose hearts they broke. In came all the young men and women employed in the business. In came the housemaid, with her cousin the baker. In came the cook, with her brother's particular friend the milkman.

There were dances and there were games, and more dances, and there was cake, and there were great pieces of cold and roast beef, and there were mince pies, and plenty of beer.

When the clock struck eleven, the ball broke up. Mr. and Mrs. Fezziwig took their stations on either side of the door, and, shaking hands with every person individually as he or she went out, wished him or her a Merry Christmas.

"A small matter," said the ghost, "to make these silly folks so full of gratitude. He has spent but a few pounds of your mortal money; three or four, perhaps. Is that so much that he deserves this praise?"

"It isn't that," said Scrooge, "it isn't that, Spirit. He has the power to render us happy or unhappy; to make our service light or burdensome; a pleasure or a toil. Say that his power lies in words and looks; in things so light and insignificant that it is impossible to add and count them up: what then? The happiness is as great as though it cost a fortune."

Scrooge awoke in his own bedroom. There was no doubt of that. But it and his own adjoining sittingroom, into which he shuffled in his slippers, were brilliant with a great light, and in easy state upon a couch there sat a Giant glorious to see, who bore a glowing torch, in shape not unlike Plenty's horn, and who raised it high to shed its light on Scrooge as he came peeping round the door.

"Come in—come in! And know me better, man. I am the Ghost of Christmas Present. Look upon me!"

"Spirit, conduct me where you will."

"Take hold of my robe!"

Scrooge did as he was told, and held it fast.

The room and its contents vanished instantly, and they stood in the city streets upon a snowy Christmas morning.

Scrooge and the Ghost passed on, invisible, straight to Scrooge's clerk, Bob Cratchit. Mrs. Cratchit, dressed out but poorly in a well-worn gown, but brave in ribbons, which are cheap and make a goodly show for sixpence, laid the cloth assisted by; Belinda Cratchit, second of her daughters, also brave in ribbons; while Master Peter Cratchit plunged a fork into the saucepan of potatoes. Two smaller Cratchits, boy and girl, came tearing in.

"What has ever got your precious father?" said Mrs. Cratchit. "And your brother, Tiny Tim! And Martha?"

"Here's Martha, mother!"

"Why, bless your heart alive, my dear, how late you are!"

"We'd a deal of work to finish up last night, and had to clear away this morning, mother."

"Well, never mind, so long as you are come. Sit ye down before the fire, my dear, and have a warm, God bless ye!"

"No, no! There's father coming home from church," cried the two young Cratchits. "Hide, Martha, hide!"

So Martha hid herself, and in came little Bob, the father, his threadbare clothes darned up and brushed, to look seasonable; and

Tiny Tim upon his shoulder. Alas for Tiny Tim, he bore a little crutch, and had his limbs supported by an iron brace!

"Why, where's our Martha?"

"Not coming!"

"Not coming?"

"No!"

"Not coming upon Christmas Day!"

Martha did not like to see him disappointed, if it were only a joke; so she came out prematurely from behind the closet door, and ran into his arms.

There never was such a goose. Its tenderness and flavor, size and cheapness, were the themes of universal admiration. Eked out by applesauce and mashed potatoes, it was a sufficient dinner for the whole family. But now, the plates being changed by Miss Belinda, Mrs. Cratchit left the room alone—too nervous to bear witnesses—to take the pudding up and bring it in.

O, a wonderful pudding! Bob Cratchit said, and calmly too, that he regarded it as the greatest success achieved by Mrs. Cratchit since their marriage. Everybody had something to say about it, but nobody thought it was at all a small pudding for a large family. Any Cratchit would have blushed to hint at such a thing.

At last the dinner was done, the cloth was cleared, the hearth swept, and the fire made up. Then all the family drew around the hearth, in what Bob Cratchit called a circle. Then Bob proposed:

"A merry Christmas to us all, my dears. God bless us!"

Which all the family reechoed.

"God bless us every one!" said Tiny Tim, the last of all.

Scrooge raised his head speedily on hearing his own name.

"Mr. Scrooge!" said Bob: "I'll salute Mr. Scrooge, the founder of the feast!"

The mention of the name cast a dark shadow on the party, which was not dispelled for a full five minutes. After it had passed away, they were ten times merrier than before, from mere relief.

It was a great surprise to Scrooge, as this scene vanished, to hear a hearty laugh. It was a much greater surprise to Scrooge to recognize it as his own nephew's, and to find himself in a bright, dry, gleaming room, with the Spirit standing smiling at his side, and looking at the same nephew.

"He said that Christmas was a humbug, as I live! He believed it, too."

"More shame for him, Fred!" said Scrooge's niece, indignantly.

"He's a comical old fellow, that's the truth; and not so pleasant as he might be. However, his offenses carry their own punishment, and I have nothing to say against him. Who suffers by his ill whims? Himself, always!"

They had just had dinner, and were clustered round the fire by lamplight.

Then there was music, and after the music there was entertainment, and Scrooge's nephew proposed a game called Yes and No, where Scrooge's nephew had to think of something, and the rest must find out what, he answering to their questions only yes or no, as the case was.

The fire of questioning to which he was exposed elicited from him that he was thinking of an animal, a live animal, rather a disagreeable animal, a savage animal, an animal that growled and grunted sometimes, and talked sometimes, and lived in London, and walked about the streets, and wasn't made a show of, and wasn't led by anybody, and didn't live in a menagerie, and was never killed in a market, and was not a horse, or an ass, or a cow, or a bull, or a tiger, or a dog, or a pig, or a cat, or a bear.

At every new question put to him, this nephew burst into a fresh roar of laughter, and was so inexpressibly tickled that he was obliged to get up off the sofa and stamp. At last one cried out:

"I have found it! I know what it is, Fred! I know what it is."

"What is it?"

"It's your uncle Scrooge!"

Which it certainly was. Admiration was the universal sentiment, though some objected that the reply to "Is it a bear?" ought to have been "Yes."

Uncle Scrooge had imperceptibly become so light of heart that he would have drunk to the company in an inaudible speech. But the whole scene passed away in the breath of the last word spoken by his nephew, and he and the Spirit were again upon their travels.

Suddenly, as they stood together in an open place, the bell struck twelve and Scrooge was alone. He saw the Ghost no more.

As the last stroke of twelve ceased to vibrate, Scrooge beheld a solemn Phantom, draped and hooded, coming like a mist along the ground towards him.

"Lead on! lead on! The night is waning fast, and it is precious time to me, I know. Lead on, Ghost of Christmas Yet to Come!"

They scarcely seemed to enter the city; for the city rather seemed to spring up about them. But there they were in the heart of it; it was the time merchants stepped outside for fresh air. The spirit stopped beside one little group of business men. Scrooge advanced and listened.

"No," said a fat man, "I don't know much about it either way. I only know he is dead."

"When did he die?"

"Last night, I believe."

"What has he done with his money?"

"I haven't heard; went into the company, perhaps. He hasn't left it to me. That's all I know. Bye, bye!"

They left this busy scene, and went into an obscure part of town, to a low shop where iron, old rags, bottles were bought. A grayhaired rascal of great age sat smoking his pipe.

Scrooge and the Phantom came into the presence of this man just as a woman with a heavy bundle slunk into the shop. But she had scarcely entered, when another woman, similarly laden, came in too; and she was closely followed by a man in faded black.

They all three burst out laughing and the first to enter cried: "Let the charwoman alone to be the first; let the laundress alone to be the second; and let the undertaker's man alone to be the third. Look here, old Joe, here's a chance! If we haven't all three met here without meaning it!"

"What have you got to sell?"

"What odds then! What odds, Mrs. Dilber?" said the other woman. "Every person has a right to take care of himself. He always did! Who's the worse for the loss of a few things like these? Not a dead man, I suppose."

"No, indeed, ma'am."

"If he wanted to keep 'em after he was dead, a wicked old screw, why wasn't he natural in his lifetime? If he had been, he'd have had somebody to look after him when he was struck with Death, instead of lying gasping out his last there, alone by himself. Open that bundle, Joe, and let me know the value of it."

"*His* blankets?"

"Whose else do you think? He isn't likely to take cold without 'em, I dare say."

Scrooge listened to this dialogue in horror.

"Spirit, I see, I see. The case of this unhappy man might be my own. My life ends that way, now. No, Spirit! Oh no, no! Spirit! hear me! I am not the man I was. Why show me this if I am past all hope? Assure me that I yet may change these shadows you have shown me by an altered life."

Holding up his hands in one last prayer to have his fate reversed, he saw an alteration in the Phantom's hood and dress. It shrunk, collapsed, and dwindled down into a bedpost. Yes, and the bedpost was his own, the room was his own. Best and happiest of all, the time before him was his own, to make amends in! The church bells were ringing out the lustiest peals he had ever heard. Running to the window, he opened it, and put his head out. No fog, no mist, no night; clear, bright, stirring, golden day.

"What's today?" cried Scrooge, calling downward to a boy in Sunday clothes.

"Today? Why, Christmas Day!"

"It's Christmas Day! I haven't missed it. Hallo, my fine fellow!"

"Hello!"

"Do you know the poultry shop, in the next street, at the corner?"

"I should hope I do."

"An intelligent boy! A remarkable boy! Do you know whether they have sold the prize turkey that was hanging up there? Not the little prize turkey—the big one?"

"What, the one as big as me?"

"What a delightful boy! It's a pleasure to talk to him. Yes, my buck!"

"It's hanging there now."

"Is it? Go and buy it, and tell 'em to bring it here, that I may give them the direction where to take it. Come back with the man and I'll give you a shilling. Come back with him in less than five minutes and I'll give you half a crown!"

The boy was off like a shot.

"I'll send it to Bob Cratchit's! He sha'n't know who sends it. It's twice the size of Tiny Tim!"

The hand in which he wrote the address was not a steady one; but write it he did, somehow, and went downstairs to open the street door, ready for the coming of the turkey.

It was a turkey! He never could have stood upon his legs, that bird. He would have snapped 'em short off in a minute, like sticks of sealing wax.

Scrooge dressed himself in his very best, and walked out into the street. By this time people were pouring forth, and walking with his hands behind him, Scrooge regarded everyone with a delighted smile. He looked so irresistibly pleasant that three or four good-humored fellows said, "Good morning, sir! A merry Christmas to you!" And Scrooge said often afterwards, that of all the lovely sounds he had ever heard, those were the loveliest to his ears.

In the afternoon he turned his steps towards his nephew's house. He passed the door a dozen times before he had the courage to go up and knock. But he made a dash and did it.

"Why, bless my soul, who's that?"

"It's I, your uncle Scrooge . . . I have come to dinner. Will you let me in?"

Let him in! It is a mercy he didn't shake his arm off. Nothing could be heartier.

His niece looked just the same. So did everyone else. Wonderful party, wonderful games, wonderful unanimity, wonderful happiness.

The next morning was a workday again. Scrooge was at the office early. If he could only be there first and catch Bob Cratchit coming late! That was the thing he had set his heart upon.

And he did it. The clock struck nine. No Bob. A quarter past. No Bob. Bob was a full eighteen minutes and a half late.

Hallo!" growled Scrooge, in his accustomed voice, as near as he could feign it. "What do you mean by coming in here at this time of day?"

"I'm sorry, sir, I am behind my time."

"You are? Yes. I think you are. Step this way, if you please."

"It's only once a year, sir. It shall not be repeated. I was making rather merry yesterday, sir."

"Now, I'll tell you what, my friend. I am not going to stand for this sort of thing any longer. And therefore," Scrooge continued, leaping from his stool and giving Bob such a dig in the waistcoat that he staggered back into the tank again—"and therefore I am about to raise your salary."

Bob trembled.

"A merry Christmas, Bob! A merry Christmas, Bob, my good fellow, merrier than I have given you for many a year! I'll raise your salary, and endeavor to assist your struggling family, and we will discuss your affairs this very afternoon, over a Christmas bowl of smoking bishop, Bob! Make up the fires, and buy a second coal-scuttle before you dot another i, Bob Cratchit!"

Scrooge was better than his word. He did all and infinitely more; and to Tiny Tim he became a second father. He became as good a friend, as good a master, and as good a man as the good old city knew, or any other good old city, town, or borough in the good old world. Some people laughed to see the alteration in him; but his own heart laughed, and that was quite enough for him.

It was always said of him, that he knew how to keep Christmas well if any man alive possessed the knowledge.

May that be truly said of us, and all of us! And so, as Tiny Tim observed, God Bless Us, Every One![63]

The Happy Howl

BY G. K. CHESTERTON

t is characteristic of Dickens that his atmospheres are more important than his stories. As with his backgrounds of gloom, so with his backgrounds of good will, in such tales as *A Christmas Carol*. The incidents change wildly; the story scarcely changes at all. *A Christmas Carol* is a kind of philanthropic dream, and enjoyable nightmare, in which the scenes shift bewilderingly and seem as miscellaneous as the pictures in a scrapbook, but in which there is one constant state of the soul, a state of rowdy benediction and a hunger for human faces. The beginning is about a winter day and a miser; yet the beginning is in no way bleak. The author starts with a kind of happy howl; he bangs on our door like a drunken carol singer; his style is festive and popular; he compares the snow and hail to philanthropists who "come down handsomely"; he compares the fog to unlimited beer.

Scrooge is not really inhuman at the beginning any more than he is at the end. There is a heartiness in his inhospitable sentiments that is akin to humor and therefore to humanity; he is only a crusty old bachelor, and had (I strongly suspect) given away turkeys secretly all his life. The beauty and the real blessing of the story do not lie in the mechanical plot of it, the repentance of Scrooge, probable or improbable; they lie in the great furnace of real happiness that glows through Scrooge and everything around him; that great furnace, the heart of

Dickens. Whether the Christmas visions would or would not convert Scrooge, they convert us. Whether or not the visions were evoked by real Spirits of the Past, Present, and Future, they were evoked by that truly exalted order of angels who are correctly called High Spirits. They are impelled and sustained by a quality which our contemporary artists ignore or almost deny, but which in a life decently lived is as normal and attainable as sleep: positive, passionate, conscious joy. The story sings from end to end like a happy man going home, and like a happy and good man, when it cannot sing it yells. It is lyric and exclamatory, from the first exclamatory words of it. It is strictly a Christmas carol.[64]

* * *

Many Christmases ago—when I was six—

I had my tonsils out over Christmas.

A neighbor asked if she could come over

and read to me. She selected The Birds'

Christmas Carol. I was mightily disappointed

when I discovered it wasn't the Scrooge story.

To make matters worse, I shed a tear or two

at the end, which embarrassed me to no end.

Now, as an adult, I recommend this

sentimental story as an all-family read.

* * *

The Birds' Christmas Carol

By Kate Douglas Wiggin

It was very early Christmas morning, and in the stillness of the dawn, with the soft snow falling on the housetops, a little child was born in the Bird household. They had intended to name the baby Lucy, if it were a girl; but they had not expected her on Christmas morning and a real Christmas baby was not to be lightly named.

Mrs. Bird lay in her room, weak, but safe and happy, with her sweet baby girl by her side.

Suddenly a sound of music poured out into the bright air and drifted into the chamber. It was the boy choir singing Christmas anthems. Higher and higher rose the clear, fresh voices, full of hope and cheer, as children's voices always are. Fuller and fuller grew the burst of melody as one glad strain fell upon another in joyful harmony:

"Carol, brothers, carol,
Carol joyfully,
Carol the good tidings,
Carol merrily!
And pray a gladsome Christmas
For all your fellow-men:
Carol, brothers, carol,
Christmas Day again."

Mrs. Bird thought, as the music floated in upon her gentle sleep, that she had slipped into heaven with her new baby, and that the angels were bidding them welcome. But the tiny bundle by her side stirred a little, and though it was scarcely more than the ruffling of a feather, she awoke; for the mother-ear is so close to the heart that it can hear the faintest whisper of a child.

"Why, my baby," whispered Mrs. Bird in soft surprise, "I had forgotten what day it was. You are a little Christmas child, and we will name you 'Carol'—mother's Christmas Carol!"

"What!" said Mr. Bird, coming in softly and closing the door behind him.

"Why, Donald, don't you think 'Carol' is a sweet name for a Christmas baby?"

"I think it is a charming name, dear heart, and sounds just like you, and I hope that, being a girl, this baby has some chance of being as lovely as her mother"—at which speech from the baby's papa, Mrs. Bird, though she was as weak and tired as she could be, blushed with happiness.

And so Carol came by her name.

Perhaps because she was born in holiday time, Carol was a very happy baby. Of course, she was too tiny to understand the joy of Christmastide, but people say there is everything in a good beginning, and she may have breathed in unconsciously the fragrance of evergreens and holiday dinners.

Her cheeks and lips were as red as hollyberries; her hair was for all the world the color of a Christmas candle-flame; her eyes were bright as stars; her laugh like a chime of Christmas-bells, and her tiny hands forever outstretched in giving.

Such a generous little creature you never saw! A spoonful of bread and milk had always to be taken by Mamma or nurse before Carol could enjoy her supper; whatever bit of cake or sweetmeat found its way into her pretty fingers was straightway broken in half to be shared with Donald, Paul, or Hugh, her brothers.

"Why does she do it?" asked Donald thoughtfully. "None of us boys ever did."

"I hardly know," said Mamma, catching her darling to her heart, "except that she is a little Christmas child, and so she has a tiny share of the blessedest birthday the world ever knew!"

It was December, ten years later.

The oldest boy, Donald, was away at college now. Paul and Hugh were great manly fellows, taller than their mother. Papa Bird had gray hairs in his whiskers; and Grandma, God bless her, had been four Christmases in heaven.

But Christmas in the Birds' Nest was scarcely as merry now as it used to be in the bygone years, for the little child, that once brought such an added blessing to the day, lay month after month a patient, helpless invalid, in the room where she was born.

The cheeks and lips that were once as red as hollyberries faded to faint pink; the star-like eyes grew softer, for they often gleamed through tears; and the gay child-laugh, that had been like a chime of Christmas bells, gave place to a smile so lovely, so touching, so tender and patient, that it haled every corner of the house with a gentle radiance that might have come from the face of the Christ-child himself.

Love could do nothing; and when we have said that we have said all, for it is stronger than anything else in the whole wide world. Mr. and Mrs. Bird were talking it over one evening, when all the children were asleep. A famous physician had visited them that day, and told them that some time, it might be in one year, it might be in more, Carol would slip quietly off into heaven, whence she came.

"It is no use to close our eyes to it any longer," said Mr. Bird, as he paced up and down the library floor; "Carol will never be well again. It almost seems as if I could not bear it when I think of that loveliest child doomed to lie there day after day, and, what is still more, to suffer pain that we are helpless to keep away from her. Merry Christmas, indeed; it gets to be the saddest day in the year to me!" and poor Mr. Bird sank into a chair by the table, and buried his face in his hands to keep his wife from seeing the tears that would come in spite of all his efforts.

"But, Donald, dear," said sweet Mrs. Bird, with trembling voice, "Christmas Day may not be so merry with us as it used, but it is very happy, and that is better, and very blessed, and that is better yet. I suffer chiefly for Carol's sake, but I have almost given up being sorrowful for my own. I am too happy in the child, and I see too clearly what she has done for us and the other children. Donald and Paul and Hugh were three strong, willful, boisterous boys, but now you seldom see such tenderness, devotion, thought for others, and self-denial in lads of their years. A quarrel or a hot word is almost unknown in this house, and why? Carol would hear it, and it would distress her, she is so full of love and goodness. The boys study with all their might and main. Why? Partly, at least, because they like to teach Carol, and amuse her by telling her what they read. When the seamstress comes, she likes to sew in Miss Carol's room, because there she forgets her own troubles, which, heaven knows, are sore enough! And as for me, Donald, I am a better woman every day for Carol's sake, I have to be her eyes, ears, feet, hands—her strength, her hope; and she, my own little child, is my example!"

"I was wrong, dear heart," said Mr. Bird more cheerfully; "we will try not to repine, but to rejoice instead, that we have an 'angel of the house.'"

"And as for her future," Mrs. Bird went on, "I think we need not be overanxious. I feel as if she did not belong altogether to us, but that when she has done what God sent her for, He will take her back to Himself—and it may not be very long!" Here it was poor Mrs. Bird's turn to break down, and Mr. Bird's turn to comfort her.

Carol herself knew nothing of motherly tears and fatherly anxieties; she lived on peacefully in the room where she was.

But you never would have known that room; for Mr. Bird had a great deal of money, and though he felt sometimes as if he wanted to throw it all in the sea, since it could not buy a strong body for his little girl, yet he was glad to make the place she lived in just as beautiful as it could be.

The room had been extended by the building of a large addition that hung out over the garden below, and was so filled with windows that it might have been a conservatory. The ones on the side were thus still nearer the Church of Our Saviour than they used to be; those in front looked out on the beautiful harbor, and those in the back commanded a view of nothing in particular but a narrow alley; nevertheless, they were pleasantest of all to Carol, for the Ruggles family lived in the alley, and the nine little, middle-sized, and big Ruggles children were a source of inexhaustible interest.

On one side of the room was a bookcase filled with hundreds—yes, I mean it—with hundreds and hundreds of books; books with gay-colored pictures, books without; books with black and white outline sketches, books with none at all; books with verses, books with stories; books that made children laugh, and some, only a few, that made them cry; books with words of one syllable for tiny boys and girls, and books with words of fearful length to puzzle wise ones.

This was Carol's "Circulating Library." Every Saturday she chose ten books, jotting their names down in a diary; into these she slipped cards that said:

> *"Please keep this book two weeks and read it.*
> *With love, Carol Bird."*

Then Mrs. Bird stepped into her carriage and took the ten books to the Children's Hospital, and brought home ten others that she had left there the fortnight before.

This was a source of great happiness; for some of the hospital children that were old enough to print or write, and were strong enough to do it, wrote Carol sweet little letters about the books, and she answered them, and they grew to be friends.

Then there was a great closet full of beautiful things to wear, but they were all dressing-gowns and slippers and shawls; and there were drawers full of toys and games, but they were such as you could play with on your lap. There were no ninepins, nor balls, nor bows and arrows, nor bean bags, nor tennis rackets; but, after all, other children needed these more than Carol Bird, for she was always happy and contented, whatever she had or whatever she lacked; and after the room had been made so lovely for her, on her eighth Christmas, she always called herself, in fun, a "Bird of Paradise."

On these particular December days she was happier than usual, for Uncle Jack was coming from England to spend the holidays. Dear, funny, jolly, loving, wise Uncle Jack, who came every two or three years, and brought so much joy with him that the world looked as black as a thundercloud for a week after he went away again.

"I want to tell you all about my plans for Christmas this year, Uncle Jack," said Carol, on the first evening of his visit, "because it will be the loveliest one I ever had. The boys laugh at me for caring so much about it; but it isn't altogether because it is Christmas, nor because it is my birthday; but long, long ago, when I first began to be ill, I used to think, the first thing when I waked on Christmas morning, 'Today is Christ's birthday—and mine!' I did not put the words close together, you know, because that made it seem to bold; but I first said, 'Christ's birthday,' out loud, and then, in a minute, softly to myself—'and mine!' 'Christ's birthday—and mine!' And so I do not quite feel about Christmas as other girls do. Now, Uncle Jack dear, I am going to try and make somebody happy every single Christmas that I live and this year it is to be the 'Ruggleses in the rear.'"

"That large and interesting brood of children in the little house at the end of the back garden?"

"Yes; isn't it nice to see so many together?—and, Uncle Jack, why do the big families always live in the small houses, and the small families in the big houses? When they first moved in, I used to sit in my window and watch them play in their back yard; they are so strong, and jolly, and good-natured—and then, one day, I had a terrible headache, and Donald asked them if they would please not scream quite so loud, and they explained that they were having a game of circus, but that they would change and play 'Deaf and Dumb Asylum' all the afternoon."

"Ha, ha, ha!" laughed Uncle Jack, "what an obliging family, to be sure!"

"Yes, we all thought it very funny, and I smiled at them from the window when I was well enough to be up again. Now, Sarah Maud comes to her door when the children come home from school, and if Mamma nods her head, 'Yes,' that means 'Carol is very well,' and then you ought to hear the little Ruggleses yell—I believe they try to see how much noise they can make; but if Mamma shakes her head, 'No,' they always play at quiet games. It is too cold now; but in warm weather I am wheeled out on my balcony, and the Ruggleses climb up and walk along our garden fence, and sit on the roof of our carriage-house. That brings them quite near, and I tell them stories. Now I'm going to give this whole Christmas to the Ruggleses; and, Uncle Jack, I earned part of the money myself."

"You, my bird; how?"

"Well, you see, it could not be my own, own Christmas if Papa gave me all the money, and I thought to really keep Christ's birthday I ought to do something of my very own; and so I talked with Mamma. Of course she thought of something lovely; she always does: Mamma's head is just brimming over with lovely thoughts—all I have to do is ask, and out pops the very one I want. This thought was to let her write down, just as I told her, a description of how a child lived in her own room for three years, and what she did to amuse herself; and we sent it to a magazine and got twenty-five dollars for it. Just think!"

"Well, well," cried Uncle Jack, "my little girl a real author! And what are you going to do with this wonderful 'own' money of yours?"

"I shall give the nine Ruggleses a grand Christmas dinner here in this very room—that will be Papa's contribution—and afterwards a beautiful Christmas tree, fairly blooming with presents—that will be my part; for I have another way of adding to my twenty-five dollars, so that I can buy nearly anything I choose. I should like it very much if you would sit at the head of the table, Uncle Jack, for nobody could ever be frightened of you, you dearest, dearest, dearest thing that ever was! Mamma is going to help us, but Papa and the boys are going to eat together downstairs for fear of making the little Ruggleses shy; and after we've had a merry time with the tree we can open my window and all listen together to the music at the evening church-service, if it comes before the children go. I have written a letter to the organist, and asked him if I might have the two songs I like best. Will you see if it is all right?"

Birds' Nest, December 21, 188—.

Dear Mr. Wilkie—I am the little girl who lives next door to the church, and, as I seldom go out, the music on practice days and Sundays is one of my greatest pleasures.

I want to know if you can have "Carol, Brothers, Carol," on Christmas night, and if the boy who sings "My Own Country" so beautifully may please sing that too. I think it is the loveliest thing in the world, but it always makes me cry; doesn't it you?

If it isn't too much trouble, I hope they can sing them both quite early, as after ten o'clock I may be asleep.

Yours respectfully,
Carol Bird

The days flew by as they always fly in holiday time, and it was Christmas Day before anybody knew it.

At 5 o'clock the nine Ruggles children went out of the back door quietly, and were presently lost to sight.

Peter rang the doorbell, and presently a servant admitted them, and, whispering something in Sarah's ear, drew her downstairs into the kitchen. The other Ruggleses stood in horror-stricken groups as the door closed behind their commanding officer; but there was no time for reflection, for a voice from above was heard, saying,

"Come right upstairs, please!"
"Theirs not to make reply,
Theirs not to reason why,
Theirs but to do or die."

Accordingly they walked upstairs, and Elfrida, the nurse, ushered them into a room more splendid than anything they had ever seen.

Carol gave them a joyful welcome.

Her bed had been moved into the farthest corner of the room, and she was lying on the outside, dressed in a wonderful dressing-gown that looked like a fleecy cloud. Her golden hair fell in fluffy curls over her white forehead and neck, her cheeks flushed delicately, her eyes beamed with joy, and the children told their mother, afterwards, that she looked as beautiful as the angels in the picture books.

There was a great bustle behind a huge screen in another part of the room, and at half past five this was taken away, and the Christmas dinner table stood revealed. What a wonderful sight it was to the poor little Ruggles children, who ate their sometimes scanty meals on the kitchen table! It blazed with tall, colored candles, it gleamed with glass and silver, it blushed with flowers, it groaned with good things to eat; so it was not strange that the Ruggleses shrieked in admiration of the fairy spectacle. But Larry's behavior was the most disgraceful, for he stood not upon the order of his going, but went at once for a high chair that pointed unmistakably to him, climbed up like a squirrel, gave a comprehensive look at the turkey, clapped his hands in ecstasy, rested his fat arms on the table, and cried with joy, "I beat the hull lot o' yer!" Carol laughed until she cried, giving orders, meanwhile— "Uncle Jack, please sit at the head, Sarah Maud at the foot, and that will leave four on each side; Mamma is going to help Elfrida, so that the children need not look after each other, but just have a good time."

A sprig of holly lay by each plate, and nothing would do but each little Ruggles must leave his seat and have it pinned on by Carol, and as each course was served, one of them pleaded to take something to her. There was hurrying to and fro, I can assure you, for it is quite a difficult matter to serve a Christmas dinner on the third floor of a great city house; but if it had been necessary to carry every dish up a rope ladder the servants would gladly have done so. There were turkey and chicken, with delicious gravy and stuffing, and there were half a dozen vegetables, with cranberry jelly, and celery, and pickles; and as for the way these delicacies were served, the Ruggleses never forgot it as long as they lived.

Peter nudged Kitty, who sat next to him, and said, "Look, will yer, ev'ry feller's got his own partic'lar butter; I s'pose that's to show you can eat that 'n' no more. No, it ain't either, for that pig of a Peory's just gettin' another helpin'!"

"Yes," whispered Kitty, "an' the napkins is marked with big red letters! I wonder if that's so nobody'll nip 'em; an' oh, Peter, look at the pictures stickin' right on the dishes! Did yer ever?"

"The plums is all took out o' my cramb'ry sarse an' it's friz to a stiff jell'!" whispered Peoria, in wild excitement.

"I declare to goodness," murmured Susan, on the other side, "there's so much to look at I can't scarcely eat nothin'!"

"Bet yer life I can!" said Peter, who had kept one servant busily employed ever since he sat down; for, luckily, no one was asked by Uncle Jack whether he would have a second helping, but the dishes were quietly passed under their noses, and not a single Ruggles refused anything that was offered him, even unto the seventh time.

Then, when Carol and Uncle Jack perceived that more turkey was a physical impossibility, the meats were taken off and the dessert was brought in—a dessert that would have frightened a strong man after such dinner as had preceded it. Not so the Ruggleses—for a strong man is nothing to a small boy—and they kindled to the dessert as if the turkey had been a dream and the six vegetables an optical delusion. There were plum-pudding, mince pie, and ice cream; and there were nuts, and raisins, and oranges. Kitty chose ice cream, explaining that she knew it "by sight, though she hadn't never tasted none"; but all the rest took the entire variety, without any regard to consequences.

"My dear child," whispered Uncle Jack, as he took Carol an orange, "there is no doubt about the necessity of this feast, but I do advise you after this to have them twice a year, or quarterly perhaps, for the way these children eat is positively dangerous; I assure you I tremble for that terrible Peoria. I'm going to run races with her after dinner."

"Never mind," laughed Carol; "let them have enough for once; it does my heart good to see them, and they shall come oftener next year."

The feast being over, the Ruggleses lay back in their chairs languidly, like little gorged boa constrictors, and the table was cleared in a trice. Then a door was opened into the next room, and there, in a corner facing Carol's bed, which had been wheeled as close as possible, stood the brilliantly lighted Christmas tree, glittering with gilded walnuts and tiny silver balloons, and wreathed with snowy chains of popcorn. The presents had been bought mostly with Carol's story-money, and were selected after long consultations with Mrs. Bird. Each girl had a blue knitted hood. and each boy a red crocheted comforter, all made by Mamma, Carol, and Elfrida ("Because if you buy everything, it doesn't show so much love," said Carol.) Then every girl had a pretty plaid dress of a different color, and every boy a warm coat of the right size. Here the useful presents stopped, and they were quite enough; but Carol had pleaded to give them something "for fun." "I know they need the clothes," she had said, when they were talking over the matter just after Thanksgiving, "but they don't care much for them, after all. Now, Papa, won't you please let me go without part of my presents this year, and give me the money they would cost, to buy something to amuse the Ruggleses?"

"You can have both," said Mr. Bird, promptly; "is there any need of my little girl's going without her own Christmas, I should like to know? Spend all the money you like."

"But that isn't the thing," objected Carol, nestling close to her father; "it wouldn't be mine. What is the use? Haven't I almost everything already, and am I not the happiest girl in the world this year, with Uncle Jack and Donald at home? You know very well it is more blessed to give than to receive; so why won't you let me do it? You never look half as happy when you are getting your presents as when you are giving us ours. Now, Papa, submit, or I shall have to be very firm and disagreeable with you!"

"Very well, your Highness, I surrender."

"That's a dear Papa! Now what were you going to give me? Confess!"

"A bronze figure of Santa Claus; and in the 'little round belly that shakes when he laughs like a bowlful of jelly,' is a wonderful clock—oh, you would never give it up if you could see it!"

"Nonsense," laughed Carol; "as I never have to get up to breakfast, nor go to bed, nor catch trains, I think my old clock will do very well! Now, Mamma, what were you going to give me?"

"Oh, I hadn't decided. A few more books, and a gold thimble, and a smelling bottle, and a music box, perhaps."

"Poor Carol," laughed the child, merrily, "she can afford to give up these lovely things, for there will still be left Uncle Jack, and Donald, and Paul, and Hugh, and Uncle Rob, and Aunt Elsie, and a dozen other people to fill her Christmas stocking!"

So Carol had her way, as she generally did; but it was usually a good way, which was fortunate, under the circumstances; and Sarah Maud had a set of Miss Alcott's books, and Peter a modest silver watch, Cornelius a tool chest, Clement a dog house for his lame puppy, Larry a magnificent Noah's ark, and each of the younger girls a beautiful doll.

You can well believe that everybody was very merry and very thankful. All the family, from Mr. Bird down to the cook, said that they had never seen so much happiness in the space of three hours; but it had to end, as all things do. The candles flickered and went out, the tree was left alone with its gilded ornaments, and Mrs. Bird sent the children downstairs at half past eight, thinking that Carol looked tired.

"Now, my darling, you have done quite enough for one day," said Mrs. Bird, getting Carol into her little nightgown. "I'm afraid you will feel worse tomorrow, and that would be a sad ending to such a charming evening."

"Oh, wasn't it a lovely, lovely time?" sighed Carol. "From first to last, everything was just right. I shall never forget Larry's face when he looked at the turkey; nor Peter's when he saw his watch; nor that sweet, sweet Kitty's smile when she kissed her dolly; nor the tears in poor, dull Sarah Maud's eyes when she thanked me for her books; nor . . ."

"But we mustn't talk any longer about it tonight," said Mrs. Bird, anxiously; "you are too tired, dear."

"I am not so very tired, Mamma. I have felt well all day; not a bit of pain anywhere. Perhaps this has done me good."

"Perhaps; I hope so. There was no noise or confusion; it was just a merry time. Now, may I close the door and leave you alone, Dear? Papa and I will steal in softly by and by to see if you are all right; but I think you need to be very quiet."

"Oh, I'm willing to stay by myself; but I am not sleepy yet, and I am going to hear the music, you know."

"Yes, I have opened the window a little, and put the screen in front of it, so that you won't feel the air."

"Good-night, Mamma. Such a happy, happy day!"

"Good-night. my precious Christmas Carol—mother's blessed Christmas child."

"Bend your head a minute, mother dear," whispered Carol, calling her mother back. "Mamma, dear, I do think that we have kept Christ's birthday this time just as He would like it. Don't you?"

"I am sure of it," said Mrs. Bird, softly.

The Ruggleses had finished a last romp in the library with Paul and Hugh, and Uncle Jack had taken them home and stayed awhile to chat with Mrs. Ruggles, who opened the door for them, her face all aglow with excitement and delight. When Kitty and Clem showed her the oranges and nuts that they had kept for her, she astonished them by saying that at six o'clock Mrs. Bird had sent her in the finest dinner she had ever seen in her life; and not only that, but a piece of dress-goods that must have cost a dollar a yard if it cost a cent.

As Uncle Jack went down the rickety steps he looked back into the window for a last glimpse of the family, as the children gathered about their mother, showing their beautiful presents again and again—and then upward to a window in the great house yonder. "A little child shall lead them," he thought. "Well, if—if anything ever happens to Carol, I will take the Ruggleses under my wing."

"Softly, Uncle Jack," whispered the boys, as he walked into the library awhile later. "We are listening to the music in the church. The choir has sung 'Carol, Brothers, Carol,' and now we think the organist is beginning to play 'My Own Country' for Carol."

"I hope she hears it," said Mrs. Bird; "but they are very late tonight, and I dare not speak to her lest she should be asleep. It is almost ten o'clock."

The boy soprano, clad in white surplice, stood in the organ loft. The light shone full upon his crown of fair hair, and his pale face, with its serious blue eyes, looked paler than usual. Perhaps it was something in the tender thrill of the voice, or in the sweet words, but there were tears in many eyes, both in the church and in the great house next door.

"I am far from my home,
I am weary aftern while
For the ranged-for home-bringin',
An' my Father's welcome smiles;
An' I'll ne'er be full content,
Until my eten do see
The golden gates o' heaven
In my own country.

"Like a bear to its mother,
A wee birdie to its nest,
I want to be holding now,
Unto my Father's breast;
For He gathers in His arms
Helpless, worthless lambs like me,
An' carries them Himself
To His own country."

There were tears in many eyes, but not in Carol's. The loving heart had quietly ceased to beat, and the "wee birdie" in the great house had flown to its "home nest."

So sad an ending to a happy day! Perhaps—to those who were left; and yet Carol's mother even in the freshness of her grief, was glad that her darling had slipped away on the loveliest day of her life, out of its glad content, into everlasting peace.[65]   ✳

Christmas Day in the Morning

BY PEARL S. BUCK

e woke suddenly and completely. It was four o'clock, the hour at which his father had always called him to get up and help with the milking. Strange how the habits of his youth clung to him still! Fifty years ago, and his father had been dead for thirty years, and yet he waked at four o'clock in the morning. He had trained himself to turn over and go to sleep, but this morning, because it was Christmas, he did not try to sleep.

Yet what was the magic of Christmas now? His childhood and youth were long past, and his own children had grown up and gone. Some of them lived only a few miles away but they had their own families, and though they would come in as usual toward the end of the day, they had explained with infinite gentleness that they wanted their children to build Christmas memories about their houses, not his. He was left alone with his wife.

Yesterday she had said, "It isn't worthwhile, perhaps—"

And he had said, "Oh, yes, Alice, even if there are only the two of us, let's have a Christmas of our own."

Then she had said, "Let's not trim the tree until tomorrow, Robert—just so it's ready when the children come. I'm tired."

He had agreed, and the tree was still out in the back entry.

He lay in his big bed in his room. The door to her room was shut because she was a light sleeper, and sometimes he had restless nights. Years ago they had decided to use separate rooms. It meant nothing, they said, except that neither of them slept as well as they once had. They had been married so long that nothing could separate them, actually.

Why did he feel so awake tonight? For it was still night, a clear and starry night. No moon, of course, but the stars were extraordinary!

Now that he thought of it, the stars seemed always large and clear before the dawn of Christmas Day. There was one star now that was certainly larger and brighter than any of the others. He could even imagine it moving, as it had seemed to him to move one night long ago.

He slipped back in time, as he did so easily nowadays. He was fifteen years old and still on his father's farm. He loved his father. He had not known it until one day a few days before Christmas, when he had overheard what his father was saying to his mother.

"Mary, I hate to call Rob in the mornings. He's growing so fast and he needs his sleep. If you could see how he sleeps when I go in to wake him up! I wish I could manage alone."

"Well, you can't, Adam." His mother's voice was brisk. "Besides, he isn't a child anymore. It's time he took his turn."

"Yes," his father said slowly. "But I sure do hate to wake him."

When he heard these words, something in him woke. His father loved him! He had never thought of it before, taking for granted the tie of their blood. Neither his father nor his mother talked about loving their children—they had no time for such things. There was always so much to do on a farm.

Now that he knew his father loved him, there would be no more loitering in the mornings and having to be called again. He got up after that, stumbling blind with sleep, and pulled on his clothes, his eyes tight shut. But he got up.

And then on the night before Christmas, that year when he was fifteen, he lay for a few minutes thinking about the next day. They were poor, and most of the excitement was in the turkey they had raised themselves and in the mince pies his mother made. His sisters sewed presents and his mother and father always bought something he needed, not only a warm jacket, maybe, but something more, such as a book. And he saved and bought them each something, too.

He wished, that Christmas he was fifteen, he had a better present for his father. As usual he had gone to the ten-cent store and bought a tie. It had seemed nice enough until he lay thinking the night before Christmas, and then he wished that he had heard his father and mother talking in time for him to save for something better.

He lay on his side, his head supported by his elbow, and looked out of his attic window. The stars were bright, much brighter than he ever remembered seeing them, and one star in particular was so bright that he wondered if it were really the Star of Bethlehem.

"Dad," he had once asked when he was a little boy, "What is a stable?"

"That's just a barn," his father had replied, "like ours."

Then Jesus had been born in a barn, and to a barn the shepherds and the Wise Men had come, bringing their Christmas gifts!

The thought struck him like a silver dagger. Why should he not give his father a special gift too, out there in the barn? He could get up early, earlier than four o'clock, and he could creep into the barn and get all the milking done. He'd do it alone, milk and clean up, and then when his father went in to start the milking, he'd see it all done. And he would know who had done it.

He laughed to himself as he gazed at the stars. It was what he would do, and he mustn't sleep too sound.

He must have waked twenty times, scratching a match each time to look at his old watch—midnight, and half past one, and then two o'clock.

At a quarter to three he got up and put on his clothes. He crept downstairs, careful of the creaky boards, and let himself out. The big star hung lower over the barn roof, a reddish gold. The cows looked at him, sleepy and surprised. It was early for them, too.

"So, boss" he whispered. They accepted him placidly, and he fetched some hay for each cow and then got the milking pail and the big milk cans.

He had never milked all alone before, but it seemed almost easy. He kept thinking about his father's surprise. His father would come in and call him, saying that he would get things started while Rob was getting dressed. He'd go to the barn, open the door, and then he'd go to get the two big empty milk cans. But they wouldn't be waiting or empty; they'd be standing in the milkhouse, filled.

"What the—" he could hear his father exclaiming.

He smiled and milked steadily, two strong streams rushing into the pail, frothing and fragrant. The cows were still surprised but acquiescent. For once they were behaving well, as though they knew it was Christmas.

The task went more easily than he had ever known it to before. Milking for once was not a chore. It was something else, a gift to his father who loved him. He finished, the two milk cans were full, and he covered them and closed the milkhouse door carefully, making sure of the latch. He put the stool in its place by the door and hung up the clean milk pail. Then he went out of the barn and barred the door behind him.

Back in his room he had only a minute to pull off his clothes in the darkness and jump into bed, for he heard his father up. He put the covers over his head to silence his quick breathing. The door opened.

"Rob!" his father called. "We have to get up, son, even if it is Christmas."

"Aw-right," he said sleepily.

"I'll go on out," his father said. "I'll get things started."

The door closed and he lay still, laughing to himself. In just a few minutes his father would know. His dancing heart was ready to jump from his body.

The minutes were endless—ten, fifteen, he did not know how many—and he heard his father's footsteps again. The door opened and he lay still.

"Yes, Dad—"

"You. . . ." His father was laughing, a queer sobbing sort of a laugh. "Thought you'd fool me, did you?" His father was standing beside his bed, feeling for him, pulling away the cover.

"It's for Christmas, Dad!"

He found his father and clutched him in a great hug. He felt his father's arms go around him. It was dark and they could not see each other's faces.

"Son, I thank you. Nobody ever did a nicer thing—"

"Oh, Dad, I want you to know—I do want to be good!" The words broke from him of their own will. He did not know what to say. His heart was bursting with love.

"Well, I reckon I can go back to bed and sleep," his father said after a moment. "No, hark—the little ones are waked up. Come to think of it, son, I've never seen you children when you first saw the Christmas tree. I was always in the barn. Come on!"

He got up and pulled on his clothes again and they went down to the Christmas tree, and soon the sun was creeping up to where the star had been. Oh, what a Christmas, and how his heart had nearly burst again with shyness and pride as his father told his mother and made the younger children listen about how he, Rob, had got up all by himself.

"The best Christmas gift I ever had, and I'll remember it, son, every year on Christmas morning, so long as I live."

They had both remembered it, and now that his father was dead he remembered it alone that blessed Christmas dawn when, alone with the cows in the barn, he had made his first gift of true love.

Outside the window now the great star slowly sank. He got up out of bed and put on his slippers and bathrobe and went softly upstairs to the attic and found the box of Christmas-tree decorations. He took them downstairs into the living room. Then he brought in the tree. It was a little one—they had not had a big tree since the children went away—but he set it in the holder and put it in the middle of the long table under the window. Then carefully he began to trim it. It was done very soon, the time passing as quickly as it had that morning long ago in the barn.

He went to his library and fetched the little box that contained his special gift to his wife, a star of diamonds, not large but dainty in design. He had written the card for it the day before. He tied the gift on the tree and then stood back. It was pretty, very pretty, and she would be surprised.

But he was not satisfied. He wanted to tell her—to tell her how much he loved her. It had been a long time since he had really told her, although he loved her in a very special way, much more than he ever had when they were young.

He had been fortunate that she had loved him—and how fortunate that he had been able to love! Ah, that was the true joy of life, the ability to love! For he was quite sure that some people were genuinely unable to love anyone. But love was alive in him, it still was.

It occurred to him suddenly that it was alive because long ago it had been born in him when he knew his father loved him. That was it: love alone could awaken love.

And he could give the gift again and again. This morning, this blessed Christmas morning, he would give it to his beloved wife. He could write it down in a letter for her to read and keep forever. He went to his desk and began his love letter to his wife. *My dearest love . . .*

When it was finished he sealed it and tied it on the tree where she would see it the first thing when she came into the room. She would read it, surprised and then moved, and realize how very much he loved her.

He put out the light and went tiptoeing up the stairs. The star in the sky was gone, and the first rays of the sun were gleaming the sky. Such a happy, happy Christmas![66]

The Joy

# of Tradition

Traditions! If there is a time of year when the traditional is expected, it's Christmas—and aren't we glad? Every generation has its Christmas tradition discussions:

"Vicki, before I ask you to marry me, I have to ask you this, do you open your gifts on Christmas Eve or in the morning?"

"I don't care what it's called, no one in our family serves shepherd's pie for Christmas dinner; first choice is ham, especially if you had turkey for Thanksgiving."

And so it goes. What are the traditions to die for? Probably the ones that make your family, your family. Real complications arise, though, when marriage is on the horizon. Pity the poor bride whose husband's mother made her turkey stuffing with sausage and mushrooms, while the frustrated newlywed's mother taught her the family recipe which used only cornbread and chestnuts.

But when all is said and done, children who have been raised with heart-felt traditions in the home are probably boys and girls who will grow up to be tradition lovers themselves, which in turn will provide the makings for a meaningful Christmas season.

Christmas Tonight

Everywhere, everywhere,
　　Christmas tonight!
Christmas in lands of the palm
　　tree and vine;
Christmas where snowpeaks stand
　　solemn and white,
Christmas where cornfields lie
　　sunny and bright.

PHILLIPS BROOKS

The Yule Log

BY DANIEL ROSELLE

*M*any years ago, in a small village in central France, there lived a beautiful little girl with the odd name of Sou-Sou. Sou-Sou had dark brown hair, large blue eyes, and a smile that warmed like the sun. She was the daughter of old Cord the village shoemaker, and each evening she helped her father as he tapped and hammered the shoes of the people of the village.

Now although old Cord worked all day and most of the night mending shoes with his hammer and nails, he was still poor. The rented cottage where he and Sou-Sou lived was very tiny. Indeed, it had for furniture only the shoemaker's round bench, two rickety chairs and two rickety beds, and a small oak table which stood by the fireplace. But even if their tiny cottage could never be mistaken for a golden castle, Sou-Sou and her father brightened the inside with green and white curtains and called it "Happy House." It was their home and they loved it very much.

One Christmas evening, when a heavy snow covered the roof of the cottage, old Cord and Sou-Sou heard the clock sound eight, which meant that it was again time for the Christmas custom of the Yule Log. They smiled at each other, hurried outside to the woodpile, and carried into the cottage a large oak log that they had saved especially for this Christmas night. Then, following the old village tradition, they sprinkled salt over it, and put the log into the fireplace. This was their Yule Log or Christmas Log. And, if it burned until morning, it meant that they would have good fortune all that year.

No sooner had their Yule Log been lighted, however, than the owner of "Happy House," Monsieur Mien, knocked gently on the door.

"Come in, come in," said old Cord, for Monsieur Mien was a good man and a close friend. He was always welcome at the cottage.

Monsieur Mien sat down on one of the rickety chairs. He shook his head sadly from side to side and looked into the fire.

"I'm afraid that I bring bad news," he said, shifting in his chair. "A rich merchant in the village has demanded that I sell him your cottage at once. I don't want to do this, of course, for you are my close friends. But you have not paid me your rent in almost a year. And it is the law."

"What law?" cried Sou-Sou, greatly frightened.

"The law that says if you don't pay your rent in a year's time and someone else wants to buy your cottage, that I must sell it to him," explained Monsieur Mien.

"But I *will* be able to pay our rent—just as soon as I finish this great pile of shoes here on the floor!" exclaimed old Cord. "In three days time I shall be done with my work. Then I promise to pay it all."

"But three days will be too late," answered Monsieur Mien. "The law cannot be changed. The year is up tomorrow morning at the very moment when your Yule Log goes out. The rent must be paid before your Yule Log goes out—or the cottage will be sold!"

So saying, Monsieur Mien sadly left the cottage.

When he had gone, old Cord slumped heavily onto his workbench, beat his right fist in the air, and cried:

"What shall we do now? The Yule Log will go out by tomorrow morning. We can never finish all these shoes by then. Our cottage will be sold. Oh, what can we do?"

Sou-Sou placed her hand on the old shoemaker's back. She waited until a tear trickled down the side of her nose, and in a soft voice answered:

"We must keep working on the shoes—that is what we must do! We must work just as if our Yule Log could burn for three days. We must not lose hope. For this is Christmas and on Christmas all things are possible!"

So all that night, while other children thought only of Christmas dinners of roast chicken and brown pudding, or dreamed happily of all the shining Christmas presents they would soon receive, Sou-Sou worked. She worked just as hard as she could to help her father as he tried to finish the shoes before the Yule Log went out.

Tap-Tap. Tap-Tap.

Nail here. Nail there.

Tap-Tap. Tap-Tap.

Hammer!

Oh, how the two of them hammered! And all the while the great log in the fireplace kept crackling noisily and burning on and on.

The next morning, when Monsieur Mien came to tell them that the time had come for the cottage to be sold, a strange and wonderful sight caught his eye. *Smoke was pouring out of the chimney! The Yule Log was still burning!*

Quickly he entered the cottage. Old Cord and Sou-Sou were sitting at the work-bench, busily mending shoes. And there, in the fireplace, the great Christmas Log was still crackling noisily and burning on and on.

Monsieur Mien could hardly believe his eyes.

"Surely," he said, "the Yule Log will go out in a little while. I'll just sit here and wait."

But the Yule Log did *not* go out all that day! And it did *not* go out the second day! And it did *not* go out the third day! And all the while old Cord and Sou-Sou, with very little sleep and even less to eat, kept working on the shoes.

Tap-Tap. Tap-Tap.

Nail here. Nail there.

Tap-Tap. Tap-Tap.

Hammer!

Smaller and smaller grew the pile of shoes. Until finally, with one last tap of her hammer, little Sou-Sou finished the last shoe!

"We're done!" cried old Cord, happily. "We've finished all the shoes! And the Yule Log is still burning! Now we can pay the rent and keep our cottage!"

And so happy were they all that old Cord, Sou-Sou, and Monsieur Mien joined hands and danced around the room.

Just as they reached the fireplace, however, they heard a sudden hissing noise and stopped at once. Then, even as they watched it with wonder, the great Yule Log in the fireplace hissed three more times, turned from bright red to cold white, and finally went out completely.

Monsieur Mien was the first to break the silence.

"But I still do not understand it," he said. "How was it possible for your Yule Log to burn for three days when it should have gone out in one?"

Sou-Sou looked at him, smiled, and answered softly.

"It's Christmas," she said. "And at Christmas all things are possible."[67]

Christmas Thoughts

Sing hey!

Sing hey!

For Christmas Day;

Twine mistletoe

and holly,

For friendship

glows

In winter snows,

And so let's all

be jolly.

AUTHOR UNKNOWN

Sing sweet as the flute,

Sing clear as the horn,

Sing joy of the children

Come Christmas the morn!

Little Christ Jesus

Our brother is born.

ELEANOR FARJEON

Come sing a hale Heigh-ho

For the Christmas long ago!—

When the old log cabin homed us

From the night of blinding snow,

Where the rarest joy held reign,

And the chimney roared amain,

With the firelight like a beacon

Through the frosty window pane.

JAMES WHITCOMB RILEY

Now Christmas is come,

Let's beat up the drum,

And call all our neighbors together,

And when they appear,

Let us make them such cheer

As will keep out the wind and the weather.

WASHINGTON IRVING

Candle, candle,

Burning bright

On our window sill tonight,

Like the shining Christmas star

Guiding shepherds from afar,

Lead some weary Traveler here,

That he may share

Our Christmas joy.

ISABEL SHAW

Let every pudding burst with plums,

And every tree bear dolls and drums,

In the week when Christmas comes.

Let every hall have boughs of green,

With berries glowing in between,

In the week when Christmas comes.

ELEANOR FARJEON

The holly's up, the house is all bright,

The tree is ready, the candles alight;

Rejoice and be glad, all children tonight.

FROM AN OLD CAROL

Then be ye glad, good people,

This night of all the year.

And light ye up your candles,

For His star it shineth clear.

FROM AN OLD CAROL

O Christmas is coming,

The geese are getting fat,

Won't you please put a penny

In a poor man's hat?

If you haven't got a penny

A ha'penny will do.

If you haven't got a ha'penny

Then God bless you!

AUTHOR UNKNOWN

Blessed by the Christmas

sunshine, our natures, per-

haps long leafless, bring

forth new love, new kindness,

new mercy, new compassion.

HELEN KELLER

December month of holly, pine, and balsam,
Of berries red, of candles' mellow light;
Of home and fireside, laughter, happy faces,
Of peace that comes upon the holy night.

FROM AN OLD CAROL

Now that the time has come wherein
Our Saviour Christ was born,
The larder's full of beef and pork,
The granary's full of corn.
As God hath plenty to thee sent,
Take comfort of thy labors,
And let it never thee repent,
To feast thy needy neighbors.

POOR ROBIN'S ALMANACK, 1700

A little child, a shiny star,
A stable rude, the door ajar.
Yet in that place so crude forlorn,
The Hope of all the world was born.

ANONYMOUS

May thy Christmas
happy be,
And naught
but joy appear,
Is now the wish
I send to thee,
And all I love
most dear.

VERSE ON VICTORIAN CARD

But give me holly,
bold and jolly,
Honest, prickly,
shining holly;
Pluck me holly
leaf and berry
For the day when
I make merry.

CHRISTINA ROSSETTI

Father, may that holy Star
Grow every year more bright,
And send its glorious beam afar
To fill the world with light.

WILLIAM CULLEN BRYANT

Merry Christmas

BY MARY H. BEAM

No words, new-coined, can ever tell
What this old greeting says so well.
Recalling other Christmas Days
With all their sweet, old-fashioned ways.

The childhood dream of sweets and toys
That were the sum of Christmas joys;
Mysterious secrets everywhere,
And snowflakes tumbling through the air.

And then the greatest thrill of all,
On Christmas Eve, as great and small,
Behind the horses gay with bells,
Glide up the hills and down the dells
To Church!

The church, bedecked with spruce and pine,
The giant tree where candles shine;
The Story of the Child (His bed,
A manger in a cattle shed):
The angels' song, the shepherds' fright;
The Wise Men traveling in the night,
To bring strange gifts from distant lands;
The star-lit path across the sands.
At long, long last, the Christmas "treat"!
Was ever candy half as sweet?

Beside the hearth to hear once more,

The Story, read from Sacred Lore,

And pray the Child will come again

And dwell within the hearts of men.

Around the organ carols sung;

In much ado, the stockings hung.

Then off to bed, for Christmas Day

Was yet some sleep-filled hours away.

Though years may come and years may go,

And every sort of wind may blow,

With "Merry Christmas" in the heart,

The joys of Christmas ne'er depart.[68]

Christmas Memories

BY HARRIET WHIPPLE

I'm thinking of Christmas as it was years ago;
To be really perfect there had to be snow.
We'd set up the manger that Mother had made
Then help with the tree while the phonograph played.

The house would be dusted and polished and clean,
And cards were displayed where each could be seen.
Our Mother's big kitchen would smell extra nice;
For days she'd been with sugar and spice.
The wind-up train waited upon its small track
For Christmas additions from Santa's big pack.

We'd get up real early while street lights were on,
For the spirit of Christmas seemed closer at dawn.
We'd look in our stockings for trinkets and treats,
Then open our presents all wrapped up so neat.

By the front parlor window where it could be seen,
Our tree would be standing so splendid and green.
There were garlands of tinsel and bright paper chains,
Some small shining bells and peppermint canes.
Some twisted wax candles were clipped on the tree;
They seldom were lighted but pretty to see.
Our time-honored angel would be in its place
And frosty glass Santa there swinging in space.
The icicles shimmered on twigs here and there
And the pretty glass fish swam high in the air.
The lights were reflected in each colored ball.
And a big golden star shone high above all.

Beneath the low branches a tiny farm grew—
With buildings and people and animals too.
Small fences and meadows, a road and some trees,
With lakes made of mirrors and boats upon these.
Some celluloid ducklings, a deer and some does,
With penny-doll people in tiniest clothes.
A woodpile and wagons and little Ford cars,
A pump and a lantern for this farm of ours.
Some years it was winter with white cotton snow,
All made and arranged by our mother each year
With extra surprises when Christmas was here.

When church bells were ringing we went down the hill
To church for a service of peace and goodwill.
If Christmas was Sunday a program was due,
With children all singing and piece-speaking too.
Or sometimes a pageant with costumes and all,
Some angels and shepherds and a star on the wall.
So nice walking homeward in new-fallen snow,
To call "Merry Christmas" to people we'd know
And to her jingling bells on each passing sleigh—
Our hearts filled with gladness for such a fine day.
Christmas in those days was simple you see
But fond recollections endear it to me.[69]

Christmas Baking

BY LOUISE WEIBERT SUTTON

Smiling, she rolled her dough with care,
Cutting the cookies, one by one:
Some into stars, and some to spare.
Shaping like Santas, just for fun.
Cinnamon, raisin, butter, spice,
Came from the oven warmly sweet;
What other smells could be so nice?
What other things so good to eat?

Filled to the brim, each cookie jar
Waited for Santa's yearly whim;
"Santa knows where the cookies are,
And leave some coffee just for him!
Maybe he'd like a midnight treat,
A chance to rock and doze a bit,
Then when he's had enough to eat
He'll start again on his happy trip."

Here, and perhaps in other lands,
Memory holds such cookie jars;
Mothers who rolled, with careful hands,
Spicy brown dough for Christmas stars,
Raisin fat Santas, ginger trees,
Coconut angels, to surprise
Happy Saint Nick, or just to please
Children who watched with shining eyes.[70]

✳ ✳ ✳

What's more traditional than Christmas

cookies? Not much! It's hard to remember

colored icing

Christmases past without recalling

sprinkles

the family decorating sugar cookies with

silver dots

colored icing, sprinkles, and silver dots,

peeled off of sheets of waxed paper.

Sugar cookies take the prize for

the most "decoratable."

✳ ✳ ✳

Traditional Sugar Cutout Cookies

A FAMILY RECIPE

1 cup (2 sticks) butter or 1/2 cup (1 stick) butter plus
    1/2 cup (1 stick) margarine, softened
1 cup sugar
2 eggs, well beaten
2 teaspoons vanilla extract
3-1/2 cups sifted all-purpose flour
2 teaspoons baking powder

Preheat oven to 375° F. Combine butter, sugar, beaten eggs and vanilla in a large mixer bowl. Cream with electric mixer until fluffy. Resift flour with baking powder and blend with other ingredients at low speed, slowly and gradually, until well mixed.

Chill dough thoroughly in refrigerator. Then tear off one-quarter to one-third of the dough, form into a ball, and roll out on lightly floured waxed paper until approximately 3/16-inch thick. Cut out Christmas shapes with floured cookie cutters.

Decorate cookies before baking with color sugar crystals, non-pareils, silver balls, and the like—or after baking with icing described below. Place on greased cookie sheet and bake for 10 to 15 minutes or until golden. Remove and cool on a wire rack. Repeat with rest of the dough. Makes about 4 dozen, depending upon size of cutters.

Icing

3 egg whites
1 teaspoon cream of tartar
1 16-ounce box confectioners' sugar
Food coloring

Beat together egg whites, cream of tartar and confectioners' sugar, mix in food coloring. Spread icing on cookies with a knife or decorate cookie using a pastry tube.

A Candy Cane for Everyone

By Bob Garrison

"*Y*our candy canes are rich in symbolism. Why don't you make enough so everyone can have them during the Christmas season?"

"Harding, you're right about the symbolism. I wish every Christian in America could realize it. But I thought you knew that candy canes are made entirely by hand, with a lot of waste. I doubt they will ever be produced commercially at a profit."

"Why not?" mused Father Harding Keller, who already held two valuable patents. "Surely someone can invent a machine to eliminate most or all of the labor."

"You do it then, Harding," responded Bob McCormick. Head of a candy manufacturing company in Albany, Georgia, McCormick was extremely fond of his brother-in-law and looked forward to his annual visits from Arkansas.

The next day Father Keller put on his old gray pants and a work shirt and went to the candy plant. There he watched the stick candy makers at work, knowing that if he was successful at inventing a machine that would make candy canes, Christmas would never be the same.

A few candy canes, mostly for local sales, had already been produced by McCormick workers. They started by combining 300 pounds of sugar with 240 pounds of corn syrup and 50 pounds of water. They put this "premelt" into a large kettle, and mixed the candy-fixings with a large boat paddle, then heated the kettle to 240 degrees to remove all the water. Then it was put into a continuous cooker, where it was heated another 48 degrees to produce a batch of candy "ropes" that were soft enough to be twisted by hand.

Men standing at each end of the table twisted the twenty-foot ropes so the stripes would spiral around the candy. Then, after a stick was cut, the cane's crook was added by hand. It was an involved, expensive, and wasteful process.

Six months later, brother-in-law Keller had invented his candy cane machine. McCormick was delighted to see the contraption actually produced candy sticks of uniform thickness, already twisted.

There was one flaw, however. Once the patented "Keller machine" moved into full speed, it scattered candy all over the room. "I fixed that problem by adding cups that counteracted the machine's centrifugal force." The inventor later explained, "Once those cups were added, my machine would twist and cut 160 sticks a minute, with very little waste. The wooden molds allowed the workers to make the sticks into canes while they were still warm." When Keller invented a mechanical device for bending the crooks, all hand labor was eliminated.

By 1959 "Bob's" was recognized as the world's largest producer of candy canes. Earlier it had taken three men a full hour to cut and twist one hundred pounds of candy. With the Keller machines, one man could twist and cut 600 pounds an hour. Production of candy canes soon soared to a previously unthinkable level of a half-million canes per eight-hour shift.

Bob McCormick, a devout churchman, launched an intensive search for the history and symbolism of the candy cane. "It's a logical piece to have around the house at Christmas," he insisted, "because it reminds us of the crooks carried by the shepherds who figure so prominently in the biblical Christmas story.

Soon after Europeans adopted the use of Christmas trees, they began to make special decorations for them. Food items predominated, with cookies and candy heavily represented. That is when straight white sticks of sugar candy came into use at Christmas, probably during the seventeenth century.

Tradition has it that some of these candies were put to use in Cologne Cathedral about 1670 while restless youngsters were attending ceremonies around the living crèche. To keep the children quiet, the choir masters persuaded craftsmen to make sticks of candy bent at the end to represent shepherds' crooks, then passed them out to boys and girls who came to the cathedral. From Cologne, the custom of handing out "souvenir" sugar crooks at living nativity scene ceremonies spread throughout Europe. Soon the white canes were embellished with sugar roses.

About 1847, a man named August Imgard of Ohio managed to decorate his Christmas tree with candy canes to entertain his nephews and nieces. Many who saw his canes went home to boil sugar and experimented with canes of their own.

It took nearly another half century before someone added stripes to the canes, though neither McCormick nor Keller ever learned the inventor's name. They did, however, find that Christmas cards produced before 1900 picture plain white canes, while striped ones appear on many cards printed early in the twentieth century.

Today's candy cane includes two large stripes and two sets of smaller stripes that spiral around the stick. "The candy cane's white background symbolizes purity," Father Keller often explains to people. "Red, which is the color of blood, reminds us of sacrifice. The wide red stripe on the cane symbolizes the sacrifice of Christ, while the smaller red ones stand for the sacrifices that must be made by His followers."

Early striped canes were sometimes flavored with wintergreen, but peppermint soon became standard. According to McCormick, even the peppermint flavor is appropriate since it is akin to the biblical herb hyssop, which represents healing.

Today's peppermint-flavored, striped candy cane is a visual reminder of the shepherd's staff and a focal point for meditation upon purity and sacrifice. The McCormick family believe and hope, that occasionally a red-striped candy cane will prod someone to find the faith centered in the Babe whose first visitors carried crooks upon their shoulders.[71]   ✳

Mistletoe

Sitting under the mistletoe
(Pale-green, fairy mistletoe),
One last candle burning low,
All the sleepy dancers gone,
Just one candle burning on,
Shadows lurking everywhere:
Someone came, and kissed me there.

Tired I was, my head would go
Nodding under the mistletoe
(Pale-green, fairy mistletoe),
No footsteps came, no voice, but only,
Just as I sat there, sleepy, lonely,
Stooped in the still and shadowy air
Lips unseen—and kissed me there.[72]

WALTER DE LA MARE

The Joy

# of Light

"They've gone out again!"

"Bother! The worse part of Christmas are these dumb tree lights."

"Aren't you going to put the outside lights up?"

"They are up. We never took them down."

"So much for the new bubble lights."

"The white candle in the center of our Advent wreath represents Jesus, the Light of the world."

"The people who walk in darkness have seen a great light."

"Yes! The electricity's back on!"

"Can you ever remember such a dark night?"

"Look, even the moon has covered his face."

"The campfire's out again."

"Look over there, you can still see the glow of Bethlehem's lights."

"Baaaaa!"

"Even the sheep hate this blackness."

"Can't see my hand in front . . ."

"The Light!"

"Glory to God in the highest."

"Let us go to Bethlehem to see."

"I am the light of the world."

And I do come home at

Christmas. We all do,

or we all should.

We all come home,

or ought to come home,

for a short holiday—the longer,

the better. . . .

CHARLES DICKENS

The Word and the Light

In the beginning was the Word, and the Word was with God, and the Word was God. He was with God in the beginning.

Through him all things were made; without him nothing was made that has been made. In him was life, and that life was the light of men. The light shines in the darkness, but the darkness has not understood it.

There came a man who was sent God; his name was John. He came as a witness to testify concerning that light, so that through him all men might believe. He himself was not the light; he came only as a witness to the light. The true light that gives light to every man was coming into the world.

JOHN 1:1-9

* * *

King George VI, of Great Britain,

quoted the first five lines of this poem

in his Christmas radio broadcast to

the World at the beginning of

the Second World War, 1939.

* * *

From the Gate of the Year

And I said to the man who stood at the gate of the year:
"Give me light, that I may tread safely into the unknown!"
And he replied:
"Go out into the darkness and put your hand in the Hand of God.
That shall be to you better than light and safer than a known way."
So, I went forth, and finding the Hand of God, trod
 gladly into the night.
And He led me toward the hills and the breaking of
the day in the lone East.
So, heart, be still!
What need our little life,
Our human life, to know,
If God hath comprehension?
In all the dizzy strife
Of things both high and low
God hideth his intention.

M. LOUISE HASKINS

Swinging Toward the Light

"I do believe the world is swinging toward the light,"
    So spoke a soul on fire with holy flame.
Amid the dark such faith pierced through the night,
    The dreamers wrought, and living fruitage came.
To give of self, and not to count the cost,
    To learn, to teach, to labor, and to pray,
To serve like Christ the least, the last, the lost—
    These were the beacon fires that lit the way.

Our light grows dim; the air is thick with doom,
    And everywhere men's souls are crushed with fears.
Yet high above the carnage and the gloom
    The call resounds across the teeming years,
"Lift high Christ's cross! Serve God and trust His might!"
    I do believe the world is swinging toward the light!

GEORGIA HARKNESS

Christmas Eve

The door is on the latch tonight,
The hearth fire is aglow;
I seem to hear soft passing feet—
The Christ Child in the snow.

My heart is open wide tonight,
For stranger, kith, or kin;
I would not bar a single door
Where love might enter in.

ANONYMOUS

As with Gladness Men of Old

As with gladness men of old
    Did the guiding star behold;
As with joy they hailed its light,
    Leading onward, beaming bright;
So, most gracious Lord, may we
    Evermore be led to Thee.

As with joyful steps they sped
    To that lowly manger-bed,
There to bend the knee before
    Him whom heaven and earth adore;
So may we with willing feet
    Ever seek thy mercy seat.

As they offered gifts most rare,
    At that manger rude and bare,
So may we with holy joy,

Pure and free from sin's alloy,
    All our costliest treasures bring,
Christ, to Thee, our heavenly King.

Holy Jesus, every day
    Keep us in the narrow way;
And, when earthly things are past,
    Bring our ransomed souls at last
Where they need no star to guide,
    Where no clouds Thy glory hide.

WILLIAM CHATTERTON DIX

ed down and

Darkness

And the Word Was Made Flesh

Light looked down and beheld Darkness.

"Thither will I go," said Light.

Peace looked down and beheld War.

"Thither will I go," said Peace.

Love looked down and saw Hatred.

"Thither will I go," said Love.

So came light and shone.

So came Peace and gave rest.

So came Love and brought Life.

LAURENCE HOUSMAN

The Christmas Lamp Is Burning

As it did once long ago:
And friendship's light is glowing
Across earth-hiding snow.
The Christmas lamp is bringing
Peace from heaven above
And messages from God, himself,
To absent ones we love.[73]

MARY WHEELER EDGERTON

Who Were the Wise Men?

Who were the Wise Men in the long ago?
 Not Herod, fearful lest he lose his throne;
 Not Pharisees too proud to claim their own;
Not priests and scribes whose province was to know;
Not money-changers running to and fro;
 But three who traveled, weary and alone,
 With dauntless faith, because before them shone
The Star that led them to a manger low.

Who are the Wise Men now, when all is told?
 Not men of science; not the great and strong;
 Not those who wear a kingly diadem;
Not those whose eager hands pile high the gold;
 But those amid the tumult and the throng
 Who follow still the Star of Bethlehem.

     — B. Y. WILLIAMS

No Candle Was There ...

FROM MATERIAL BY MAYMIE R. KRYTHE

"No candle was there . . ." so a Christmas song tells us, in the stable of Bethlehem. But from ancient times candles have been used at winter feasts. Today candles are universally used as Yuletide decorations.

The Christian use of candles is symbolic of Christ, the "Light of the World." At first, tallow candles were chiefly used for church services, because of the high cost of wax tapers. When the wax became cheaper, they were favored as an emblem of the Virgin Mary's purity. Wax is the product of virgin bees. An early writer, Durandus, said the wax represented Christ's body; the wick, His soul; and the flame, His divine nature.

In medieval Europe, it was customary to light a candle "of monstrous size, called the Christmas candle," so that it could shed its glow on the festivities. This burned each evening until Twelfth Night [Remember the "Twelve Days of Christmas"?]

Martin Luther is credited with starting the practice of placing candles on Christmas trees; and soon others followed his example.

Bayberry candles with their delicate odor are popular at Christmas, and are said to bring good fortune to a home. Also there is a belief that if sweethearts (who are separated at Christmas) light bayberry candles, the scent will be wafted from one to the other, even across the world, if they are truly in love.

In certain lands, it was the habit to place candles in windows to guide the Christ Child, or weary travelers, to shelter; many thought He would knock, in the guise of a stranger, to test their hospitality. Therefore, no one was turned away; and several stories have been based on this idea.

The Irish would place a candle in the window, and then leave the door open to attract the Holy Family, searching for lodgings on their way to Bethlehem. So strangers were always given food and shelter for the night. Also in Ireland, only girls named Mary had the right to put the candle in the churches on Christmas Eve.

In the Scandinavian countries, the mother always lights the candles on Christmas Eve, while the boys and girls sing carols around the tree. Norwegians believed that Yule candles bestowed blessings; therefore, they used to spread out food and clothing, and set out their silver and pewter that the light might shine in benediction on them.

Swedish people have always featured candles at the Yuletide; they placed them at their windows, burned small tapers on their trees, and at their Christmas gift exchange, used them to melt the wax with which packages were sealed.

In Spain each family places a burning taper above its door, while in Italy the candles on the window sill to light the Holy Child on His way. On Christmas Eve, in Italian homes, small wax tapers surround the nativity scene; and a large one lights the supper table where the family gathers after their twenty-four hour fast.

Bulgarians went to their stables with lighted candles and greeted the domestic animals with "The Child is born and blesses you tonight."

Candles were popular in England, too, at Christmas. On the first Sunday in Advent, in many English homes, an Advent wreath with four tapers (two red and two white) was placed in the window. Just before the evening meal, the first candle was set aflame. On the second Advent Sunday, two were lighted, and so on, until the four were burning. In English villages years ago, boys and girls took candles to school to give to their teachers on the day before Christmas. Grocers presented candles to their customers.

In the United States, candlelight church services, especially carols by candlelight, have become very popular. One of the most impressive meetings of this kind has taken place each year since 1741 at the Central Moravian church in Bethlehem, Pennsylvania. At the first service the Moravian leader, Count Nicholas von Zinzendorf, with a lighted candle in his hand, led his people into a nearby stable. There, all joined together singing the old carol:

> Not stately Jerusalem,
> Rather humble Bethlehem
> Giveth that which maketh life rich. . . .

So they named their settlement Bethlehem, to honor the Christ Child.

There was a time when every fire station in San Francisco was decorated and illuminated for Christmas. The Country Club Plaza, a suburban shopping area in Kansas City, Missouri, outlines all of the shops and buildings in the 10-square block area with 50 thousand light bulbs and more than 60 miles of wiring. This display remains burning for five weeks.

According to rather outdated statistics, Americans spend more than $13,000,000 in buying more than 250,000,000 candles each year. All across the world, Christmas has become a festival of light; the soft glow of candles, the festive sparkle of electric lights, and the warm beauty of southwestern illuminarios—paper bags holding lighted candles anchored in sand. What are they? Some decorators idea of display? No! Christmas lights are the constant reminder that Christ, is the light of the world.[74]

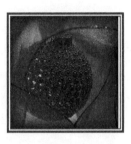

O Father, may that holy Star

Grow every year more bright,

And send its glorious beam afar

To fill the world with light.

WILLIAM CULLEN BRYANT

The Luminous Christ

BY ALBERT W. BEAVEN

The real Christmas experience for anyone is the turning on of the light within, which comes from the spirit of the indwelling Christ. It is still his incoming that makes the difference between a darkened inn and a glorified stable. Before we go on with our Christmas preparation, let us ask ourselves whether the real Christmas has come to us; whether what we are going through is just a form, a bartering of gifts, a forced holiday, or whether we have a real experience that makes Christmas a joy and not a bore. Christ taken in and then given out, that makes it a genuine Christmas for us and for others; for "God shined in our hearts" that the light might be passed on. All about us are those who wait for our coming: lonely people, discouraged people, heart-sick people with little love and joy. Christmas opens our eyes and challenges us to let our light shine outside our own little circle and give cheer where it is needed most.[75]

＊　＊　＊

Good news from heaven

the angels bring,

Glad tidings to

the earth they sing:

To us this day a

child is given,

To crown us with

the joy of heaven.

MARTIN LUTHER

＊　＊　＊

* * *

The stars shone bright

that Christmas night,

When Jesus lay on His bed of hay.

The shepherds came from far away

To find the place where the baby lay.

The wise men brought their gifts

of love;Led by the star

that shown from above.

E. WEBSTER

* * *

* * *

What star is this,

with beams so bright,

Which shames the sun's

less radiant light?

It shines to announce

a newborn King,

Glad tidings of our God

to bring.

TRANSLATED FROM LATIN, BY REV. J. CHANDLER

* * *

of the *World*

In Western Samoa, in the warm, flower-scented dawn, clocks are striking six—Christmas Day has begun. At this same moment it is seven A.M. in wintry Alaska, where children tumble from warm beds and scamper to their stockings to see what's under the tree. Along the east coast of the United States it is noon. Families are gathering at laden tables, where golden-skinned turkeys wait to be carved. And in England other families are sitting down to late afternoon tea. Already dusk has fallen in the Holy Land, where it is seven P.M. The first stars have appeared in the sky, another Christmas is drawing to its close. In every time zone Christ's birthday is celebrated. Those celebrations vary from country to country, but they have one thing very much in common, the Baby Jesus. The gifts, the foods, the languages in which carols are sung, the source of radiance, the religious ceremonies, differ only in detail. Everywhere there is some form of giving, feasting, and song. Everywhere there is light. Everywhere—or at least this day—peace and goodwill prevail among men.

Nativity

Within a native hut, ere stirred the dawn,
Unto the Pure One was an infant born,
Wrapped in a blue lappah that His mother dyed,
Laid on His father's home-tanned deerskin hide,
The baby still slept, by all things glorified
Spirits of black bards burst their bonds and sang
"Peace upon earth" until the heavens rang.
All the black babies who from earth had fled
Peeped through the clouds, then gathered round His head.
Telling of things a baby needs to do,
When first he opens his eyes on wonders new,
Telling Him that to sleep was sweeter rest,
All comfort came from His black mother's breast.
Their gifts were of Love, caught from the spring sod,
Whilest tears and laughter were the gifts of God.
Then all the Wise Men of the past stood forth,
Filling the air East, West, South and North,
And told Him of the joys that wisdom brings
To mortals in their earthly wanderings.
The children of the past shook down each bough,
Wreathed frangipani blossoms for His brow,
They put pink lilies in His mother's hand,
And heaped for both the first fruits of the land.
His father cut some palm fronds, that the air
Be coaxed to zephyrs while He rested there.
Birds trilled their hallelujahs; and the dew
Trembled with laughter, till the Babe laughed too.
All the black women brought their love so wise,
And kissed their motherhood into His mother's eyes.[76]

GLADYS MAY CASELY HAYFORD

Go Tell It on the Mountain

Go tell it on the mountain,
Over the hills and everywhere,
Go tell it on the mountain,
That Jesus Christ is born.

When I was a sinner
I prayed both night and day,
I asked the Lord to help me,
And He showed me the way.

While sheperds kept their watching
O'er silent flocks by night
Behold, throughout the heavens
There shown a holy light.

Down in a lowly manger
The humble Christ was born,
And God sent out salvation
That blessed Christmas morn.

Go tell it on the mountain,
Over the hills and everywhere,
Go tell it on the mountain,
That Jesus Christ is born.

AMERICAN BLACK SPIRITUAL

One of the oldest recorded Christmas folk

stories, based on the biblical Nativity story,

comes from Spain. Here, in the Basque

country, shepherds have been held in high

esteem for hundreds of years.

The Shepherds

You who keep Christmas, who keep the holy-tide, have you ever thought why a child needs must be born in the world to save it? Here is a Christmas story about God, meaning Good. It begins far back when the world was first created.

In the beginning God had two favorite archangels: one was called Lucifer, meaning Light, and one called Michael, meaning Strength. They led the heavenly hosts; they stood, one on the right hand and one on the left hand of God's throne. They were His chosen messengers.

Now the Archangel Michael served God with his whole heart and angelic soul. There was no task too great for him to perform, no thousand years of service too long. But the Archangel Lucifer chafed at serving any power higher than his own. As one thousand years swept after another thousand years—each as a day—he became bitter in his service and jealous of God.

The appointed time came for God to create the Universe. He made the sun, the moon, the stars. He made earth and water, and separated them. He made trees and flowers and grass to grow; He made creatures to walk the earth and eat thereof; and He made birds for the air and fish for the waters. And when all else was created, He made a man and called him Adam, and a woman and called her Eve. It took Him six heavenly days to create this Universe; and at the end He was tired and rested.

While the Creation was coming to pass and God was occupied most enormously, Lucifer went stealthily about Heaven. He spoke with this angel and with that, whispering, whispering. He spoke with the cherubim and seraphim—to all and everyone who would give him an attending ear. And what he whispered was this: "Why should God rule supreme? Why should He be the only one to create and to say what shall be created? We are powerful. We are worthy to rule. What say you?"

He whispered throughout the six days of Creation; and when God rested Lucifer led a host of rebellious angels against God; they drew their flaming swords and laid siege to God's throne. But the Archangel Michael drew his flaming sword; he led God's true angels to defend Heaven. The army of Lucifer was put to rout and his captains were taken prisoner and led before God's throne. And God said: "I cannot take life from you, for you are celestial beings. But you shall no longer be known as the hosts of light; you shall be the hosts of darkness. You, Lucifer, shall bear the name of Satan. You and those who have rebelled must seek a kingdom elsewhere. But I command you this— leave this Earth, which I have but freshly made, alone. Molest not my handiwork." So spoke God.

So Lucifer was banished with his minions; and henceforth he was known as Satan. He established a kingdom under the Earth and called it Hell. But because God had commanded him to leave Earth untouched, he straightway coveted Earth for his own. He sent his spirits abroad to tempt and make evil those born upon Earth. So it came to pass that the people of Earth knew at last the power of evil as well as of good; they felt the long reach of darkness even while they lifted their eyes to the Face of Light.

And now the years became millions. Earth became peopled in its four corners; and God looked down upon it and sorrowed. He called Archangel Michael to Him and spoke: "It has come to pass that Satan's power upon Earth is great. No longer can my angels prevail. A kingdom of destruction, of greed, of hate, and of false-witnessing has been set up among my people on the Earth I have created. Their hearts have grown dark with evil; their eyes no longer see the light. I must send to Earth my own spirit that evil may be conquered. He shall be one conceived of Heaven and born of Earth, none less than my own beloved Son." So spoke God.

Earth had been divided into countries, some great and powerful, some small and weak. And the strong reached out even with their armies and took the weak. Now such a one, taken, was called Judea. Within its rolling hills, its olive groves, its high pastures and twisting rivers, men had built a little city called Bethlehem—King David's city. And to this city the conquering Romans had ordered all of the tribe of Jesse to come and render tribute unto Caesar.

Beyond the city, on the high pastures, many shepherds herded their sheep. And it came to pass that God chose Bethlehem to be the place of birth for His Son; and the time to be the taxing time of the year. He chose to reveal the coming to the shepherds, they being men of simple faith and pure hearts. And God sent forth a star to show them the way, and commanded angels to sing to them of the glad tidings.

The night had grown late. High in the pastures the shepherds had built fires to keep themselves warm, to frighten off stray wolves or robbers. All slept but Esteban, the boy. He alone saw the angel, heard the tidings; and straightway he woke the sleeping ones: "Lo, an angel has but now come among us, singing. Wake—wake, all of you! I think this night must have great meaning for us."

Now at this time Satan stood at the gateway of Hell. Of late he had been troubled in mind, a sense of impending doom moved him. And as he gazed abroad upon the Earth he saw the angel appear. Then did his troubled mind grow fearful. He summoned his hosts of Hell, commanding them to make ready: "Tonight I think again we defy God's power over the Universe. We fight, I think, for Earth, to make it ours. I go to it now. Come when I smite the ground."

Swift as his thought Satan reached the Earth. He came as a wanderer, upon his head a wide sombrero, about his shoulders and falling to the ground a cloak, in his hand a staff. Across the Earth he traveled even as the lightning crosses the sky. He was here—he was beyond.

And so he came to the high pastures of Judea and stood at one of the fires about which the shepherds watched. Again the angel came, shouting God's tidings: "Fear not! For unto you is born this day in the city of David a Messiah!"

Satan covered his face and spoke: "What means that message?"

The shepherds cowered. "We know not."

"What is that Saviour—that Messiah yonder apparition shouts of?"

"We know not."

Satan dropped his cloak that they might see the fire that damns and burns shining even in his eyes: "I command you to know!"

It was Benito, the oldest shepherd, who asked: "In the name of God, who are you?"

And Satan answered: "In my own name I am a wanderer. Once I had taken from me a mighty kingdom. I am here to restore it unto myself."

Could this be the Saviour of whom the angels sang? The shepherds drew close—close. They looked. And to each came terror. Here truly was darkness, not light; here was nameless evil, not good. Here was one who had denied the name of God. Together they shouted: "Begone!" They drew brands from the fire and crossed them, making fiery crosses to burn between themselves and Satan.

While they had been talking among themselves Esteban, the boy, had gone far off seeking stray lambs. Now Satan sought him out. "You heard the angel sing. Where is this City of David?"

"I know not."

"Who is this Messiah?"

"You speak of Mahas?" The boy was stupid with fear. "You mean my mother's brother, a shepherd, wise and faithful? But he is ill. I tend his sheep."

"Idiot! Dolt! Fool!" The voice of Satan rose like a whirlwind. "In your great stupidness you sin against me, and that is more terrible than sinning against God. For this you die!"

The boy tried to open his mouth to shriek for mercy. Before words could come, before Satan's hand could smite him, there came between them, out of the vast spaces of the Universe, one who thrust a flaming sword between the Devil and the boy; while through the vast dome of Heaven rang a voice: "Thou shalt not take the innocent!"

It was the voice of the Archangel Michael. He stood now, all in shining armor, beside Esteban, his sword shielding him. And again he spoke: "How dare you break God's command!"

"I dare do more than that." Satan spoke with mockery. "God's Earth is no longer His but mine. My minions rule it. But tonight I shall fight you for it. I shall take it from you by right of sword and mightier hosts."

He stamped the ground. It split asunder, and from its very bowels came forth rank after rank of devils, waving their double-bladed swords forged in Hell's own fires. Then Michael thrust his sword aloft and behold a mighty stairway, even like Jacob's ladder, was built between Earth and Heaven. Down its shining way came rank on rank of the heavenly hosts. Across the sky rang the shout of "Combat!"

Then such a battle was fought between the armies of darkness and the armies of light as had not been waged since the beginning of all things. And Michael's sword pinioned Satan to the ground so that he could not rise; and Michael's hosts put Satan's to rout, so that the Earth's crust broke with them and they were swallowed in belching flames. And when the Earth was rid of them, Michael spoke to Satan: "You have asked of many this night who is the Saviour—the Messiah. I will answer you, defeated. He is God's Son, and Man's. He is Peace. He is Love. He is one against whom your evil cannot prevail. For next to God He is supreme."

The face of Archangel Michael shone with the light of conquering Heaven, all goodness, all strength. And Satan, crawling to his feet, looked upon it and hated it. "I am conquered now. But wait another thousand years, two thousand!"

Meanwhile the boy Esteban watched. And with the crawling of Satan back to Hell, Michael commanded Esteban to lead the shepherds to Bethlehem that they might look upon the face of their Saviour, and worship Him.

And as the boy joined the shepherds about their fires, there came the angel again, the third time; and with it was a multitude of the heavenly host, praising God and singing hallelujahs! While over all shone a star of a magnitude never seen by them before in all the heavens.

But of the many watching their flocks that night only a few heeded. These wrapped their cloaks about them and followed the boy Esteban. As they walked he pointed out the roadsides, guarded by rank on rank of angels in shining armor. But none saw them save the boy.

Yet a great joy welled up in each heart, so that every shepherd needs must raise his voice in song. Benito, the oldest, gave them words for the beginning:

Yonder star in the skies marks the manger where He lies.

Then Andres caught the air and gave them the second verse to sing:

Joy and laughter,

    song and mirth

herald in

    our Saviour's birth.

Miguel lifted his voice in a great swelling tumult of thanksgiving:

Now good will

    unto all men.

Shout it, brothers,

    shout again!

Carlos caught from him the song and threw it back to the others with gladness:

Peace then be

    among us all;

upon great nations

    and on small!

It was Esteban who gave the words for the last, singing them down the end of the road, leading them to the stable opening:

Let each shepherd
     raise his voice
till the whole world
     shall rejoice;
till in one voice
     all shall sing—
Glory to our
     Saviour—King!

The star overhead lighted the way into the stable. Within they found a young woman, very fair, and on the straw beside her a small, newborn child. Benito spoke the questions that were on the minds of all: "What is thy name, woman?"

"They call me Mary."

"And his—the child's?"

"He is called Jesus."

Benito knelt. "Nene Jesus—Baby Jesus, the angels have sent us to worship thee. We bring what poor gifts are ours. Here is a young cockerel for thee." Benito laid it on the straw beside the child, then rose and called: "Andres, it is thy turn."

Andres knelt. "I, Andres, bring thee a lamb." He put it with the cockerel, rose, and said: "Miguel, give thine."

Miguel knelt. "I bring thee a basket of figs, little one. Carlos, thy turn."

Carlos knelt and held out shepherd-pipes. "I have made them. Thou shalt play on them when thou art grown. Juan, what hast thou?"

Juan knelt. "Here is some cheese—good goats' cheese."

In turn they knelt, each shepherd, until all but Esteban, the boy, had given his gift. "Alas, Nene Jesus, I have little for thee. But here are the ribbons from my cap. Thou likest them, yes? And now I make a prayer: 'Bless all shepherds. Give us to teach others the love for all gentle and small things that is in our hearts. Give us to see thy star always on this, the night of thy birth. And keep our eyes lifted eternally to the far hills.' "

And having made the prayer, and all having given their gifts, the shepherds departed into the night, singing.[77]   ✳

The Mountains of Papa Morelli

By Natala de la Fere

"Will you come with me to the Piazza Navona, Signora?" asked Papa Morelli one evening a week before Christmas.

"Gladly," I replied, "but why especially the Piazza Navona?"

"I know . . . another figure," suggested his twelve-year-old daughter Maria Grazia.

"Yes, I expect that's it—another figure," agreed his older daughter Teresa.

Signora Morelli said nothing but slowly nodded her head in silence.

"Another figure?" I queried with curiosity.

"Yes of course, they know," explained Papa Morelli seriously. "Every year another figure is added to our crib at Christmas and I am the one who must choose it in the market for Christmas figures in the Piazza Navona."

"But why so especially there?" I asked in my unpardonable ignorance.

"Why?" repeated Signora Morelli, amazed, "because that is where they have the special market every year for figures and everything else for Christmas cribs."

"Why don't you buy the mountains this year, babbo?" asked Maria Grazia with what I thought was an exaggeratedly casual air.

"Yes, haven't we enough figures?" went on Teresa. (Did I imagine a quick sidelong look at her mother?) "We must have more than thirty figures now."

Papa Morelli did not answer; it was as if he had not heard. It was his wife who answered loyally:

"Your father will buy the mountains when he is ready, and not before."

But I thought I detected a note of resignation in her voice. And when he glanced at her somewhat sheepishly, the mystery of the mountains seemed real enough to me.

Quietly he got up and said, "Shall we go now, Signora?"

I jumped up with alacrity, partly to dispel what I felt sure was an "atmosphere," even if only a light one, and partly because I really was eager to see this market which sounded quite unique.

In the crowded bus we did not have a chance to speak, so I let my mind dwell affectionately on this little family, so simple, united and open-hearted and so kind to have invited me to spend my first Christmas in Rome with them.

The Piazza Navona is one of the oldest squares in Rome and so well hidden by a maze of narrow little streets that if you do not know about it you could live in the city almost indefinitely without ever seeing it. Actually it is not a square, but a long rectangle with a fabulous Bernini fountain in the centre and two others, less grandiose, at either end. Completely surrounded by houses that have remained unchanged for centuries, it is unlike any other square in Rome. And the week before Christmas, unlike any other square in the world.

When Papa Morelli and I emerged from one of the tiny streets into the piazza, I could only stand and marvel. Both its sides were tightly lined with stalls, peopled by a multitude of miniatures.

Thousands of figures of the Virgin Mary, Saint Joseph, the Infant Jesus, shepherds, kings, peasants, asses, oxen, camels, and sheep arranged in groups or in processions or just jumbled anyhow, stretched right down to the far end. Music blared forth from loudspeakers; sweet stalls where the traditional nougat was made and sold in slabs up to almost any length and weight, did a roaring trade. The nougat was the only merchandise allowed to be sold apart from the figures.

Carefully, lovingly, and beautifully made, either in wood or plaster, these saintly biblical characters quietly knelt, sat, or stood in silent testimony to the greatest event in the history of man. Hanging all around them were replicas, big and small, of the holy stable; glittering stars of Bethlehem and comets swung on high and range after range of papier mâché painted mountains completed the decor. Every stall was arranged according to the individual taste of its owner and some of the effects were dramatic and imposing.

The noise and gaiety increased as the square became more and more crowded. Children stood wide-eyed pointing to the figures they wanted their parents to buy for the crib at home.

Papa Morelli pulled my arm gently. "Why so silent, Signora? You haven't spoken a word since we came."

How could I explain the deep impression made upon me by myriads of figures so beautifully fashioned and so dignified in their attitudes of mute adoration? It seemed almost sacrilegious to watch them being bought for a few lire, wrapped up in newspaper and thrust into baskets by the milling, shouting throng which then crowded round the nougat stalls to complete traditional Christmas purchases.

"Which one are you going to buy this year?" I asked Papa Morelli, at last.

We walked along inspecting each stall carefully.

"I have all the principal ones," he said. "The Virgin, Saint Joseph, the Child, of course, the Three Kings and some shepherds, but I need a few peasants . . . yes, I think that peasant woman in her wide red skirt and the man over there kneeling, holding a sheep."

"Are they the right size?" I asked.

"Oh yes, about ten centimeters . . . yes, they'll match the others nicely."

We bought them and he stuffed them in his pockets.

"There," he said happily, "they will just fill that empty corner in front nicely."

I longed to offer to buy some mountains for his crib, but remembering the mysterious "atmosphere" earlier in the evening when they had been mentioned, I refrained and, as events turned out, I did not know whether to be glad or sorry for having held back.

As we were turning away to go to the nearby nougat stall I was struck by the figure of a tiny Madonna holding the Child. She was not looking down at Him in the usual way but upwards, as if to thank God in His Heaven for this wondrous miracle. She was carved out of wood, and her delicate colouring and ecstatic expression enhanced by the soft light of a paper-covered bulb so captivated me that I did not hesitate for a second. I bought her, handing over my lire quickly with a curious sense of shame for the inglorious gesture, and snatched her out of reach of the proffered sheet of newspaper. Slipping the carving inside my coat, I held it against my heart for the rest of the evening.

Two days before Christmas Papa Morelli came home from the office with a busy air and shut himself in the front room with a request that he was not to be disturbed. The family and I had supper in the kitchen and his was kept warm in the oven.

"Well . . . it's Christmas again," sighed the Signora.

"And the crib," sighed Maria Grazia.

"And the crib," echoed Teresa hopelessly.

Tentatively I tried to discover why the making of the Christmas crib should cast such a gloom over this happy household every year.

"It'll begin soon now," said Signora Morelli softly, towards ten o'clock.

Just as I was about to ask some indiscreet questions, we heard the key turn in the lock and Papa Morelli crossed the hall and came in with a broad, satisfied smile.

"My love," he turned to his wife with a courtly gesture, "you will be the first to see it."

Signora Morelli rose calmly and with a significant look at all of us left the room with her husband.

"What is behind all this?" I asked Teresa, throwing discretion to the wind.

"It's the mountains," she explained, "every year it's the mountains."

"And it'll be the same again this year, you'll see," said Maria Grazia slowly.

"What's the matter with the mountains?" I asked bluntly.

"We don't know—yet."

"Last year they were too high."

"And the year before that they were too low."

"And I remember one year when they looked more like a stormy sea than mountains."

"He will make them himself," went on Maria Grazia, "he loves making them. He collects stiff brown paper for weeks beforehand and we always have such a mess of paint to clear up afterwards. "

"But the real trouble is Mother, she can never stop herself saying what she thinks of the mountains, and it's always wrong. Then there's an awful row—you'll see."

"That's the trouble," Teresa explained further. "If only Mother would let him do what he likes with his mountains and admire them whatever they look like."

In a few moments their worst forebodings were confirmed. Voices raised in argument came from the closed room, Papa Morelli's in a sharp, gradual crescendo, and Signora Morelli's in shrill and excited trills. The girls looked at each other and then at me. Then they sat hunched up waiting for the eruption. It came inevitably. The door opposite was flung open and then slammed. Signora Morelli burst into the kitchen very pink-cheeked.

"They are too dark, I said so because they are. How can I say what isn't true? They are too dark!"

Once more we heard the key turned deliberately in the lock of the front room door. Teresa got up resignedly and turned off the oven. Signora Morelli slept with the girls that night.

The next evening was Christmas Eve. Nobody had seen Papa Morelli since the day before, but we heard him returning from the office very early. He stumped down the corridor and then, after much grunting and heaving, went back to the front room staggering under the burden of the large linen cupboard door. He had heaved it off its hinges leaving the shelves of linen exposed to public view. Then he locked himself in again.

The rest of us passed the time quietly playing cards in the kitchen. Supper time came and went.

"He'll come out just before it's time to go to midnight Mass, I suppose," said Signora Morelli.

"Hasn't he had anything to eat since yesterday?" I inquired anxiously.

"Of course," she laughed. "I heard him come in here very late in the night, and this morning I saw he'd eaten up everything. He'll go hungry!"

About an hour later the door opened and we all concentrated very hard on our cards.

"Signora," he said quietly.

I looked up feigning surprise.

"Me, Signore?"

"Certainly, Signora, as our guest I want you to be the first to see my crib."

As I went with him the family gave me encouraging looks and nods.

A moment later I stood facing a virtual work of art. Papa Morelli had used the linen cupboard door as a base supported by trestles. On it he had designed and built a corner of the Bethlehem countryside. Sparse tufts of grass and stony patches through which twisted paths led up to the stable were realistically reproduced in paper and cardboard truthfully painted, and perfectly arranged in natural disorder. Peasants standing at the doors of their huts with their animals grazing or resting nearby, filled the foreground. The steep, narrow paths all converged upon the stable. The Three Kings leading their laden camels were resplendent in brilliant costumes and head-dresses, while simple shepherds knelt in prayer surrounded by their sheep. Inside the dim stable I could discern the shadowy ox and ass. Saint Joseph in an attitude of devout humility was bending over the Virgin in her blue mantle, seated in the center looking at her empty arms.

"The Child is not born yet," whispered Papa Morelli softly. "He will be put in her arms when we come back from Mass."

I raised my eyes to the glittering tinsel star of Bethlehem shining over the stable roof. Rising in sombre, majestic splendour along the whole background were the dark—the "too dark"—mountains. Only, for me they were not too dark.

"Papa Morelli," I said softly, "it is one of the loveliest things I have ever seen. It is perfect."

He pressed my hand. "And the mountains, Signora, are they too dark?"

I wished he had not asked me that. I did not want to upset Signora Morelli any more than I wanted to hurt him. I hesitated. He himself saved me from my dilemma.

"How can they be too dark when I have little lights hidden everywhere to light it all up? It's the first year I've had them, and you'll see what a wonderful surprise it will be." He came closer and whispered in my ear. "They don't know."

He went to the door and shouted: "Well? Are you coming to see the crib or aren't you?"

They filed into the room obediently and with quiet, serious expressions gazed on the masterpiece. Then, suddenly, Papa Morelli reestablished a true, happy Christmas Eve. He put his arms round his wife and kissed her. "Tell me it is beautiful, *tesoro* . . . my treasure. Just say it for me, and then I shall show you how light the mountains really are."

She laughed happily and stroked his cheek. "Why, of course, Gino, of course it's beautiful, you shouldn't listen to me."

"Ah, but you were right then, darling, quite right, it was I who would not admit it, but watch now!"

He stepped to the switch in the wainscoting and bent down. "Now you will see your light mountains," he pronounced proudly.

He turned on the switch and—we were in complete darkness. Every light in the apartment had fused. For a moment there was a bitter silence.

"Santa Madonna," he wailed, "Santa Madonna, now look what I've done!"

Immediately we all rallied to his aid. "Why, it's nothing, nothing at all, only a little fuse that can be put right in no time," I cried.

"Gino, I'm sure it's wonderful all lit up," his wife encouraged him, "we'll get it fixed quickly before it's time to go to Mass. Teresa, go and find the candle . . . Maria Grazia, get some matches . . . I'll get the step-ladder."

We all sprang into action, feeling our way in the dark. Bumping and jostling each other, we scrambled about in the kitchen opening cupboards and drawers, fumbling badly in our haste to help him remedy the situation and enjoy his triumph.

"What could have gone wrong?" we heard him muttering to himself all alone in the dark front room.

"Don't worry, don't get excited," Signora Morelli called out to him. "We are finding everything, just one minute more, *tesoro*."

At last the candle was lit, the step-ladder fixed under the fuse-box, and the candle held on high to light his way. He climbed up and fiddled for what seemed an endless time. Then, with a relieved *"finalmente,"* he clambered down and we switched on the light in the hall. Tactfully we left him alone to readjust his precious wires, as he shouted a triumphant, *"Ecco!* Done!"

Now, in the surrounding darkness, the little holy scene lay revealed in dramatic light and shade; the figures cast life-like shadows and had they really moved I don't think I would have been surprised; the star of Bethlehem shone like a real star and the still childless Virgin sat serenely in a golden aura. The glorious moment was at hand.

When we returned from Mass, Papa Morelli laid the Child reverently in His mother's arms, and a little later we went to our rooms to sleep with His message of peace and goodwill in our hearts.[78] ✳

* * *

Fans of A. A. Milne are legion. Pooh,

Christopher Robin, Kanga, Roo, and all the

rest have become household names where there

are children. The poetry of Milne is equally

loved by kids of every age. Milne wonderfully

exemplifies England in this international

Christmas chapter.

* * *

King John's Christmas

King John was not a good man—
　　He had his little ways.
And sometimes no one spoke to him
　　For days and days and days.
And men who came across him,
　　When walking in the town,
Gave him a supercilious stare,
Or passed with noses in the air—
And bad King John stood dumbly there,
　　Blushing beneath his crown.

King John was not a good man,
　　And no good friends had he.
He stayed in every afternoon . . .
　　But no one came to tea.
and round about December,
　　The cards upon his shelf
Which wish him lots of Christmas cheer,
And fortune in the coming year,
Were never from his near and dear,
　　But only from himself.

King John was not a good man,
    Yet had his hopes and fears.
They'd given him no present now
    For years and years and years.
But every year at Christmas,
    While minstrels stood about,
Collecting tribute from the young
For all the songs they might have sung,
He stole away upstairs and hung
    A hopeful stocking out.

King John was not a good man,
    He lived his life aloof;
Alone he thought a message out
    While climbing up the roof.
He wrote it down and propped it
Against the chimney stack:
"TO ALL AND SUNDRY—NEAR AND FAR—
F. CHRISTMAS IN PARTICULAR."
And signed it not "Johannes R."
    But very humbly, "JACK."

"I want some crackers,
       And I want some candy;
I think a box of chocolates
       Would come in handy;
       I don't mind oranges,
       I do like nuts!
And I SHOULD like a pocket-knife
       That really cuts.
And, oh! Father Christmas, if you love me at all,
Bring me a big, red, india-rubber ball!"

       King John was not a good man—
       He wrote this message out,
And got him to his room again,
       Descending by the spout.
And all that night he lay there,
       A prey to hopes and fears.
"I think that's him a-coming now."
(Anxiety bedewed his brow.)
"He'll bring one present, anyhow—
       The first I've had for years."

"Forget about the crackers,
    And forget about the candy;
I'm sure a box of chocolates
    Would never come in handy;
I don't like oranges,
    I don't want nuts,
And I HAVE got a pocket-knife
    That almost cuts.
But, oh! Father Christmas, if you love me at all,
Bring me a big, red india-rubber ball!"

    King John was not a good man—
        Next morning when the sun
Rose up to tell a waiting world
        That Christmas had begun,
And people seized their stockings,
        And opened them with glee,
And crackers, toys and games appeared,
And lips with sticky sweets were smeared,
King John said grimly; "As I feared,
        Nothing again for me!"

    "I did want crackers,
        And I did want candy;
I KNOW A BOX OF CHOCOLATES
        Would come in handy;

I do love oranges,
I did want nuts.
I haven't got a pocket-knife—
Not one that cuts.
And, Oh! if Father Christmas had loved me at all,
He would have brought a big, red, india-rubber ball."

King John stood by the window,
        And frowned to see below
The happy bands of boys and girls
        All playing in the snow.
And while he stood there watching,
        And envying them all . . .
When through the window big and red
There hurtled by his royal head,
And bounced and fell upon the bed,
        And india-rubber ball!

AND, OH, FATHER CHRISTMAS,
MY BLESSINGS ON YOU FALL
        FOR BRINGING HIM
        A BIG, RED,
        INDIA-RUBBER
        BALL![79]

A. A. MILNE

Like a bell, with solemn, sweet

vibrations, I hear once more the

voice of Christ say "Peace!"

HENRY W. LONGFELLOW

The Lord gives strength

to all his people;

the Lord blesses his people

with peace.

PSALM 29:11 NIV

Children at Christmastime Around the World

BY ROBINA BECKLES WILLSON

CHRISTMAS FOR THE ANIMALS

Animals are part of Christmas celebrations in many countries of the world. There are many fables and stories told about the friendly animals in the stable where Jesus was born.

It is said that the cow did not eat the fresh hay which was put in the manger, so Mary could use the hay for the baby's bed. The cow also helped to keep the Holy Child warm by breathing on Him and warming Him with her breath.

The sheep gave Mary some wool so that she could weave a soft blanket, while the doves cooed Jesus to sleep.

Not only the shepherds were pleased to see Jesus. A robin sheltering in the stable roof sang for joy with the angels. Because it was the first bird song Jesus heard, he rewarded the robin by making its voice sweeter still, and especially so in winter, at Christmastime.

A very small brown beetle crept into the stable that joyful night. When at last it reached the manger, only Jesus noticed the beetle, because it was so small. But Jesus touched it with His finger. And ever since then the glow-worm has shone with a tiny light, to guide travelers through the dark night.

It is also told that on Christmas Eve, at midnight, every farm animal has been given the gift of human speech. It is bad luck to disturb them, however, so no one has ever reported overhearing them.

Even the bees are said to give homage to the Christ Child, by humming a psalm. "Give thanks to Him and bless His name," they sing in remembrance of the baby who was born in a manger.

CHRISTMAS IN GERMANY

In Germany, children start getting ready for Christmas at the beginning of December with Advent calendars. Advent means "coming" and it is the time when people prepare for the coming of Christ.

As with other birthdays, it is exciting to count the days up to the birthday of Christ. An Advent calendar has twenty-four numbered doors to open, one for each day of December up to Christmas Eve. Inside each door is a Christmas picture.

Another kind of Advent calendar is made of a wreath of fir branches on which twenty-four little boxes are hung. Each box, wrapped in brightly-colored paper, has a number on the outside and a tiny present inside. One box is opened on every day of Advent.

Other children will help make an Advent wreath of fir branches bound together to make a circle. This is decorated with four red or yellow candles, set into metal cups. One candle is lit on the first Sunday of Advent, two on the second, and so on up to Christmas Day.

In some parts of Germany children write to the Christ Child, asking for presents.

To make the letters sparkle and catch the Christ Child's eye as He passes, the children sprinkle the envelope with sugar. They spread a little glue on each one, then, while it is still sticky, they shake sugar on to it. The glittering envelopes are left on the window sill, and the children go to bed on Christmas Eve, hoping for presents the next day.

Sometimes on Christmas Eve presents are given secretly. While the family is settled at home, the door is suddenly pushed open just wide enough for small presents to be tossed inside onto the floor. Each member of the family opens a package to find inside another package bearing the name of someone else. Packages are passed back and forth until at last each gift reaches the person for whom it was intended. No one must ever find out who sent the presents.

For German children, one of the most exciting moments of the holiday is Christmas Eve, when they see their Christmas tree for the first time. It is usually decorated secretly by the mother of the family.

One traditional story often told on Christmas Eve is about a woodman and his family. As they sat snugly by the fire, they heard a knock at the door. They were surprised to see a small boy standing outside in the snowy forest, all by himself. So they took him in, and gave him warm food and drink and a bed for the night.

The next morning they were awakened by singing. It was a choir of angels, whose presence filled the cottage with light.

The woodman and his family realized then that they had given shelter to the Christ Child.

"You cared for me," said Jesus. "This will remind you of my visit." He touched a little fir tree by the door. "May this tree glow to warm your hearts. And may it carry presents, so that you are as kind to one another as you were to me."

Another well-beloved German Christmas fable tells how a widow was secretly decorating a tree for her children. When she had gone to bed, spiders spun their webs all over it. The Christ Child, passing by, turned the webs to silver, to delight them all on Christmas morning. That is why we put tinsel on our trees.

Christmas in Italy

Saint Francis of Assisi has a special place in Christmas celebrations in Italy. He loved all living creatures and called animals his brothers and sisters.

Hundreds of years after Jesus was born, Francis visited Bethlehem, and saw the place where the stable had been.

The following Christmas, at home in Greccio in Italy, he decided to re-enact the story of the baby born in a manger. He did so to remind his people that Jesus was not rich, but born into a poor family, in a humble stable. He took a live ox and a donkey into a cave, and built a manger there, with wood and straw. Village people played the parts of Mary, Joseph, and the shepherds. A little figure was carved of the baby Jesus.

Many people came, lighting their way with candles, to hear Francis tell the story of Jesus' birth. One man reported he thought he saw the baby open his eyes when Francis looked into the manger.

Other churches in Italy copied Saint Francis' idea for a Christmas crèche [miniature manger scene]. Then Italian families began making crèches in their own homes, and now families in countries all over the world have taken up the custom.

An old custom for Italian children is to go before Christmas from house to house playing songs on shepherds' pipes, and wearing shepherds' sandals and hats. They are given money to buy Christmas food.

But on Christmas Eve, Italians do without food for a whole day. Then, that night, after a midnight service, they have as grand and delectable feast as they can manage which will include the special Italian Christmas cake called *panetone*.

Italian children have to wait for their Christmas presents until Twelfth Night, the Epiphany. This is when the three kings arrived in Bethlehem to worship the Christ Child. That night, children wait for the *la Bafana* to come down their chimney. Bad children find pieces of charcoal inn their shoes, but good ones find presents.

CHRISTMAS IN SWEDEN

In Sweden, December 13th is a special day for this is the feast of Saint Lucia, whose goodness is remembered every year in towns and villages all over the country.

Lucia was an early follower of Jesus. In those days, Christians were sometimes cruelly treated. They met to pray, hiding in underground caves. Lucia secretly took them food in the night, so they would not go hungry. On her head she wore a crown of candles. In this way, with both hands free to carry the food and drink, she was able to see her way in the dark.

One day, she was caught and killed by the Roman Emperor's men. But her kindness has never been forgotten and her story continues to bring brightness to the long dark winter nights.

Many Swedish children begin thinking of Saint Lucia on December 12th, when they cook special Lucia buns and ginger snaps. The next morning all the children get up early and the youngest girl dresses up as Saint Lucia in a long white dress with a red sash. Her brothers may act as "Star Boys," in white shirts. On the girl's head will be a crown of evergreens with candles in it to light her way in the darkness, just like brave Saint Lucia. In her hands she carries a tray of coffee and Lucia buns to her family while they are still in bed.

Today, Swedish children often have a billy goat made of straw to guard the Christmas tree. He keeps away wicked spirits.

Even before Jesus was born, straw seemed to some to have some sort of special properties. Farmers, for instance, spread it over fields to make crops grow better. Because baby Jesus lay in a manger on straw, people began to use it for Christmas decorations for the Christmas tree. Other popular Christmas tree ornaments are little heart-shaped baskets which can be filled with candies.[80]

Tastes of the Season

Here's a quote from Charles Dickens' Christmas classic:

"The raisins were so plentiful and rare, the almonds so extremely white, the sticks of cinnamon so long and straight, the other spices so delicious, the candied fruits so caked and spotted with molten sugar as to make the coldest lookers-on feel faint and subsequently bilious. Nor was it that the figs were moist and pulpy, or that the French plums blushed in modest tartness from their highly-decorated boxes, or that everything was good to eat and in its Christmas dress. . . ."

The Early Church designated Christmas as a day of fasting and meditation. But this official position quickly met with opposition. After all, food and special occasions were fused in many traditions; why should Christmas be an exception? Most celebrants disregarded Church sanctions, although some honored meatless "fasts" during Advent.

The following are traditional international menus for Christmas Eve suppers:

DENMARK

Dinner begins with rice pudding, then goose with prune-apple stuffing, potatoes browned in sugar, and sweet red cabbage.

AUSTRIA

Fish soup, carp, potato salad, and sacher torte are served.

SICILY

A twenty-four hour fast precedes *Il Cenone*, an elaborate meal which may include as many as twenty fish dishes! Eel is a popular entrée. Seasonal vegetables, plaited breads, fresh fruit, spumoni, cookies, roasted chestnuts, hazelnuts, almonds, and walnuts are holiday favorites. Strong coffee are the finishing touch to this festive occasion

BOLIVIA

Picana—a stew consisting of three to four types of meat and several vegetables is traditionally served after Midnight Mass on Christmas Eve.

PERU

Pachamancha—pork, lamb, chicken, and potatoes are wrapped in banana leaves and cooked over heated stones.

NEW ZEALAND

Hanga—lamb is stuffed with sweet potato and pumpkin, then barbecued.

NORWAY

A home-brewed special Christmas beer is served with pork as the main Yule dish.

CZECHOSLOVAKIA

Masika—a fruit stew which accompanies plaited white Christmas bread.

THE UKRAINE

A twelve-course dinner commemorates the Twelve Apostles. The meal begins with *kutya*, boiled wheat with honey and poppy seed. After blessing this special dish, the head of the family takes a spoonful and throws it against the ceiling for good fortune.

ENGLAND

Plum pudding began as a frumentary (wheat boiled and seasoned with spices and sugar). It was a fasting dish, but over the years, meat, eggs, dried fruits, and liqueurs were added. The burning brandy on the plum symbolizes the sun's rebirth.

AMERICAN FRONTIER

One Christmas feast on the American frontier featured:
Roast wild goose
Potatoes, turnips, and bread
Boiled buffalo rump
Boiled buffalo calf
A dish of dried moose nose
White fish fried in buffalo marrow
Buffalo tongue
Beaver tail[81]

It Came Upon the Midnight Clear

By Maymie R. Krythe

The Origin and development of our modern Christmas

*W*hen the angels appeared to the wondering shepherds, as they kept watch over their sheep, in the fields near Bethlehem, the celestial chorus sang "that glorious song of old," "Glory to God in the highest, and on earth peace, good will toward men." So began our most beloved religious festival Christmas, or Christes Mass. Now, all over the world, this holiday is celebrated in various ways, under such names as *KerstMisse* in Holland; Noel in France; *Il Natale* in Italy; *Welknachten* in Germany; and *El Natal* in Spain.

A celebration, at the time of the winter solstice, when all were looking forward to the coming of spring, was not an original idea with the Christians. For, many years before Christ's birth, other religious groups had held festivals (connected with the earth's fertility) at this same season. The Romans, for example, observed the lavish Saturnalia honoring Saturn, their god of agriculture—from the middle of December to the beginning of the new year. They exchanged gifts, and indulged in much eating, drinking, gaming, and visiting. Masked revelers on the streets often went to great excess during this riotous celebration.

Since primitive peoples realized their dependence upon the sun as the source of light and life, sun worship was prevalent among them. In Persia at the winter solstice, they observed a notable feast to show their reverence for the sun, and they kindled great fires in homage to Mithra, their deity of light.

In Northern Europe, the pagan Teutonic tribes (whose new year began at the time of the winter solstice) met at that period, to honor their "All Father," Woden (or Odin). After gathering their harvests, they slaughtered animals for meat during the following months. This was the natural time for feasting and general rejoicing. By the light of bonfires, they consumed quantities of food and drink during their "Yuletide" season, the rebirth of the sun.

When Emperor Constantine established Christianity as the state religion of the Roman Empire, the persecution of the Christians came to an end. At first, Christ's birthday was not observed by His followers, for the Church fathers did not want this sacred occasion put on a par with pagan carnivals. One official, Origen, especially declared against such a practice, asserting that it was sinful to keep Christ's birthday "as though He were a King Pharaoh."

Although in the early centuries of the Christian era the exact date of the nativity was not known, by the third century some had been observing the event on these varying dates: January 6, February 2, March 25, April 19, May 20, and November 7. (At this period there were five different systems of reckoning time.)

Finally, according to St. Chrysostomat at the request of St. Cyril of Jerusalem, Julius I (Pope or Bishop of Rome from A.D. 337 to 352) made an investigation into the matter of the date. In A.D. 350, December 25 was set as the most probable time. The Feast of the Nativity was first observed on this day at Rome, perhaps in 353; and from then on the custom spread eastward.

About a century later (440) the Pope at Jerusalem also accepted this ruling, as did most of the other Christians, except the Armenians, who still observe Christmas on January 6. Various scholars had wanted the date established as January 1, March 21, March 29, April 9, or September 29. Although authorities did not agree and this time may not be the correct one, the world will no doubt continue to celebrate the holy festival on December 25.

It is interesting to note that different sources have suggested reasons why the early Church officials selected this particular date. Many of the Roman soldiers were adherents of Mithraism, a religion that for a time was a strong rival to Christianity in the Empire. Its most important feast day, Dies Solis Invicti Nati (Birth of the Unconquered Sun), occurred on December 25. Also, the Roman Saturnalia came at this time, as did the Jewish Feast of Dedication of the Temple. The latter, one of their most important sacred days, commemorated the cleansing of the temple after its profanation by Antiochus Epiphanes in the second century.

The Church authorities may have set the date of Christ's birth to correspond to celebrations already in vogue through earlier beliefs. Perhaps they thought it wise to give a sacred meaning to pagan observances, rather than antagonize new converts by doing away completely with old customs. For instance, instead of thanking a heathen deity for the rebirth of the year, the Christians were inspired to show their gratitude to the one and only true God.

Pope Gregory once wrote St. Augustine, advising him about the wisest way of converting the Anglo-Saxons. The prelate was in favor of allowing them to continue their heathen practice of slaughtering oxen, but to do so to the glory of God, rather than to Woden, as had formerly been their practice.

But attempts to combine pagan and Christian events led to difficulties. In Rome, for example, where the Saturnalian ideas still were strong at this season, many Christians were guilty of conduct frowned upon by the Church. St. Gregory (who died in 389) urged his people to celebrate Christmas "after a heavenly and not an earthly manner"; and he warned them against excessive indulgence in gluttony, dancing, etc. Taking part in plays and other secular spectacles, dressing in grotesque costumes, such as animals' skins, were also forbidden.

The actions of some unruly converts in Rome had a strong influence, even on the distant Teutonic tribes. St. Boniface, "The Apostle to Germany," wrote to the Pope, complaining that his efforts were frustrated by the conduct some northern visitors had witnessed near the great Church of St. Peter at Rome.

This caused embarrassment to the prelate; and by repeated bans he tried to restrain Roman Christians from going to excess at the winter festival. And, as the early Church found itself unable to abolish former customs entirely, it did the next best thing; it took over certain ones, "Christianized" them after purging them of their three worst features, and incorporated them into the Christian observance of Christmas.

Such traditions as using greenery and candles, or other lights, for decorating homes and churches, bringing in and burning the Yule log, singing carols, giving presents, feasting happily together, amid general rejoicing—all these have become integral parts of our Yuletide festivities. Although, at first, Christians were supposed to observe the day of the nativity only as a religious holiday, gradually secular elements were added. Therefore, our modern Christmas, in which varied elements are successfully combined, is indeed "the feast of all mankind."

In the United States we now have an unusually complicated celebration, one that is truly "a strange medley of Christian and pagan rites." For our land was settled by men of differing religious ideas, men from various countries, each of which had its own characteristic customs and traditions.

Before reviewing the influence of other lands on our holiday festival, it may be interesting to note how the first Christmas was spent here in the New World by a white man—its discoverer, Christopher Columbus. This has been described by Vincent Edwards, who tells us the explorer had planned to spend the feast day in 1492 with an Indian chief, ruler of the island of Haiti. But on Christmas Eve, Columbus's flagship, the Santa Maria, was wrecked on a coral reef, so he and his men had to go aboard the Niña.

At once the chief sent natives to remove all the valuables from the wreck. Then on Christmas the Spaniards dined with the Indian ruler. Columbus had planned to start the first Spanish colony here, so he built a small fortress on the island naming it La Navidad (the nativity) as they had been wrecked at this season.

Since so many early American settlers came here from "Merrie England," we are naturally greatly indebted to her for many of our cherished Yuletide traditions.

In England—so the story goes—Christmas was first observed as a holiday in A.D. 521, when King Arthur celebrated his victory in retaking York. Many guests sat at his famous Round Table, and enjoyed a bounteous meal. They were entertained by wandering minstrels, who sang of the mighty deeds of their national heroes. Jugglers, harpists, and pipe players added to the enjoyment; also such pastimes as gambling, playing dice or backgammon, along with hunting, hawking, and jousting, were popular when the Anglo-Saxons got together for their winter celebrations. At this season, the council, or Witenagemot met to attend to affairs of state, wherever the king and his courtiers happened to be.

During the ninth century, seven petty kingdoms in Britain were united under Alfred the Great, who annually set aside twelve days for Yule festivities. In 878, while he and his court were feasting in lavish style, their enemies, the Danes, suddenly rode through the land of the West Saxons and made a surprise attack. Alfred's army was scattered; and the King, with a small band, fled to the forest. According to one account, Alfred, in order to discover the Danish strength, disguised himself as a Christmas minstrel. He spent several days in their camp, where he pleased them with his ability as an entertainer, and left without their learning his identity.

After the Normans had conquered England in 1066, they built great castles and introduced their feudal system with its strict division of people into various classes, from the king and his luxury-loving nobles, down to the meanest serf. Christmas became gayer than ever before; each great lord kept open house; and food and drink were given to all who entered his walls during the holy season. This entertaining and revelry continued until Twelfth Night, January 6.

In the spacious manor halls, great fires blazed on wide hearths, lighting the walls, high ceilings, and decorations of holiday greenery. The "Lord of Misrule," a person who was well paid for his services, presided over his subjects during the Yule period with absolute power. He planned the entertainment with the assistance of jesters, mummers, and musicians, who played on their bagpipes, harps, drums, fiddles, or flageolets. Games, such as snapdragon, dancing, and caroling were the order of the time.

During the Middle Ages, Christmas was England's most popular holiday with everyone, from the king to beggars, taking part. All who could do so quit work, and gave themselves entirely to pleasure. And no people ever entered more heartily into the joys of the Yule season than the Britons did.

Christmas was elaborately observed by English monarchs of this epoch; and several outstanding events occurred on the holiday. On Christmas, 1085, William the Conqueror met with his Great Council, when they decided to make that noted survey of England contained in the *Domesday Book*. Henry II was crowned on Christmas, 1154; and on the same date in 1214, barons demanded that King John sign the Magna Carta. During the Yule of 1348, Edward III established the senior order of chivalry, that of the famous Garter. A few years later, this same ruler had, as his Christmas guests, the kings of Scotland and Cyprus.

Tournaments, staged at the winter holidays such as Richard II gave for his visitor, the king of Armenia, were lavish and expensive affairs. Holiday entertainment also included the presentation of sumptuous pageants and masques, put on by actors, dancers, and tumblers. Some of the productions were of religious origin; but the performers often added bits of comic relief. In one popular play, the shepherd Mak stole a sheep and hid it in a child's bed in his home. When his fellow shepherds discovered his deceit, they tossed Mak in a canvas; this horseplay, of course, delighted the audiences of that period.

The English stage owes much to early holiday customs, for the first British comedy was written for a Yuletide performance. Also the earliest tragedy, *Gorbuduc,* was performed at Christmas, 1561. During the reigns of the Tudors, holiday productions reached their zenith. Since Henry VIII loved buffoonery, he furnished the actors with expensive costumes, paid them well, and encouraged his subjects in their fondness for theatrical entertainment.

His daughter, Queen Elizabeth, organized companies of actors, and sponsored Christmas plays at Greenwich and at Hampton Court; thus the modern English stage got its start. In addition to court productions, it had, for some time, been customary for the lawyers (members of the Inns of Court) to put on expensive stage performances at Christmastime.

Similar celebrations continued under the Stuart Kings; but the Reformation was having its effect. The Calvinists declared that observing Christ's birthday was a human invention. They disapproved of it, not only because of its pagan origin, but because of the excesses to which too many Christmas celebrants went. In some places, groups of holiday revelers, under their "Lord of Misrule," even took possession of towns and caused much trouble for the authorities.

When the Civil War broke out (1642) and the Puritans came into power under Oliver Cromwell, their ministers preached strongly against Christmas observance as a "heathen" practice. They asserted that Christ would not have approved of it, for it merely furnished excuse for wrongdoing.

As soon as the new regime felt secure in its position, Parliament passed an act forbidding the celebration of Christ's nativity and other religious festivals, including Whitsuntide and Easter. Everyone was ordered to go on with his work as usual; shops were to stay open on Christmas Day; and no one was allowed to light Christmas candles or to eat holiday cakes. In many places on Christmas Eve the town criers went around and called out loudly so that all might hear, "No Christmas! No Christmas!"

This edict caused rioting on the streets between the two factions—in Ealing and Canterbury, for example. But many Englishmen continued to observe the day in spite of the Puritanic law. Some ministers, with members of their congregations, were actually arrested for attending services on Christmas. The Puritans went about their daily business on former Church holidays; and their Parliament met on Christmas Day as usual.

With the Restoration of the monarchy under Charles II (1660), old Yuletide customs "emerged from hiding." However, from this time on, holiday observance never reached its former extravagance. During his exile, Charles had known poverty, so he discouraged his lords from putting on the expensive pre-Cromwellian masques. Gradually the "Lord of Misrule" disappeared from the scene; the "Age of Cards" arrived; and this became a favorite holiday pastime. Some of the nobles still kept open house for their tenants; people of the middle class enjoyed their Christmas dinners; and in remote rural districts many of the old customs continued in use.

A characteristically British holiday tradition that survives today came into existence during the eighteenth century—the Christmas pantomime.

In December, 1717, Edmund Rich, who held the license for the theater at Lincoln's Inn Fields, put on *Harlequin Executed*, the first English pantomime. During the next forty-five years—until his death in 1761—Rich kept producing these annual performances with their fantastic stories, spectacular stage effects, singing, and dancing.

In the Victorian period Charles Dickens, who reveled in Christmas lore and traditions of his native England, revived former customs, and many of his countrymen joined him. Dickens' influence, through his incomparable *Christmas Carol* and other holiday classics, was also felt strongly here in the United States.

With the settlement of America by both Puritan and Cavalier types, naturally the attitudes of each group in regard to Yuletide traditions and observances had their effects upon the development of our chief holiday.

The Puritans, of course, brought their hatred of such festivities with them. That first Christmas on the bleak New England shore must have been a gloomy one, with all merriment banned. The men went ashore from the Mayflower to fell and carry lumber, and worked the entire day. Governor Bradford reported in his diary that on "ye 25th day began to erect ye first house for common use to receive them and their goods."

Next year, 1621, the governor again insisted that work be continued as usual, and permitted no religious observance. That Christmas Day, some young men who had come on the Fortune (after the arrival of the Mayflower) excused themselves from work for religious reasons. Later that day, when the governor found them on the street, playing ball, he became very angry and stopped their sport, declaring it went against *his* conscience to see them at play while others were laboring. He added that if it were "a matter of devotion," they should stay indoors. (Even though the Pilgrims did not take any notice of Christmas, their Thanksgiving Day with its feasting and sports, really took its place, when they joined in festive celebrations with friendly Indian neighbors.)

In 1659, because of their continued enmity toward holiday joys, the Pilgrims passed this law:

Whosoever shall be found observing any such day as Christmas and the like, either by forbearing labor, feasting, or any other way upon such account as aforesaid, every such person so offending shall pay for each Dense five shillings as a fine to the country.

Despite this decree, there was some celebrating in Massachusetts, for members of the Church of England were also settling there. After a long struggle the law was repealed in 1681. Five years later Governor Andros conducted a service in the Boston Town Hall; and this may have been the first legal Christmas held in the colony. However, the holiday did not become lawful in Massachusetts until 1856; and New England did not enter wholeheartedly into Christmas celebrations until late in the nineteenth century.

In marked contrast to these stern Puritans was the attitude of the jolly Dutch settlers in nearby New Amsterdam, later New York. They loved Yuletide feasting and merriment; and from their "Sant Nikolass" evolved our modern Santa Claus.

Christmas has been properly observed in Virginia from the time of Captain John Smith, when he and his men feasted on fish, oysters, and game they had caught. As the colony grew and prospered, visiting and gay festivities went on at the stately colonial mansions. Many of the settlers in Virginia were descendants of the pleasure-loving Cavaliers. So from "Merrie England" they brought with them such holiday customs as ringing bells, burning a Yule log, dining elaborately, dancing, playing games, and singing carols. Their homes and churches were lavishly decorated with garlands of evergreens, while hundreds of candles furnished illumination for long-remembered holiday balls, where handsomely dressed ladies and gentlemen danced the stately minuet.

(During the Revolution, General Washington knew that the German mercenary soldiers, the Hessians, whom George III had sent across the Atlantic to fight his rebellious colonists, would be celebrating Christmas as they had done at their homes in the Old World. So he took advantage of this fact, crossed the Delaware in 1776, and attacked the redcoats while they were sleeping off the effects of too much holiday food and drink.)

Today, in beautifully restored Williamsburg, Virginia, the gracious eighteenth century customs have been revived. Many visitors join with the townspeople in Yule log ceremonies, candlelight concerts, square dancing, and caroling. And on Christmas Day open house is held at the old Raleigh Tavern; and at other hotels in this unique city, delicious Southern dishes are served with the same grace that distinguished the Christmas dinners of colonial days.

In the South many persons continue the characteristic Yule habit of shooting firearms or firecrackers. Some sources say this custom originated in early days when settlers wished to send Christmas greetings to distant neighbors. Others believe the idea goes back to the ancient habit of making noises to frighten away evil spirits.

In Theriot, Louisiana, the holiday is kept in the middle of February, for during the regular Christmas season the men are away on the marshes trapping. In some parts of the South, "Old Christmas" is celebrated on January fifth, or seventh, a date related to the visit of the Magi, or Wise Men, to the Holy Babe.

During the holidays, Florida becomes closely connected with all the other states through the mails. Near Orlando there is a small town, Christmas, with about 250 inhabitants. It was formerly a fort and was so named because it was completed on Christmas, 1835. At one time its postmistress, Mrs. Juanita Tucker, kept busy stamping cards, letters, and packages (sent from all parts of our country) with "Christmas, Florida," and remailing them. In one year alone, her small post office handled more than 300,000 pieces of mail. And to live up to its name, the town has a permanent Christmas tree set up, with weatherproof ornaments.

In Pennsylvania, many persons observe the old holiday traditions of their Moravian ancestors, while, at various places in the Middle West, Scandinavian customs still prevail. And the same special dishes are enjoyed that were served generations ago by their European ancestors.

The Spanish influence in our great Southwest has strongly affected Christmas celebrations. An ancient Spanish nativity play, *Los Pastores*, reached this section from Spain, by way of Old Mexico. In its complete form, it took about five hours for one performance, and was usually given out of doors. It has been played in Texas and in Los Angeles.

Los Pastores (The Shepherds) is an old miracle play with its theme the eternal struggle between Good and Evil. One of its chief features is the attempt of the Devil (El Diablo) to prevent the shepherds' going to Bethlehem to worship the Christ Child. But with the aid of the Archangel, St. Michael, the Devil is put to rout; and the shepherds reach the stable, kneel devoutly before El Nina, and present Him their gifts.

Before the American conquest of California, *Los Pastores* was very popular in the pueblo of Los Angeles. Men and boys from a nearby rancho practiced their parts for weeks before Christmas. Then, on Christmas Eve, they came into town, stopped at various homes around the Plaza, and gave their play, often adding some humor to the speeches. These performances continued until Twelfth Night in town and at outlying ranchos.

Las Posadas (The Lodgings) is one episode of *Los Pastores*, depicting the journey of Mary and Joseph from Nazareth to Bethlehem, and their fruitless search for an inn in the crowded town. In recent years this play has been a special feature of the holidays on Olvera Street in Los Angeles, beginning on December sixteenth and continuing until Christmas Eve. Each evening four Mexicans carry a small cart, containing wax figures of Joseph and Mary. They are followed by a procession of men, women, and children in colorful garb with lighted candles and gaily decorated shepherds' crooks.

When they knock at a door, they chant "The Litany of Loretto," and ask for admission, which at first is refused. When the owner finally relents, all enter and kneel before the manger, or *nacimiento*. This pageant is repeated at a different home each night; after the religious ceremony, the evening is spent playing games, dancing and feasting together. On Christmas Eve the climax is reached when an image of the Christ Child is gently placed in the empty cradle.

At Mexican Christmas parties in our Southwest a popular feature is the *pinata*, a large earthenware jug, filled with candy and nuts. It hangs on a rope from the ceiling; and a blindfolded child is given a bat, and allowed three "tries" at breaking the *pinata*. As the jug can be pulled up and down by the rope, the game often continues for some time, before the youngster succeeds in breaking it. There is a wild scramble when the children get down on the floor to gather the goodies scattered over it.

So, today, wherever you travel over this great country, you'll find interesting, varied customs and ways of celebrating our modern Christmas. All these traditions are a valuable heritage from different periods of time and from faraway places; and they combine to make our Yuletide unique. Here in the United States all kinds of individuals from widely diverse backgrounds join in homage to the Christ Child.[82]   ✳

The Joy

New

of New Life

FIRST SHEPHERD: Amos?

SECOND SHEPHERD: Yeah, Obie?

FIRST SHEPHERD: Did you really think the job would pan out like this?

SECOND SHEPHERD: Whataya mean Obie?

FIRST SHEPHERD: I'm not sure. But answer me this, aren't you tired of mucking around with this mangy bunch of sheep?

SECOND SHEPHERD: It's better than donkeys, Obediah.

FIRST SHEPHERD: Yeah, but . . . Amos?

SECOND SHEPHERD: Uh huh?

FIRST SHEPHERD: Did'ya ever wish you could start all over again?

SECOND SHEPHERD: Ya mean, like get born all over again?

FIRST SHEPHERD: Sort of, I guess. . . .

SECOND SHEPHERD: I can't see how. . . .

ANGEL: Today a baby has been born in Bethlehem. He will be your Savior, and make all things new!

FIRST SHEPHERD: For such a Savior I have waited all my life. Now, that's real newness!

Comfort, comfort my people,

says your God. . . .

Prepare the way for the LORD;

Make straight in the wilderness a

highway for our God. . . .

And the glory of the Lord will be

revealed, and all mankind

together will see it.

ISAIAH 40:1, 3, 5 NIV

The Door

"He that entereth in by the door is the shepherd of the sheep."
He came to us
Himself a Star!
He spoke to us
Himself a song!

The entrance to His place of birth
    Was by a little Door,
So humble all might find Him there,
    The wise, the rich, the poor.

A little Door, where cows had passed,
Opened to a King!
The Shepherds and the Wise Men bent
    To see so fair a thing.

The talking trees upon the Door
    Their chequered shadows cast
"Ah, who shall know, and who shall know,
    How He will go at last?"

Somewhere upon a far-off hill
At Christmas time,
    At Christmas time,
A little Door creaks open still,—
    It opens still.[83]

HELEN SLACK WICKENDEN

Many poets have brought the truth

of Easter into their Christmas verse.

To the spiritually minded Bethlehem and

Jerusalem cannot be separated.

The purpose of Bethlehem was Jerusalem.

The purpose of Jerusalem was new life.

A Nativity

RUDYARD KIPLING

The Babe was laid in the Manger
Between the gentle kine—
All safe from cold and danger—
"But it was not so with mine,"
(With mine! With mine!)

"Is it well with the child, is it well?"
The waiting mother prayed.
"For I know not how he fell,
And I know not where he is laid."

A star stood forth in Heaven;
The Watchers ran to see
The Sign of the Promise given—
"But there comes no sign to me."
(To me! To me!)

"My child died in the dark.
Is it well with the child, is it well?
There was none to tend him or mark,
And I know not how he fell."

The Cross was raised on high;
The Mother grieved beside—
"But the Mother saw Him die
And took Him when He died."
(He died! He died!)

"Seemly and undefiled
His burial-place was made—
Is it well, is it well with the child?
For I know not where he is laid."

On the dawning of Easter Day
Come Mary Magdalene;
But the stone was rolled away,
And the Body was not within—
(Within! Within!)

"Ah, who will answer my word?"
The broken mother prayed.
"They have taken away my Lord,
And I know not where He is laid."
The Star stands forth in Heaven.
The watchers watch in vain
For Sign of the Promise given
Of peace on earth again—
(Again! Again!)

"But I know for Whom he fell"—
The steadfast mother smiled,
"Is it well with the child—is it well?
It is well—it is well with the child."[84]

* * *

Can any of us live through

the fun and fervor of Christmas

and not feel again the newness that

the Babe of Bethlehem brought to the world?

To your family? To your heart?

* * *

Christmas Night

BY MAX LUCADO

It's Christmas night. The house is quiet. Even the crackle is gone from the fireplace. Warm coals issue a lighthouse glow in the darkened den. Stockings hang empty on the mantle. The tree stands naked in the corner. Christmas cards, tinsel, and memories remind Christmas night of Christmas Day.

It's Christmas night. What a day it has been! Spiced tea. Santa Claus. Cranberry sauce. "Thank you so much." "You shouldn't have!" "Grandma is on the phone." Knee deep wrapping paper. "It just fits." Flashing cameras.

It's Christmas night. The girls are in bed. Jenna dreams of her talking Big Bird and clutches her new purse. Andrea sleeps in her new Santa pajamas.

It's Christmas night. The tree that only yesterday grew from soil made of gifts, again grows from the Christmas tree stand. Presents are now possessions. Wrapping paper is bagged and in the dumpster. The dishes are washed and leftover turkey awaits next week's sandwiches.

It's Christmas night. The last of the carolers appeared on the ten o'clock news. The last of the apple pie was eaten by my brother-in-law. And the last of the Christmas albums have been stored away having dutifully performed their annual rendition of chestnuts, white Christmases, and red-nosed reindeers.

It's Christmas night.

The midnight hour has chimed and I should be asleep, but I'm awake. I'm kept awake by one stunning thought. The world was different this week. It was temporarily transformed.

The magical dust of Christmas glittered on the cheeks of humanity ever so briefly, reminding us of what is worth having and what we were intended to be. We forgot our compulsion with winning, wooing, and warring. We put away our ladders and ledgers, we hung up our stopwatches and weapons. We stepped off our racetracks and roller coasters and looked outward toward the star of Bethlehem.

It's the season to be jolly because, more that at any other time, we think of Him. More than in any other season, His name is on our lips.

And the results? For a few precious hours our heavenly yearnings intermesh and we become a chorus. A ragtag chorus of longshoremen, Boston lawyers, illegal immigrants, housewives, and a thousand other peculiar persons who are banking that Bethlehem's mystery is in reality, a reality. "Come and behold Him" we sing, stirring even the sleepiest of shepherds and pointing them toward the Christ-child.

For a few precious hours, He is beheld. Christ the Lord. Those who pass the year without seeing Him, suddenly see Him. People who have been accustomed to using His name in vain, pause to use it in praise. Eyes, now free of the blinders of self, marvel at His majesty.

All of a sudden He's everywhere.

In the grin of the policeman as he drives the paddy wagon full of presents to the orphanage.

In the twinkle in the eyes of the Taiwanese waiter as he tells of his upcoming Christmas trip to see his children.

In the emotion of the father who is too thankful to finish the dinner table prayer.

He's in the tear of the mother as she welcomes home her son from overseas.

He's in the heart of the man who spent Christmas morning on skid row giving away cold baloney sandwiches and warm wishes.

He's in the solemn silence of the crowd of shopping mall shoppers as the elementary school chorus sings "Away in a Manger."

Emmanuel. He is with us. God came near.

It's Christmas night. In a few hours the cleanup will begin—lights will come down, trees will be thrown out. Size thirty-six will be exchanged for size forty, eggnog will be on sale for half price. Soon life will be normal again. December's generosity will become January's payments and the magic will begin to fade.

But for the moment, the magic is still in the air. Maybe that's why I'm still awake. I want to savor the spirit just a bit more. I want to pray that those who beheld Him today will look for Him next August. And I can't help but linger on one fanciful thought: if He can do so much with such timid prayers offered in December, how much more could He do if we thought of Him every day?[85]

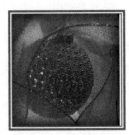

I Heard a Bird Sing

I heard a bird sing
    In the dark of December
A magical thing
    And sweet to remember.

"We are nearer to Spring
    Than we were in September,"
I heard a bird sing
    In the dark of December.[86]

OLIVER HERFORD

Born Anew

The legend tells that when Jesus was born
the sun danced in the sky, the aged trees
straightened themselves and put on leaves
and sent forth the fragrance of blossoms.
These are the symbols of what takes place
in our hearts when the Christ Child is born
anew in each of us.

ROBERT LOUIS STEVENSON

Christmas Prayer

O God, our loving Father,
help us rightly to remember the birth of Jesus,
that we may share in the song of the angels,
the gladness of the shepherds,
and the worship of the wise men. . . .
May the Christmas morning make us happy
to be thy children
and the Christmas evening bring us to our beds
with grateful thoughts,
forgiving and forgiven, for Jesus' sake.

Amen

ROBERT LOUIS STEVENSON

The Night Amahl Met Jesus

BY PAUL M. MILLER

For many of us one of the great joys of Christmas is one of the theatre or concert hall masterpieces. Young dance students anticipate their opportunities as *Nutcracker* mice or soldiers. Actors look to community stagings of Dickens' *A Christmas Carol*, while *Messiah* performances draw the voice student or instrumentalist.

My most memorable Christmas performance opportunity happened quite a few years ago, but oh, I wish it would happen again. Oh, I enjoy narrating church cantatas and reading the background Scriptures for Handel's *Messiah*, I have no desire to play Ebenezer Scrooge—but I do want to direct another staging of Gian Carlo Mennoti's Christmas opera, *Amahl and the Night Visitors*. The one and only time I've been involved with an *Amahl* production is when I directed the staging and acting for a church performance in Berkeley, California. Thereby hangs the story that is the basis of this piece.

While a graduate student in Berkeley, I gave two months of my life to help breathe life into an amateur cast of actor-singers consisting of a twelve year old small-for-his-age boy with an unchanged voice who played Amahl the crippled shepherd boy; his overworked mother; the Three Wise Men with their gold and gifts; the Magi's servant; and a dozen dancing villagers, most of whom were rhythmically deficient.

To this day I recall the second *Amahl* dress rehearsal. Mother and the Kings had just sang their dramatic "I know a child the color of wheat, the color of Gold" duet, when I called for a ten minute break. Our Amahl. Bobby Cole was curled up on his pallet feigning sleep. When he heard me call for ten, he jumped up and bounded over to me.

"Can we talk, Paul?"

"Sure, Bobby. What's on your mind?"

Bobby suddenly looked bashful. He projected such confidence on stage, that it was easy to forget he was your typical junior high kid with all the usual questions.

"Well, you know I'm playing Amahl . . ."

"I know, Bobby."

"You know how I'm . . . rather Amahl is healed and can walk again?"

"I remember, Bobby."

"Yeah, I know you do. Anyway, could this really happen?"

"What?"

"You know, did God really do that for Amahl?"

"Well, this is only a story, but God has always been able to do things like that."

I glanced at my watch. "Bobby?" I asked, "Can we finish this later? I need to get the rehearsal started."

We finished working through the scene where Amahl asks the hard-of-hearing King if he has anything in his box of gifts that could heal a crippled boy, and the hard-of-hearing King replies, "Eh?" causing Amahl to reply, "Oh, nothing," as he hobbles away on his crutch. This is a heart wrenching scene, second only to the boy and his mother's "Goodbye" duet, when he joins the three Kings to take his crutch as a gift to the Christ child.

The rehearsal hall emptied quickly—except for Bobby Cole. He stood over at the humming Coke machine, a target of the music director's ire, because "it hummed in the wrong key."

"Kinda tough being the only kid in the show?" I asked, dropping fifteen cents in the machine.

"No, I like talking to adults," Bobby answered wiping Pepsi off his mouth. "That's why I need to ask you something."

"What's on your mind, Bob?"

"I want God to help me like he helped Amahl."

"Whata you mean, Bobby?"

Bobby, set his Pepsi bottle down and walked over to the prop table, where he picked up his crutch. He put it under his shoulder and hobbled over to me like he did in the show.

"I want to give Christ a gift this Christmas."

"Oh? What do you have in mind?"

Bobby looked down at his shoes. Then kicked at a spot on the floor. Finally, he looked up at me, and with tears in his eyes he announced, "I want to give Him me!"

I suggested, "Why don't we have a prayer?" We went up into the church sanctuary and knelt side by side. Bobby opened up a reservoir of guilt and shame. Then I helped him turn the weight of his guilt and shame over to Jesus Christ, not the baby in the manger, but the man who died on a cross and was brought back to life on Easter.

The youngster's weekend performances were outstanding. The *Oakland Tribune* praised the production, especially Bobby Cole. (Not a word about the direction.) When a reporter from one of the Berkeley papers asked Bobby what he got out of his *Amahl* performances, he immediately answered, with a wink at me, "God's love." Then when pressed, he provided the expected answers.

That summer I directed Bobby again. This time it was an outdoor children's theatre performance of "The Wizard of Oz" in Mosswood Park. Bobby was one of the Munchkins who welcomed Dorothy on the other side of the rainbow. Today Bobby is a middle-aged man living with his wife Amy in Lafayette, California. Since my family lived in the next town in Contra Costa county, I've visited the Coles in their home. On the first visit I was surprised to discover a framed photo of Bobby as Amahl hanging in his den.

"It's a reminder of what happened to me at Christmas in 1956. I have *Amahl* and you to thank for my new life."

Hush, All Ye Sounds of Love

Hush, all ye sounds of war,
   Ye nations all be still,
A voice of heav'nly joy steals over vale and hill,
   O hear the angels sing the captive world's release,
This day is born in Bethlehem the Prince of Peace.

No more divided be,
   Ye families of men,
Old enmity forget, old friendships knit again,
   In the new year of God let brother's love increase,
This day is born in Bethlehem the Prince of Peace.

WILLIAM H. DRAPER

The excuse of the innkeeper in this poem reflects the universal rejection of the Christ of Christmas.

The Inn That
Missed Its Chance

AMOS R. WELLS

(The Landlord speaks—A.D. 28)
What could be done? The inn was full of folks:
His honor Marcus Lucius, and his scribes
Who made the census; honorable men
From Farthest Galilee, come hitherward
To be enrolled; high ladies and their lords;
The rich, the rabbis, such a noble throng
As Bethlehem had never seen before
And may not see again. And there they were,
Close-herded with their servants, till the inn
Was like a hive at swarming time, and I
I was fairly crazed among them.

Could I know
That they were so important? Just the two,
No servants, just a workman sort of a man,
Leading a donkey, and his wife thereon
Drooping and pale,—I saw them not myself,
My servants must have driven them away;
But had I seen them,—how was I to know?
Were inns to welcome stragglers, up and down
In all our towns from Beersheba to Dan,
Till He should come? And how were men to know?
There was a sign, they say, a heavenly light

Resplendent: but I had no time for stars,
And there were songs of angels in the air
Out on the hills; but how was I to hear
Amid the thousand clamors of an inn?

Of course, if I had known them, who they were,
And who was He that should be born that night—
For now I learn that they will make him King,
A second David, who will ransom us
From these Philistine Romans—who but he
That feeds an army with a loaf of bread,
And if a soldier falls, he touches him
And up he leaps, uninjured?—Had I known,
I would have turned the whole inn upside down,
His honor, Marcus Lucius, and the rest,
And sent them all to stables.

So you have seen him, stranger, and perhaps
Again may see him? Prithee say for me
I did not know; and if he comes again,
As he will surely come, with retinue,
And banners, and an army—tell him my Lord
That all my inn is his to make amends.
(Exit Traveler)
Alas, alas! to miss a chance like that!
This inn that might be chief among them all—
The birthplace of the MESSIAH—had I known![87]

＊　＊　＊

Just because a wilting tree is on the curb

with fluttering wisps of tinsel, you

cannot leave the Babe of Bethlehem in

the manger. He became a grown man,

Who gave his life so the world might

have eternal life. That includes you.

＊　＊　＊

After Christmas

Gone is that errant star. The shepherds rise
And, packed in buses, go their separate ways
To bench and counter where their flocks will graze
On winter grass, no bonus of sweet hay.
The myrrh, the frankincense fade from memory:
Another year of waiting for the day.

Still in his palace Herod waits for orders;
Arrests, an edict, more judicial murders,
New taxes, reinforcements for the borders.
Still high priests preach decorum, rebels rage
At Caesar battening on their heritage
And a few prophets mourn a godless age.

The Magi in three chauffeur-driven cars
Begin their homeward journey round the wars,
Each to his capital, the stocks and shares,
Whose constellations, flickering into place,
Must guide him through a vaster wilderness
Than did the star absconded out of space.

The golden thread winds back upon the spool.
A bird's dry carcass and an empty bottle
Beside the dustbin, vomit of goodwill,
Pale streets, pale faces and a paler sky;
A paper Bethlehem, a rootless tree
Soon to be stripped, dismembered, put away,

Burnt on the grate . . . and dressed in candlelight
When next the shepherds turn their flocks about,
The three wise kings recall their second state
And from the smaller circle of the year,
Axle and weighted hub, look high and far
To pierce their weekday heaven that hides the star.

MICHAEL HAMBURGER

Loving Father, help us remember the birth of Jesus, that we may share in the song of the angels, the gladness of the shepherds, and the worship of the wise men.

Close the door of hate and open the door of love all over the world.

Let kindness come with every gift and good desires with every greeting.

Deliver us from evil by the blessing which Christ brings, and teach us to be merry with clear hearts.

May the Christmas morning make us happy to be Thy children, and the Christmas evening bring us to our beds with grateful thoughts, forgiving and forgiven, for Jesus sake. Amen!

ROBERT LOUIS STEVENSON

O holy Child of Bethlehem!

Descend to us, we pray,

Cast out our sin, and enter in,

Be born in us today.

PHILLIPS BROOKS

ENDNOTES
* * *

1. From *A Celebration of Christmas* (Gillian Cooke, Ed.), "Shepherds, Shake Off Your Drowsy Sleep" by Eleanor Farjeon in *The Oxford Book of Carols* (New York, NY: G. P. Putnam's Sons, 1980).

2. From *The Finishing Touch*, "A Christmas List" by Charles R. Swindoll (Dallas, TX: Word Publishing, 1994).

3. From *Christmas* (Robert H. Schauffler, Ed.), *"A Christmas Carol"* by James Russell Lowell (New York, NY: Dodd, Mead, & Co., 1958).

4. From *Little House in the Ozarks: A Laura Ingalls Wilder Sampler, The Rediscovered Writings*, "Christmas When I Was Sixteen" by Laura Ingalls Wilder (Nashville, TN: Thomas Nelson, Inc., 1991 by Stephen W. Hines, Ed.).

5. *"The Meaning of Christmas"* by Francis Cardinal Spellman (Pleasantville, NY: Reader's Digest Association, Inc.), p. 423.

6. From *Wrappings* (A Monologue for Gabriel), "The Word Is Given" by Lawrence G. Enscoe (Reprinted by permission of Lillenas Publishing Co., Kansas City, MO, 1969, 1993).

7. From *A Family Christmas*, "Mr. Edwards Meets Santa Claus" by Laura Ingalls Wilder (Pleasantville, NY: Reader's Digest Association, Inc., 1984), 208-215.

8. From *"Let's Keep Christmas"* (A Sermon), with Introduction by Catherine Marshall (McGraw-Hill Book Co., 1952, 1953).

9. From *Christ and the Fine Arts* (Cynthia Pearl Maus, Ed.), "The Shepherd Speaks" by John Erskine (New York, NY: Harper & Brothers, Publishers, 1938).

10. From *Christ and the Fine Arts* (Cynthia Pearl Maus, Ed.), "How Far to Bethlehem?" by Madeleine Sweeny Miller (New York, NY: Harper & Brothers, Publishers, 1938).

11. From *Christmas in My Heart* (Joe Wheeler, Compiler & Editor), "A Gift from the Heart" by Norman Vincent Peale (New York, NY: Doubleday, 1996), 82-88.

12. From *Masterpieces of Religious Verse* (James Dalton Morrison, Ed.), "The Road to Bethlehem" by Watson Kirkconnell (New York, NY: Harper & Brothers, Publishers).

13. From *God Came Near* by Max Lucado, "Mary's Prayer" (Multnomah Press, 1987), 35-37.

14. From *Masterpieces of Religious Verse* (James Dalton Morrison, Ed.), "Judean Hills Are Holy" by William L. Stidger (New York, NY: Harper & Brothers, Publishers).

15. From *Masterpieces of Religious Verse* (James Dalton Morrison, Ed.), "Christmas Prayer" by Ralph Spaulding Cushman (New York, NY: Harper & Brothers, Publishers).

16. From *Christmas* (Robert H. Schauffler, Ed.), "An Offertory" by Mary Mapes Dodge (New York, NY: Dodd, Mead, & Co., 1958).

17. From *Ideals*, "Dear God" by Deborah Killip (Milwaukee, WI: Ideals Publishing Corp., 1956).

18. From *Christ and the Fine Arts* (Cynthia Pearl Maus, Ed.), "The Consecration of the Common Way" by Edwin Markham (New York, NY: Harper & Brothers, Publishers, 1938).

19. From *The Literature of Christmas*, "The Gift of the Magi" by O. Henry (Pleasantville, NY: Reader's Digest Association, Inc.), 113-117.

20. From *Ideals*, "Christmas Gifts" by Betty Cooke (Milwaukee, WI: Ideals Publishing Corp., 1976).

21. From *Christmas* (Robert Haven Schauffler, Ed.), "A Simple Bill of Fare for a Christmas Dinner" by H. H. (New York, NY: Dodd, Mead & Co., 1907, 1958), 223-225.

22. From *Ideals*, "And for as Long as I Can Remember" by Catherine Otten (Milwaukee, WI: Ideals Publishing Corp., 1976.)

23. From *Heart Throbs*, Vol. 2, "In the Glow of Christmas," by Joe Mitchell Chapple (New York, NY: Grosset & Dunlap, 1911), 93.

24. From *Christmas in My Heart* (Joe Wheeler, Compiler & Editor), "My Christmas Miracle" by Taylor Caldwell (New York, NY: Doubleday, 1996).

25. From *Thirty-Nine Christmas Ideals*, "The ABC's of Christmas" by Jeanne Blomquest (Milwaukee, WI: Ideals Publishing Corp.).

26. From *Christmas Tales for Reading Aloud* (Robert Lohan, Compiler & Adapter), "The Fir Tree" by Hans Christian Andersen (New York, NY: Stephen Daye Press, 1946, 1956).

27. From *A Celebration of Christmas* (Gillian Cooke, Ed.), "A Visit from St. Nicholas," Clement C. Moore (New York, NY: G. P. Putnam's Sons, 1980).

28. From *Sketches in Prose* (Robert Haven Schauffler, Ed.), "God Bless Us Every One" by James Whitcomb Riley (Bobbs-Merrill Co., 1900; Dodd, Mead & Co., New York, 1907, 1958).

29. From *One Thousand Beautiful Things* (Compiled by Marjorie Barrows), "Christmas in the Heart" by Rachel Field (Chicago, IL: Peoples Book Club, Inc., 1947), 414-420.

30. From *One Thousand Beautiful Things* (Compiled by Marjorie Barrows), "Christmas Morning" by Elizabeth Madox Roberts (Chicago, IL: Peoples Book Club, Inc., 1947).

31. From *A Christmas Sampler* (E. A. Crawford & Teresa Kennedy, Eds.), "Christmas Every Day" by William Dean Howells (New York, NY: Hyperion, 1992), 93-97.

32. From *Christmas Tales for Reading Aloud* (Robert Lohan, Compiler & Adapter), "The Life of Our Lord" by Charles Dickens (New York, NY: Stephen Daye Press, 1946, 1956), 21-23.

33. From *Happy Christmas* (William Kean Seymour & John Smith, Compilers), "The Trouble with Presents" by John Smith (Philadelphia, PA: The Westminster Press, 1968), 130-133.

34. From *The Book of Christmas*, "Christmas Tree" by E. E. Cummings (Pleasantville, NY: Reader's Digest Association, Inc.).

35. From *Christ and the Fine Arts* (Cynthia Pearl Maus, Ed.), "The Mystery of the Incarnation" by Harold Francis Branch (New York, NY: Harper & Brothers, Publishers, 1938).

36. "The Prayer of the Children of Provence" (Pleasantville, NY: The Reader's Digest Association, Inc.).

37. From *Ideals*, "Christmas Is a Book" by Margaret Cousins (Milwaukee, WI: Ideals Publishing Corp.).

38. From *The Fireside Book of Christmas Stories* (Edward Wagenknecht, Ed.), "Snow for Christmas" by Vincent Starrett (New York, NY: Grosset & Dunlap, Publishers, 1945), 582-596.

39. From *1001 Christmas Facts and Fancies*, Alfred Carl Hottes, "Silent Night, Holy Night" (New York, NY: A. T. De La Mare Co., Inc., 1937).

40. From *Ideals*, "The Miracle of Silent Night" by Dorothy Travers Zisa (Milwaukee, WI: Ideals Publishing Corp., 1982).

41. From *Christmas Tales for Reading Aloud* (Robert Lohan, Compiler & Adapter), "In the Bleak Mid-Winter" by Christina Georgina Rossetti (New York, NY: Stephen Daye Press, 1946, 1956).

42. From *Christmas Ideals*, "Songs of Christmas" by Peggy Milcuch (Milwaukee, WI: Ideals Publishing Corp.).

43. From *Sing to the Lord Hymnal*, "What Child Is This?" by Richard Dix (Reprinted with permission of Lillenas Publishing Co., Kansas City, MO, 1993).

44. From *Sing to the Lord Hymnal*, "I Heard the Bells on Christmas Day" by Henry Wadsworth Longfellow (Reprinted with permission of Lillenas Publishing Co., Kansas City, MO, 1985, 1993).

45. From *Sing to the Lord Hymnal*, "O Little Town of Bethlehem" by Phillips Brooks (Reprinted with permission of Lillenas Publishing Co., Kansas City, MO, 1985, 1993).

46. From *Masterpieces of Religious Verse* (James Dalton Morrison, Ed.), "A Christmas Hymn" by Richard Watson Gilder (New York, NY: Harper & Brothers, Publishers).

47. From *Christmas Ideals*, "Christmas Caroling" by Alice Kennelly Roberts (Milwaukee, WI: Ideals Publishing Corp., 1974).

48. From *The Book of Christmas*, "Carol of the Brown King" by Langston Hughes (Pleasantville, NY: Reader's Digest Association, Inc.).

49. From *Happy Christmas* (William Kean Seymour & John Smith, Compilers), "The Computer's First Christmas Card" by Edwin Morgan (Philadelphia, PA: Westminster Press, 1968).

50. From *I Wouldn't Have Missed It*, "A Carol for Children" by Ogden Nash (Boston, MA: Little, Brown & Co., 1902-1971), 106-107.

51. From *Christmas Tales for Reading Aloud* (Robert Lohan, Compiler & Adapter), "A Miserable Merry Christmas" by Lincoln Steffens (New York, NY: Stephen Daye Press, 1946, 1956).

52. From *Christmas in My Heart* (Joe Wheeler, Compiler & Editor), "Trouble at the Inn" by Dina Donohue (New York, NY: Doubleday, 1996), 42-45.

53. From *Christmas Tales for Reading Aloud* (Robert Lohan, Compiler & Adapter), "Jest 'fore Christmas" by Eugene Field (New York, NY: Stephen Daye Press, 1946, 1956).

54. From *The Great American Christmas Almanac*, "Fruitcake Is Forever" by Russell Baker (New York, NY: Viking Studio Books, 1983), 24-25.

55. From *Christmas Tales for Reading Aloud* (Robert Lohan, Compiler & Adapter), "The Thieves Who Couldn't Help Sneezing" by Thomas Hardy (New York, NY: Stephen Daye Press, 1946, 1956), 297-304.

56. From *The Christmas Book* (Lewis & Heseltine, Eds.), "The Stock Exchange Carol" by J. B. Morton (London: J.M. Dent & Sons, 1928).

57. From *Wrappings*, "Christmas Scenes from Warmwater, Illinois" by Lawrence G. Enscoe (Reprinted with permission of Lillenas Publishing Co., Kansas City, MO, 1985).

58. From *The Fireside Book of Christmas Stories* (Edward Wagenknecht, Ed.), "Christmas At Orchard House" by Louisa May Alcott (New York, NY: Grosset & Dunlap, Publishers, 1945), 471-482.

59. From *The Fireside Book of Christmas Stories* (Edward Wagenknecht, Ed.), "The Christmas Play" by Louisa May Alcott (New York, NY: Grosset & Dunlap, Publishers, 1945).

60. From *The Fireside Book of Christmas Stories* (Edward Wagenknecht, Ed.), "Merry Christmas" by Jake Falstaff (New York, NY: Grosset & Dunlap, Publishers, 1945).

61. From *Christmas Tales for Reading Aloud* (Robert Lohan, Compiler & Adapter), "A Christmas Carol" by Charles Dickens (New York, NY: Stephen Daye Press, 1946, 1956).

62. From *Celebrate the Wonder*, Kristin M. Tucker & Rebecca Love Warren, "Family Christmas Finances" (New York, NY: Ballantine Books, 1988).

63. From *Christmas Tales for Reading Aloud* (Robert Lohan, Compiler & Adapter), "A Christmas Carol" by Charles Dickens (New York, NY: Stephen Daye Press, 1946, 1956), 97-109.

64. From *A Christmas Book* (D. B. Ulyndham & G. C. Heseltine), "The Happy Howl" by G. K. Chesterton (New York, NY: E. P. Dutton & Co., 1928, 1951).

65. From *Christmas Tales for Reading Aloud* (Robert Lohan, Compiler & Adapter), "The Birds' Christmas Carol" by Kate Douglas Wiggin (New York, NY: Stephen Daye Press, 1946, 1956), 111-126, Public Domain.

66. From *The Book of Christmas*, "Christmas Day in the Morning" by Pearl S. Buck (Pleasantville, NY: Reader's Digest Association, Inc.).

67. From *Christmas Ideals*, "The Yule Log" by Daniel Roselle (Milwaukee, WI: Ideals Publishing Corp., 1954).

68. From *Christmas Ideals*, "Merry Christmas" by Mary H. Beam (Milwaukee, WI: Ideals Publishing Corp., 1954).

69. From *Christmas Ideals*, "Christmas Memories" by Harriet Whipple (Milwaukee, WI: Ideals Publishing Corp., 1976).

70. From *Christmas Ideals*, "Christmas Baking" by Louise Weibert Sutton (Milwaukee, WI: Ideals Publishing Corp., 1976).

71. From *A Treasury of Christmas Stories,* "A Candy Cane for Everyone" by Webb Garrison (Nashville, TN: Rutledge Hill Press, 1990), 127.

72. From *A Family Christmas,* "Mistletoe" by Walter De La Mare (Pleasantville, NY: Reader's Digest Association, Inc. 1934).

73. From *Christmas Ideals,* "The Christmas Lamp Is Burning" by Mary Wheeler Edgerton (Milwaukee, WI: Ideals Publishing Corp., 1982).

74. From *All About Christmas,* "No Candle Was There . . ." by Maymie R. Krythe (New York, NY: Harper & Brothers, 1954).

75. From *Worship Resources for the Christian Year,* "The Luminous Christ" by Albert W. Beaven.

76. From *West African Melodies,* "Nativity" by Gladys May Casely Hayford (The Atlantic Monthly Co., 1927, 1956).

77. From *The Long Christmas,* "The Shepherds" by Ruth Sawyer (New York, NY: The Viking Press, 1941, 1960), 21-31.

78. From *Happy Christmas,* "The Mountains of Papa Morelli" by Natala de la Fere (Philadelphia, PA: Westminster Press, 1968), 104-110.

79. From *Now We Are Six,* "King John's Christmas" by A. A. Milne (E. P. Dutton & Co., Inc., 1927, A. A. Milne, 1955), 460-464.

80. From *Merry Christmas, Children at Christmastime Around the World,* "Christmas for the Animals" and "Christmas in Germany" by Robina Beckles Willson (New York, NY: Philomel Books, 1983).

81. From *Celebrate the Wonder, A Family Christmas Treasury,* "Tastes of the Season" by Kristin M. Tucker & Rebecca Lowe Warren (New York, NY: Ballantine Books, 1988).

82. From *All About Christmas,* "It Came Upon the Midnight Clear" by Maymie R. Krythe (New York, NY: Harper & Brothers, 1954), 1-2,113-119.

83. From *Christ and the Fine Arts* (Cynthia Pearl Maus, Ed.), "The Door" by Helen Slack Wickenden (Harper & Brothers, Publishers, 1938).

84. From *Rudyard Kipling's Verse: Definitive Edition,* "A Nativity" by Rudyard Kipling (Bantum Doubleday Dell).

85. From *God Came Near,* "Christmas Night" by Max Lucado (Multnomah Press/Questar, 1987), 45-47.

86. From *The Book of Christmas,* "I Heard a Bird Sing" by Oliver Herford (Pleasantville, NY: Reader's Digest Association, Inc., 1935), 117.

87. From *Christ and the Fine Arts* (Cynthia Pearl Maus, Ed.), "The Inn That Missed Its Chance" by Amos R. Wells (New York, NY: Harper & Brothers, Publishers, 1938).

$\mathcal{T}$ITLE INDEX

✻ ✻ ✻

AUTHOR INDEX

* * *

Additional copies of this book are available
from your local bookstore.

Other titles in the Honor Books *Treasury* series:

God's Treasury of Virtues:
An Inspirational Collection of Stories, Quotes,
Hymns, Scriptures, and Poems

Treasury of Love and Romance:
A Classic Collection of Stories, Quotes,
Ballads, Verses, and Poems

If you have enjoyed this book, or if it has impacted your life,
we would like to hear from you. Please contact us at:

HONOR BOOKS
Department E
P.O. Box 55388
Tulsa, Oklahoma 74155
Or by e-mail at info@honorbooks.com